The Political Economy of Livelihoods in Contemporary Zimbabwe

Since the introduction of the fast track land reform programme in 2000, Zimbabwe has undergone major economic and political shifts and these have had a profound impact on both urban and rural livelihoods. This book provides rich empirical studies that examine a range of multi-faceted and contested livelihoods within the context of systemic crises. Taking a broad political economy approach, the chapters advance a grounded and in-depth understanding of emerging and shifting livelihood processes, strategies and resilience that foregrounds agency at household level.

Highlighting an emergent scholarship amongst young black scholars in Zimbabwe, and providing an understanding of how people and communities respond to socio-economic challenges, this book is an important read for scholars of African political economy, southern African studies and livelihoods.

Kirk Helliker is Director of the Unit of Zimbabwean Studies, Rhodes University, South Africa.

Manase Kudzai Chiweshe is a Senior Lecturer at Chinhoyi University of Technology, Zimbabwe.

Sandra Bhatasara is a Senior Lecturer at the University of Zimbabwe.

Routledge Studies on the Political Economy of Africa

1 **The Political Economy of Energy in Sub-Saharan Africa**
   Edited by Lucky E. Asuelime and Andrew E. Okem

2 **The Political Economy of Land and Agrarian Development in Ethiopia**
   The Arssi Region since 1941
   Ketebo Abdiyo Ensene

3 **The Political Economy of Livelihoods in Contemporary Zimbabwe**
   Edited by Kirk Helliker, Manase Kudzai Chiweshe and Sandra Bhatasara

The Political Economy of Livelihoods in Contemporary Zimbabwe

**Edited by
Kirk Helliker,
Manase Kudzai Chiweshe
and Sandra Bhatasara**

Routledge
Taylor & Francis Group

LONDON AND NEW YORK

First published 2018
by Routledge

2 Park Square, Milton Park, Abingdon, Oxfordshire OX14 4RN
52 Vanderbilt Avenue, New York, NY 10017

Routledge is an imprint of the Taylor & Francis Group, an informa business

First issued in paperback 2020

British Library Cataloguing in Publication Data
A catalogue record for this book is available from the British Library

Library of Congress Cataloging in Publication Data
Names: Helliker, Kirk, editor, contributor. | Chiweshe, Manase Kudzai,
editor, contributor. | Bhatasara, Sandra, editor, contributor.
Title: The political economy of livelihood in contemporary Zimbabwe /
edited by Kirk Helliker, Manase Kudzai Chiweshe and Sandra Bhatasara.
Other titles: Routledge studies on the political economy of Africa ; 3.
Description: New York, NY : Routledge, 2018. | Series: Routledge studies
on the political economy of Africa ; 3 | Includes bibliographical references
and index.
Identifiers: LCCN 2017043837| ISBN 9781138574717 (hardback) |
ISBN 9781351273244 (ebook)Subjects: LCSH: Income–Zimbabwe. |
Households–Economic aspects–Zimbabwe. | Zimbabwe–Economic
conditions–21st century–Case studies. | Zimbabwe–Rural conditions. |
Land tenure–Zimbabwe. | Fast Track Land Reform Programme
(Zimbabwe)
Classification: LCC HC910.Z9 I526 2018 | DDC 330.96891–dc23
LC record available at https://lccn.loc.gov/2017043837

ISBN: 978-1-138-57471-7 (hbk)
ISBN: 978-0-367-59340-7 (pbk)

Typeset in Times New Roman
by Wearset Ltd, Boldon, Tyne and Wear

To Sam Moyo, your legacy will endure across generations of scholars, activists and policy makers.

Contents

List of illustrations   ix
Preface   x
Notes on contributors   xi

1 **Introduction: theorising the political economy of livelihoods in contemporary Zimbabwe**   1
SANDRA BHATASARA, MANASE KUDZAI CHIWESHE AND KIRK HELLIKER

2 **Livelihood strategies of urban women: emerging evidence from Magaba, Harare**   26
TAKUNDA CHIRAU

3 **Livelihood strategies in Harare: the case of low-income households in Budiriro**   42
TAFADZWA CHEVO

4 **Sex work as a livelihood strategy in the border town of Beitbridge**   57
WADZANAI TAKAWIRA AND KIRK HELLIKER

5 **Migration-based livelihoods in post-2000 Zimbabwe**   74
MANASE KUDZAI CHIWESHE

6 **Agricultural production systems of small-scale farmers in Hwedza in the context of innovation platforms**   91
INNOCENT MAHIYA

7 **Development NGOs: understanding participatory methods, accountability and effectiveness of World Vision in Umzingwane District**   107
KAYLA KNIGHT WAGHORN

 8 **A critical analysis of community participation at the
    primary level of the health system in Goromonzi District** 124
    RACHEL GONDO

 9 **Climate variability in local scales: narratives and
    ambivalences from Mutoko District** 139
    SANDRA BHATASARA

10 **Livelihoods vulnerability among riverbed farmers in
    Negande, NyamiNyami District** 154
    FELIX TOMBINDO

11 **"Let them starve so that they 'hear' us": differing
    perspectives on unresolved land occupations and
    livelihoods at Mushandike smallholder irrigation scheme,
    Masvingo District** 170
    JONATHAN MAFUKIDZE

12 **"Other people inherit property, but I inherit people and
    their problems": the role of kinship and social capital in
    providing care and support for the HIV infected and AIDS
    affected, Chivanhu informal settlement, Masvingo Province** 184
    LOVENESS MAKONESE

13 **Insecure land tenure and natural resource use in a post-fast
    track area of Zimbabwe** 198
    TAKUNDA CHABATA

14 **Fast track land reform programme and women in
    Goromonzi District** 213
    LOVENESS CHAKONA AND MANASE KUDZAI CHIWESHE

    Index 230

Illustrations

Figure

12.1 Machekeche Cluster showing kinship networks and movement
 of the chronically ill and orphans over time   188

Tables

3.1 Wealth index of Budiriro households   45
3.2 Types of employment for household heads   46
3.3 Types of household business enterprises (HBEs)   47
3.4 Recipients and non-recipients of household business income   49
3.5 Practicing and non-practicing agriculture households   50
3.6 Livestock ownership   51
3.7 Recipients and non-recipients of rental income   53
7.1 Projects in Umzingwane   117

Preface

This book has emerged out of the Unit of Zimbabwean Studies in the Department of Sociology, Rhodes University in South Africa. Though the Unit was formed only at the beginning of 2015, the Director of the Unit (Professor Kirk Helliker) has been involved in Zimbabwean-focused research projects at the university since 2009. As well as pursuing his own research, he has supervised many PhD and master's degree students from Zimbabwe. The other two editors of this book, Dr. Manase Kudzai Chiweshe and Dr. Sandra Bhatasara, both graduated from Rhodes University with doctorates under Prof. Helliker's supervision. All of the contributors to this book are either current or former PhD and master's degree students supervised by Prof. Helliker, and all the chapters (except one) draw upon their PhD and master's degree theses. In this regard, the editors would like to acknowledge any funding received from Rhodes University for these PhD and master's degree students.

As editors of this book, we have been influenced by a number of Zimbabwean scholars. Of particular importance is Sam Moyo, the former Director of the African Institute for Agrarian Studies in Harare until his tragic death in late 2015. He was also a member of the Advisory Board for the Unit of Zimbabwean Studies at the time of his death. Because of the way in which he has inspired us, we dedicate this book to Sam, the person, the activist and the scholar.

Contributors

Sandra Bhatasara is a Senior Lecturer in the Sociology Department, University of Zimbabwe. She researches and writes on agrarian issues, rural and environmental sociology and women's studies. Some of her recent publications include interrogating women's experiences in fast track land reform in Zimbabwe (*Africa Review*) and sociology of adaptation to rainfall variability amongst smallholder farmers in rural Zimbabwe (*Fudan Journal of the Humanities and Social Sciences*).

Takunda Chabata is a holder of a Master of Science degree in Sociology and Social Anthropology and a Bachelor of Science honours degree in Sociology, both from the University of Zimbabwe. Currently, he is reading towards a doctoral degree in Sociology with Rhodes University. Since 2010, he has been with Women's University in Africa in Harare where he works as a Sociology lecturer and programme coordinator in Sociology. His research interests include natural resources management, rural livelihoods, family and gender studies.

Loveness Chakona completed an honours degree at the University of Zimbabwe and a master's degree in Sociology at Rhodes University, where she studied the position of women on fast track farms in Goromonzi District in Zimbabwe in the context of local patriarchal systems.

Tafadzwa Chevo is a Lecturer in the Department of Sociology at the University of Zimbabwe in Harare. He undertook his master's degree at this university and is now currently registered for a PhD in the Department of Sociology at Rhodes University where he is undertaking research on urban livelihoods in Zimbabwe.

Takunda Chirau did his master's degree and PhD studies at Rhodes University in the Sociology Department. He obtained his first degree in Social Sciences at the University of Fort Hare in 2009 and earned an Honours in Sociology there in 2010. His ongoing research interests lie in gender, rural and urban sociology (particularly on livelihoods). Currently, he is finalising his postgraduate diploma in Monitoring and Evaluation at the University of Stellenbosch. His experience involves consultancy, and monitoring and evaluation of local non-governmental organisation programmes in South Africa.

Manase Kudzai Chiweshe is a Senior Lecturer in the Institute of Lifelong Learning and Development Studies at Chinhoyi University of Technology and winner of the 2015 Gerti Hessling Award for the best paper in African studies. He has over 50 papers in peer reviewed journals and book chapters and he has co-edited a book entitled *Perspectives in Sustainable Development in Zimbabwe* (2017). His has interest in African agrarian studies: land, livelihoods, football, gender and youth studies. His work revolves around the sociology of everyday life in African spaces with special focus on promoting African ways of knowing.

Rachel Gondo holds a master's degree in Social Sciences from Rhodes University in South Africa. She is a Zimbabwean scholar and avid activist for social change in southern Africa and currently works for the Public Service Accountability Monitor located at Rhodes University. Her research interests include health systems strengthening, gender budgeting, and participation in governance for social accountability.

Kirk Helliker is an Associate Professor in the Department of Sociology at Rhodes University in South Africa. He is also Director of the Unit of Zimbabwean Studies in the Department. Over the past ten years, he has co-edited three books focusing on questions of land and civil society in Zimbabwe, South Africa and southern Africa more broadly. These are as follows: *The Promise of Land: Undoing a Century of Dispossession in South Africa* (2013), *Land Struggles and Civil Society in Southern Africa* (2011), and *Contested Terrain: Land Reform and Civil Society* (2008). He supervises a large number of PhD students working on diverse topics in contemporary Zimbabwe. His current research on Zimbabwe focuses on the land occupation movement in the year 2000, primarily in Mashonaland Central Province.

Kayla Knight Waghorn holds a Master of Arts in Sociology from Rhodes University. She has worked recently in rural development and education in Zimbabwe with Falcon College, and founded the Umzingwane District Maths and Science Forum. Her research interests include rural development, non-governmental organisations and education in rural Zimbabwe.

Jonathan Mafukidze is a PhD in Sociology candidate at Rhodes University, researching land and water politics. He obtained a Master of Science and a BSc honours degree in Sociology and Social Anthropology from the University of Zimbabwe. He has been researching xenophobia, identity, migration, housing and land management in South Africa for more than a decade now, and has published on these issues.

Innocent Mahiya has a PhD in Sociology from Rhodes University where he studied food security among small-scale farmers in Hwedza, Zimbabwe. He holds a master's degree in Sociology and Social Anthropology from the University of Zimbabwe. He is currently a departmental chairperson at the Women's University in Africa in Harare where he also teaches Sociology of Agriculture. He has expertise in rural development and food security issues with reference to Zimbabwean communal areas. He has published in academic journals.

Loveness Makonese obtained her PhD from Rhodes University's Department of Sociology. Her thesis focused on how people cope with HIV and AIDS in marginalised settlements. Loveness holds an MPhil from the University of Western Cape in South Africa and a Bachelor of Science honours degree in Sociology from the University of Zimbabwe. She specialises in development specifically on livelihoods, gender and HIV and AIDS and has experience in working in the public and development sector. She has worked for the Ministry of Finance and the Ministry of Health in Zimbabwe, CARE International, Goal International and Plan International, and is currently working for the UN Food and Agriculture Organization.

Wadzanai Takawira completed both her honours and master's degrees in Sociology at Rhodes University. Her master's thesis involved an in-depth study of the lives and livelihoods of female sex workers in the border town of Beitbridge along the Zimbabwean-South African border.

Felix Tombindo is a final year master's degree student in the Sociology Department at Rhodes University. He obtained his first degree in Social Anthropology at Great Zimbabwe University in 2012. He undertook his honours in Sociology at Rhodes University in 2014. His ongoing research interests lie in land and agrarian studies, rural sociology (centring mainly on livelihoods), China–Africa studies, belonging and citizenship politics.

1 Introduction

Theorising the political economy of livelihoods in contemporary Zimbabwe

Sandra Bhatasara, Manase Kudzai Chiweshe and Kirk Helliker

Introduction

In the context of multiple crises, this book examines livelihoods in post-2000 Zimbabwe through diverse case studies, and it provides an understanding of how people and communities act in the face of deepening socio-economic challenges. All of the chapters are firmly rooted in empirical research and, individually and combined, they weave together a rich tapestry of stories which enable analyses of various forms of localised agency – despite systemic crises – in both rural and urban spaces. Some of the themes included are: climate variability, HIV and AIDS, gender inequalities, food insecurities, primary health care, non-governmental organisations, informal employment and poverty. Importantly, the chapters in this book highlight an emergent scholarship amongst young black scholars in Zimbabwe. Broadly speaking, each chapter is informed in some way, at least implicitly, by the Livelihoods Framework, also known as the Sustainable Livelihoods Framework.

This introductory chapter theorises about livelihoods with particular reference to the Livelihoods Framework, and it offers an analysis of the political economy of post-2000 Zimbabwe within which we locate the chapter-based studies. The case studies come from research undertaken since 2010, but an understanding of the livelihoods examined in the chapters requires a historical focus at least as far back as 2000 – the year the Zimbabwean state's controversial fast track land reform programme was introduced. At the same time, we recognise that a fuller analysis of contemporary crises and livelihoods requires a *longue durée* approach to unfolding events. Undoubtedly though, post-2000 Zimbabwe has undergone major economic and political shifts and these have had a profound impact on both rural and urban livelihoods and continue to do so.

The in-depth and multi-faceted micro-level livelihood studies in this book are crucial in order to provide a grounded understanding of emerging and changing livelihood processes, patterns and strategies in Zimbabwe. This, we would argue, ensures that this book makes a significant contribution to literature on post-2000 Zimbabwe. But, alone, micro-studies are insufficient unless they are properly contextualised. For this reason, the purpose of this introductory chapter is two-fold. First of all, it offers a critical analysis of the Livelihoods Framework and examines how it can be augmented and strengthened by macro-sociological theorising. Second, and in this context, it examines the political economy of Zimbabwe. On this basis, we provide a brief review of livelihoods literature on Zimbabwe, and show broadly how each livelihood case study presented in this book can be more fully understood in the context of post-2000 political and economic restructuring. In this regard, each chapter tends to focus almost exclusively on a livelihood case study, including the empirical setting and research methods, with the introductory chapter setting the broad contextual stage for the livelihood studies.

Critical appraisal of the Livelihoods Framework

There is voluminous academic literature available on the basic principles and concepts of the Livelihoods Framework (LF). Because such ample literature exists, we make no attempt to provide a basic or comprehensive overview of the LF. The framework has been subjected to significant criticism in recent years, but in a manner which seeks to re-energise and revitalise it. Considering that this edited collection seeks to contribute to the LF (with specific reference to Zimbabwean studies), our discussion of the LF in this introductory chapter is primarily concerned with the ways in which the framework can be given a more critical analytical edge.

Livelihoods framework

From mainly the 1990s, strong advocacy for programmatic interventions designed to ensure sustainable livelihoods when pursuing socio-economic development arose (Chambers and Conway 1992, Scoones 1998, Carney 1998, 2002, Ashley and Carney 1999). The LF, as an analytical perspective, came increasingly to the fore alongside this programmatic initiative and indeed was deeply intertwined with it. The framework for instance sometimes became part of the planning phase for a development intervention via policy or for a specific development project. Development agencies such as the United Nations Development Programme, Oxfam and CARE soon adopted the concept of sustainable livelihoods (Solesbury 2003). In this context, the LF sought to examine peoples' current livelihoods and then assess what was necessary for a livelihood 'enhancement', and one which would be sustainable across generations (Morse and McNamara 2013).

The roots of the concept of 'sustainable livelihoods' can be traced analytically, at least indirectly, to the works for example of Sen's (1981) classic focus on entitlements and Long's (1984) actor-oriented perspective as well as, more programmatically, to the World Commission on Environment and Development's Brundtland advisory panel report (WCED 1987) and other international forums. But the framework is more directly linked to the seminal work by Chambers and Conway (1992), as the current notion of 'sustainable livelihoods' derives from this. Drawing upon insights from previous academic research on food security and agro-ecological sustainability, they put livelihoods, and in particular 'sustainable livelihoods', at centre stage within the worldwide development system and also within scholarly work. Soon, other important insights fed directly into the livelihoods framework, including those around environmental entitlements (Leach *et al.* 1999, Scoones 1998, Carney 1998) and the diversification of livelihood activities (Ellis 1998). Initially, the focus was on rural livelihoods but later the LF became useful for urban-based studies.

In terms of the framework (Chambers and Conway 1992, Scoones 1998), the crucial focus is livelihood assets, including both material and social resources, and activities or strategies that form the basis of a means of living or livelihood. A livelihood is said to be sustainable when it can cope with (and recover from) stresses and shocks, and maintain or enhance its capabilities and assets while not undermining the natural resource base. Overall, the LF encompasses analysis of the context in which people live (i.e. their socio-economic, technological, demographic, agro-ecological and political context); their access to natural, human, social, physical and financial capitals or assets (and their ability to put these capitals to productive use); the institutions, policies and organisations which determine people's access to these assets and the returns they can achieve on assets; and the priorities that people identify in confronting the problems, including stresses and shocks, which they face as well as the different strategies (even of only a coping character) they adopt in pursuit of these priorities (Ashley and Carney 1999). The framework therefore links inputs ('capitals' or 'assets') and outputs (livelihood strategies), which are connected in turn to livelihood outcomes (Scoones 2009). Households and individuals living under conditions of poverty – in both rural and urban settings – juggle 'capital assets' in actively seeking (hopefully) positive livelihood outcomes, and this juggling is mediated through different structures and processes which may either constrain or enable livelihood activities (Batterbury 2008, Scoones 2009).

Undoubtedly, the LF has contributed to a deeper and more integrated understanding of how marginalised groups and households make their living under adverse and dynamic conditions by highlighting their agency and ingenuity in the context of a multiplicity of vulnerabilities (Levine 2014). In doing so, according to Serrat (2008), the framework is able to, at least potentially: examine changing combinations of modes of livelihood in fluid historical and social contexts; go beyond narrow sectoral approaches in allowing for a holistic analysis of household-based livelihoods; and, though focusing on the local, show the ways in which the local is linked to broader national and even global processes. Though such positive appraisals have a certain degree of validity, the more critical literature on the LF raises a range of weaknesses which, if able to be addressed, would enhance the analytical weight of the framework.

Reinvigorating the framework

In considering the means for strengthening the LF, two points are particularly important. First of all, the LF needs to be more sensitive to the political economy of capitalist development. In this respect, Cowen and Shenton (1998) make a distinction between small *d* and big *d* development (see also Bebbington *et al.* 2007). The former refers to the immanent development processes intrinsic to capitalism as a political-economic system, which takes on various forms over time and is uneven in its character and effects spatially. The latter refers to the current international development system (or industry) and speaks to the existence of intentional and directed development interventions and practices. Clearly, small *d* development is a broader social process which incorporates big *d* development, such that the current period of neo-liberal capitalist development is characterised by specific forms of big *d* development interventions. In terms of its emergence, as indicated earlier, the LF was linked to big *d* development; such that the programmatic interventions associated with the LF fail to address the global and national forms of domination and inequality inherent within capitalism. Analytically, the LF is marked by weaknesses when it comes to properly and fully locating livelihood studies within small *d* capitalist development. For instance, the central notion of sustainability is rarely if ever rooted in an analysis of capitalism (Fuchs 2017). In the end, this means that the LF, as a kind of actor-oriented perspective, needs to be grounded in a political economy analysis (Scoones 2009, Banks 2015). In the later section on the political economy of Zimbabwe, we seek to ensure that the chapter-based micro-studies in this volume are properly conceptualised on this basis, such that power and inequality are foregrounded.

The second main issue is that the framework is in effect a middle-level theory that is not explicitly located within broader macro-sociological theorising or a "social theoretical foundation" (Thieme 2008:56). As a form of middle-level theorising, rooted it seems in rational choice theory (van Dijk 2011), it implicitly makes a range of problematic methodological claims, both epistemological and ontological, which need to be articulated and addressed. Of particular importance, as noted below, is the question of structure-agency and the stratified character of social reality. A higher level of theorising, we would argue, would also go some way in enhancing the framework's acknowledgement of small *d* development and therefore strengthen and enrich the analytical power of the LF without involving a complete rejection of it. We discuss the importance of macro-theorising for the LF in the balance of this section.

As it originally emerged, the LF is now identified as the 'mainstream' livelihoods perspective (Prowse 2010) because of its subjection to significant criticisms and subsequent revisions. At first sight, it appears that the framework focuses on both structure and agency, and in a balanced manner, but the framework is flawed in this respect (Sakdapolrak 2014). On the one hand, households are seen as enacting agency by deploying available assets in constructing and pursuing livelihoods. On the other hand, the framework notes the existence of a structural context within which livelihood activities are undertaken, a context involving 'policies, institutions and processes' and characterised by vulnerability. However, it is generally recognised that agency takes precedence over structure in the framework, or at least structural constraints are downplayed. Further, the conceptualisations of both agency and structure are problematic.

In the case of agency, as argued by van Dijk (2011), there is an implicit methodological individualism permeating the livelihoods approach, with the notion of rational and strategic actors using their assets in order to maximise their utilities in pursuing seemingly clearly-defined ends. Thus, households are seen as discrete rational actors carefully weighing their available options in enhancing livelihood outcomes, and it appears acting on occasion almost outside or beyond structures as free-floating agents. As Banks (2015:270) argues, "actor-oriented frameworks [such as the SL] overestimate a household's autonomy in devising and mobilising strategies". In this way, households come across as highly reflexive, on a constant basis and quite explicitly so. At the same time, the household as the main unit of analysis is treated as a unitary whole and, as such, the framework fails to unpack the power differentials existing within households, particularly in terms of patriarchal practices.

Some sympathetic critics of the LF (Thieme 2008, Speranza *et al.* 2014, Sakdapolrak 2014) argue that the work of Pierre Bourdieu (Bourdieu 1977, 1990), and his notions of habitus and field in particular, is an important corrective to the livelihood framework's conception of agency. This is because habitus highlights the ways in which society becomes embodied in human subjects so that they act, in an almost non-reflective but reasonable manner, according to historically-conditioned socialised dispositions. Because of this, from a Bourdieusian perspective, human agency is not reducible to the rationalising actor. Certainly more forcefully than the LF, habitus brings to the fore the importance of structure in inhibiting the agency of households living under conditions of vulnerability, such that households become almost pre-set along particular livelihood pathways not of their choosing, and thus they are "rooted in collective histories inscribed in their *habitus*" (Sakdapolrak 2014:23). The work of Margaret Archer (Archer 1995, 2003) based on critical realism, may however allow for an ongoing retention of reflexivity in livelihoods analyses, as Lyon and Parkins (2013) suggest. Her morphogenetic approach would recognise the ways in which rationalising agents, with personal concerns and projects (such as livelihood activities), often end up reproducing their prevailing conditions of existence.

A related issue is the central notion of 'assets' in the livelihoods framework, with assets (or resources or capitals) conceived as things or stock owned, possessed and used by rational actors in building livelihoods. Though the world of capitalism may appear in fetishised form as a conglomeration of interacting things, the framework – in treating assets as things – fails to recognise that society is profoundly relational. This 'thingology' view of the world, in which assets are also regularly viewed in very economistic and materialistic terms (White and Ellison 2006), thus depicts assets as objective facts (Wood 2003) rather than as being endowed with cultural and social meanings and subject to contestation. In the end, 'things' are the embodiment of, and are embedded in, complex and tension-riddled social relationships, and the presence and character of assets at household 'level' represent the fluid manifestation of a range of nested power relations existing locally, nationally and globally (Bebbington 1999, Wilshusen 2012). From Bourdieu's perspective, as highlighted by

Sakdapolrak (2014:24), "capital does not have an intrinsic value, but rather its value is linked to the logics of fields" as sites of domination and struggle. In offering in large part a de-politicised conception of assets, power is simply treated as context rather than as central to livelihoods analyses (Scoones 2009).

In this context, livelihoods analysis has been criticised for insufficient inquiry into spatial and temporal dynamics. Regarding questions of space and place, many livelihood scholars now recognise that livelihoods are deeply immersed in intensified local-global networks of interaction and that global processes increasingly have ramifications for local livelihoods, even in deep rural spaces (Sakdapolrak 2014, Scoones 2009). This also includes the importance of considering the existence of multi-local and trans-local livelihoods beyond specific localities (de Haan and Zoomers 2003, Zoomers and Westen 2011), or what has been called the "contemporary hybridities of rural and urban ... livelihoods" (Fairbairn *et al.* 2014:661) such that the urban–rural dualism in terms of livelihoods becomes problematic. In this respect, Bebbington and Batterbury (2001:373–375) call for "more attention to the embeddedness of livelihoods within both trans-local and trans-national structures, networks and spaces, and [for] examining the effects of this connectedness".

In terms of temporality, Scoones (2009) observes that the livelihoods approach tends to focus on how people pursue their livelihoods within current circumstances without addressing particular livelihoods historically. Because of this, stability, durability and resilience, even in times of systemic crises, tend to be taken for granted. Temporal dynamics, including historical shifts in livelihoods because of long-term social changes and socio-ecological transformations, have not been extensively analysed (Sakdapolrak 2014), including "long-term shifts in rural economies and wider questions about agrarian change" (Scoones 2009:182). This also implies "a lack of rigorous attempts to deal with long-term secular change in environmental conditions" (Scoones 2009:182) in which climate change and variation around temperature and rainfall patterns become particularly important. For this reason, the LF has been criticised as being static and ahistorical. As noted by Scoones and Wolmer (2002:27), "livelihoods emerge out of past actions and decisions are made within specific historical and agro-ecological conditions, and are constantly shaped by institutions and social arrangements".

Another recurrent criticism of the LF is the downplaying if not ignoring of power and politics, including structures and processes of extraction, exploitation and domination (Scoones 2009). The framework privileges the power of households to access assets and to act as they rationally pursue and construct livelihoods optimally, but this claim does not derive from any theory of power including Michael Foucault's notion that power is everywhere. Rather, the 'power to act' emerges from the LF's pronounced methodological individualism and its underestimation of the constraining effects of power. It may be that at times household livelihoods are enabled in and through power relations at localised levels, and that there are cracks and crevices in local political economies in which households can manoeuvre strategically. But, ultimately, power relations imply modes of domination in which there are winners and losers, with more privileged groups gaining at the expense of others (Harriss 1997). Because of ongoing political contestations, which may in fact deepen conditions of vulnerability, there are bound to be reversals in livelihood trajectories and pathways, and not simply incremental advances.

We would like to suggest tentatively that a turn to Roy Bhaskar's critical realism (Bhaskar 1978) may provide the strongest basis for re-energising the LF and more firmly rooting it in sociological theorising, a point which van Dijk (2011) brings to the fore. Of overall importance in this regard is that the livelihoods framework tends to operate at particular 'levels' of social reality, and fails to appreciate in full the stratified character of reality. In a manner similar to Marxism and its critical political economy, Bhaskar's critical realism speaks about ontological depth, distinguishing between 'the real' (involving structures and mechanisms), 'the actual' (events) and 'the empirical' (experiences). The LF does not delve properly if at all into the deep ('real') relational structures of society, such as capitalism, colonialism and patriarchy, and the ways in which underlying structures and mechanisms give rise to events and experiences – with events and particularly experiences in effect being the focus of livelihoods studies. Because of this, capitals – their form and extent – are treated as having causal effects when they themselves need to be explained. As van Dijk (2011:102) argues, livelihoods are "constituted by arrangements" and these are "fragile but path-dependent emergent properties of the web of structures households operate in". In seeking to show the validity of Bhaskar's critical realism for livelihoods studies, Prowse (2010) indicates that these causal-type mechanisms do not act in a deterministic manner. Rather, they represent tendencies subject to time and space specificities and thus merely set the conditions for particular livelihood events and experiences.

This ontological limitation of the LF leads to epistemological positions which inhibit deep explanatory analysis. For instance, treating assets as 'things', and households as rational actors, in large part arises from concentrating on the experiential level – or sphere – of reality, without understanding how experiences are generated through underlying processes and mechanisms marked by power, and thus how the world of households is, if only in mediated form, a manifestation of these deep structures. Likewise, events in the lives of households, including troubling events which may intensify conditions of vulnerability, are only accessible to explanation through a focus on 'the real'. This perspective does not reduce households to simple bearers of structures, but it does emphasise, if understood as well in terms of Archer's morphogenetic approach, that the capacity for households to transform their lives is often trumped by the mere reproduction of their lives and the relationships of domination and inequality which prevail.

Zimbabwe's political economy

In this section, we do not seek to provide a comprehensive overview of the political economy of Zimbabwe since the year 2000. Rather, we seek to highlight key developments which are of particular relevance to the livelihood case studies contained in this volume. We first provide a historical narrative and then turn briefly to attempts to theorise the on-going crisis.

Before 2000

Following the first democratic elections in sovereign Zimbabwe in 1980, the Zimbabwe African National Union-Patriotic Front (ZANU-PF) assumed power, after a prolonged guerrilla war. Politically, during the early years of independence, the post-colonial government sought to engage in national reconciliation and reconstruction, to bring about civil and political democracy, and to enact various progressive reforms, including labour reforms and state decentralisation. At the same time, the government embarked on restructuring the economy to integrate it into the world economy (after years of sanctions against the Rhodesian regime). This involved significant state intervention in the economy, including positive commodity pricing, better access to loans and credits, and the revitalisation of goods markets. In terms of the economy, the country registered an average Gross Domestic Product (GDP) growth rate of 5.5% during the 1980s (Brown *et al.* 2012). A significant redistributive programme involving the delivery of social services and infrastructure also took place, particularly in relation to roads, health clinics, boreholes, sanitation and education in the former Tribal Trust Lands – now communal areas.

However, "the legacies of enclavity and dualism remained intact" (Kanyenze *et al.* 2011:18). Hence, the ZANU-PF government maintained the colonial spatial geography of the country, as it did not for example challenge the existence of communal areas. Though civil government was introduced into these areas, the chieftainship system remained influential. Nevertheless, the government provided important forms of agricultural assistance to communal farmers during the first decade. At independence, white commercial farmers possessed 45% of the prime land in the country, and were supplying 90% of the country's marketed food. Black farmers living in the Tribal Trust Lands had been subjected to overcrowding, absence of state support and growing degradation of the land. The compromise Lancaster House Constitution, which formed the basis of the post-colonial state in Zimbabwe, provided white farmers with the investment security they viewed as indispensable for their farms by the adoption of a 'willing-buyer willing-seller' land redistribution agreement (Southall 2011). On this basis, the Zimbabwean state implemented only minimal land redistribution during the 1980s directed primarily at reducing rural poverty.

Despite the claims put forward by the ruling party about reconciliation and democratic transition, the 1980s were marked by pronounced state intolerance, authoritarianism and coercion. This was exemplified most vividly by the *Gukurahundi* killings undertaken by the 5th Brigade in Matabeleland against supposed Ndebele rebels in the mid-1980s, the subsequent incorporation of the Matabeleland-based party known as the Zimbabwe African People's Union within ZANU-PF, the seeming efforts of ZANU-PF to create a one-party state, and the creation of the post of executive president. Arguably, these developments marked significant continuity with the mode of political domination bequeathed by the colonial state.

For reasons that continue to be debated, the Zimbabwean government in 1991 adopted a standard structural adjustment programme known as the Economic Structural Adjustment Programme (ESAP). This purported to liberalise the economy and bolster economic growth but, significantly, it undermined many social and economic gains for both workers and communal farmers attained during the first decade of independence. The cardinal weakness of ESAP was its failure to provide meaningful safety nets to buffer those groups deeply affected by neo-liberal restructuring (Raftopoulos 2001). The effects within the social sectors were very prevalent. For instance, because of declining health care, infant mortality (which had decreased from 86 to 49 per 1,000 live births between 1980 and 1990) increased to 53 per 1,000 live births by 1994 (Parliament of Zimbabwe 2010). Alongside this was the scourge of HIV and AIDS – in this respect, life expectancy at birth averaged 56 years in the 1980s and had risen to 60 in 1990, but diminished to 40 by 2000 (Nyazema 2010). As well, pronounced de-industrialisation of the manufacturing sector and rising urban unemployment took place, rural poverty in communal areas escalated, and national and rural income inequalities were amplified (Muzondidya 2009, Laakso 2003). Because of the neo-liberal trajectory, land redistribution dropped considerably during the 1990s, and any land reforms focused on maximising productivity on redistributed farms. In the meantime, white commercial farmers were able to diversify into the lucrative export market through exotic vegetables, fruits and flowers. However an overall economic decline took place, with the GDP growth rate declining sharply from a peak of 7% in 1990 to an average 1.5% per annum between 1991 and 1995 (Government of Zimbabwe 2010).

During the 1990s, if the national power structure did not entail a one-party state, it certainly was marked by a dominant party state, in the form of ZANU-PF with on-going authoritarian tendencies. The 1990s witnessed the emergence of an autonomous national trade union federation, the Zimbabwe Congress of Trade Unions, which previously had operated as a subservient wing of the ruling party. It became extremely vocal against ESAP such that the decade was marked by a steep rise in strike action. Simultaneously, in seeking to counter what it considered as an authoritarian state and to defend eroding civil and political liberties, a significant urban civic movement emerged, most notably the National Constitutional Assembly (NCA) (Sutcliffe 2012), which was heavily funded by international donors. As a result of the deepening political restlessness, disgruntlement and dissatisfaction within the union and civic movements, a new opposition political party emerged in 1999, namely, the Movement for Democratic Change (MDC) (Mawere 2011). Its formation was to set in motion a series of developments that continue to work themselves out.

After 2000

There is evidence that the ruling party was becoming increasingly radicalised during the late 1990s, with attempts for instance to bring about land redistribution through expropriation. While subject to pressure from the growing civic and union movements, there was agitation by marginalised war veterans (ex-guerrillas) against ZANU-PF, which led to war veterans being granted unbudgeted gratuities and the consequent crash of the Zimbabwean dollar in 1997 (Nyathi 2004). Both the civic movement led by the NCA and the ruling party itself was also pursuing constitutional reform. This resulted in a proposed new constitution, as formulated by the ruling party, which was put to a referendum vote in February 2000. Key constitutional changes involved enhancing the powers of the executive president and a move towards land expropriation. The MDC campaigned vigorously for a 'no' vote, and indeed this was the outcome. ZANU-PF's dominant party position seemed to be in jeopardy. Soon afterwards, war veterans mobilised people (mainly from communal areas) to occupy commercial land throughout the country. In July 2000, in the midst of the land occupations, ZANU-PF implemented the fast track land reform programme, which in effect legitimised the occupations.

There is no doubt that the disruption of the white commercial agricultural sector was immediate and substantial, leading to major declines in the production by white farmers of key agricultural commodities including maize, soya beans, wheat and tobacco. In the early years of fast track (between 2001 and 2002), maize output slumped from 800,000 tons to about 80,000 tons, wheat from 225,000 tons to about 100,000 tons, tobacco from 230 million kilogrammes to 70 million kilogrammes, and soya bean production plunged by 50%. The overall macro-level evidence is that fast track was followed by a contraction of the Zimbabwean economy (Chikozho 2010). In the first seven years after fast track (2000 to 2007), the GDP fell by a cumulative 40%. By 2010, agricultural output had deteriorated by 51% and industrial production by 47%. There is a direct causal link between fast track, agricultural decline and economic contraction, a point that is emphasised most forcefully by the MDC (Biti 2009). But the international sanctions imposed on Zimbabwe post-2000 were also of some significance with regard to economic performance (Nyamwanza 2012), as were incessant annual droughts.

By the year 2008, the country was pronounced as a net importer of food, with a large proportion of the population depending upon food aid. Urban poverty levels rose markedly and, as economic growth continued to slump, so did levels of employment. This involved further de-industrialisation, the increased informalisation of the economy and a growth in the feminisation of poverty. Chagutah (2010) claims that humanitarian aid for 2008 was a monumental US$490 million, against a backdrop of over 90% unemployment and the worst crop failure in the country's history. More women (53%) were involved in the informal sector than men (47%), with 44% of those in the informal sector living below the total consumption poverty line, compared to 36% in the formal sector. Overall, poverty in the country increased from 30% in 1990 to 80% by 2008, and unemployment moved from 15% in 1990 to 94% by December 2008 (Tevera 2008). Another outstanding consequence of the economic crisis was the massive migration of highly skilled workers to neighbouring countries in southern Africa and beyond (Mandaza 2016).

In the meantime, farmers resettled on heavily subdivided A1 fast track farms received only minimal post-settlement support from the state. However, some micro-level assessments demonstrate that the amount of land planted under cereals had actually increased (for instance by 9% from 2001 to 2002), with the area planted with maize increasing by 14% mostly as a result of expansion in the fast track resettlement areas (Mukherjee 2002). In other words, though national agricultural production declined, there may have been enhanced agricultural production for home-consumption and hence for rural livelihoods (if analysed at household level) particularly on A1 fast track farms. Agricultural production in communal areas, which had been only partially decongested through fast track, remained in large part stagnant. Rural development non-governmental organisations, which had a major presence in communal areas since the early 1980s, continued to work in these areas but, on instructions from their donors, refrained from engaging with the fast track farms.

The overall waning national economic performance became associated with pronounced economic mismanagement, insufficient public sector management, and the general loss of international support amongst key multilateral and bilateral donors. Simultaneously, subsequent to the June 2000 parliamentary elections in which the MDC did extremely well, the MDC continued to stridently oppose the ruling party within the electoral system, including in the presidential elections of 2002, and parliamentary and senatorial elections of 2005. The disputed harmonised presidential and parliamentary/senatorial elections of 2008, in which the MDC received a parliamentary majority but lost in a presidential run-off, resulted in the formation of the Government of National Unity (GNU) in 2009. ZANU-PF constantly sought to undermine the MDC, and its urban civic supporters, prior to the GNU. Behind the facade of a vibrant two-party system based on constitutional democracy, there existed a semi-authoritarian party state involved in the prohibition of democratic space and the severe infringement of human rights and the rule of law (Muzondidya 2009). The Public Order and Security Act and the Access to Information and Protection of Privacy Act, both from 2002, testify to this. Additionally, with the MDC gaining local government control of urban centres, including the metropolitan areas of Harare and Bulawayo, the ruling party used its access to the national state to undercut the MDC urban councils. Bulawayo, as historically a centre of support for ZAPU and later the MDC, and as symbolic of the history of Matabeleland more broadly, was effectively seen as a 'rebel city'. Overall, ZANU-PF ceaselessly, ruthlessly and violently machinated state power to confront the challenge presented by the MDC, and the various elections since 2000 have been grossly manipulated to continue the ruling party in power. The 2008 election in fact has been described by Sachikonye (2011:68) as "the most violent in the annals of Zimbabwe's post-independence history".

Urban centres in particular, as MDC strongholds, became the target under the military-style Operation Restore Order (Operation *Murambatsvina*) in 2005, which focused on informal housing and trading structures and operations in urban spaces. It entailed the destruction of illegal structures in towns and cities that produced a major humanitarian crisis, as an estimated 700,000 people across the country lost their homes or sources of livelihood. Vambe (2008:10) contends that the operation "pronounced the authoring of a new political (im)morality where violence is instrumentally escalated to foil the manoeuvre of internal enemies". As the economic hardships deepened, the government's intolerance and repressive tendencies also heightened. This is evident in further military-style operations, for instance against 'illegal' rural miners (2006–2008), profiteers in a price control blitz (2007) and during the 2008 presidential elections against those who were no longer subscribing to the 'vanguard' claims of the ZANU-PF party (Moyo and Yeros 2011). Thus, regimentation, as opposed to mobilisation, became the order of the day through a combination of state-driven violence (or the threat of it) and state-sponsored patronage (Mandaza 2016), with claims for example of any food aid aimed specifically at ZANU-PF supporters.

Indeed, for this period, corruption constantly rears its ugly head when discussions arise about the politicking of the ruling party and its unfettered control of state resources. Corruption took on various characteristics, from petty bureaucratic corruption to grand forms implicating high level party and state officials. As argued by Chene (2015), corruption in Zimbabwe manifested itself through a deeply entrenched cultural system of political patronage and clientelism, a tight grip by ZANU-PF on the security forces, and political violence, repression, and manipulation (Moyo 2014, Ndlovu-Gatsheni 2011). While corruption existed from 1980, the predominant forms of corruption in the early years were largely opportunistic or driven by greed, but since the late 1990s this has been transformed into network-based corruption which involves highly-connected politicians and elites plundering national resources because of their status and class (Shana 2006). This relates to the fact that corruption is the product of the dependence for accumulation and class formation on state power and public resources (Sachikonye 2015), as evidenced for instance in privileged access by elites to A2 commercial farms under the fast track programme as well as to mineral ventures – with significant losses of gold and diamonds through illicit mineral and financial flows outside the country. But corruption and political patronage also played itself out within ZANU-PF because of its pronounced internal factionalism. Writing on the economic costs of corruption, Chitambara (2015) speaks of much lower foreign direct investment inflows, less private domestic investment, the lowering of domestic savings, lower levels of institutional quality and even lower levels of life expectancy. Even in terms of the everyday lives of ordinary Zimbabweans, including with reference to the social sector, the paying of bribes became endemic for accessing services, which aggravated inequality and injustice (Bhatasara 2015).

Following the March 2008 elections and the presidential run-off in which the MDC declined to take part (following widespread violence and intimidation), a political impasse ensued. Nonetheless, after negotiations expedited by the Southern African Development Community and the African Union, a Global Political Agreement (GPA) was signed in September 2008 and accordingly a coalition government constituting MDC (now divided into two separate parties) and ZANU-PF was forged in February 2009. Deep instability in the political and macro-economic environment had clearly existed before this, and some normalisation occurred during the coalition government that ended in 2013. On-the-ground confrontations between ordinary members of the contending political parties declined, but major political struggles existed between the parties within the GNU, such as contestations between the branches of the state bureaucracy (Moyo and Yeros 2011).

Under the GNU, the national economy grew by 5.8% in 2009, 8.1% in 2010 and 9.3% in 2011. Inflation, which had reached astronomical levels after the year 2000 (500 billion percent in September 2008), came under reasonable control; and agricultural production to some extent recuperated after the significant downfall arising from fast track land reform (Gasana *et al.* 2011, Sachikonye 2011). The adoption of a multi-currency regime (involving the dollarisation of the national currency) in early 2009 (Manjengwa *et al.* 2012) was important in this regard. The surrender of monetary policy by ZANU-PF under the GNU (as the finance ministry was controlled by the MDC), decontrol of agricultural markets, privatisation of state enterprises, loosening of the capital account and trade liberalisation were regarded as progressive moves under the GNU. However, normalisation was also marked by failures on the part of the MDC because of its inability to confront sanctions, land reform and the mining sector controlled by ZANU-PF. Overall, the MDC parties were the subservient partners in the GNU and ZANU-PF used successfully its experience of state capture to further its power base (Bratton 2016, Mwonzora 2016) and to inhibit electoral, judicial and security reforms. The GNU ended after the election on 31 July 2013 that involved an overwhelming defeat of MDC by ZANU-PF in the harmonised presidential and parliamentary/senatorial elections. Since then, ZANU-PF has returned to its status as the dominant party, though subject to internal fissures and breakaways.

Theorising Zimbabwe

In the context of this historical narrative, we note briefly the acrimonious debate which emerged within Zimbabwean studies about the historical origins, character and trajectory of the multiple crises since 2000. This debate has tended to subside in recent years – since the late 2000s – but it remains significant in that the two sides of the debate captured the tension-riddled and contradictory processes embedded in the crisis. Though often articulated as two alternative understandings, if considered in combination, the two renderings of the crisis facilitate an analysis of the overall political economy of crisis in Zimbabwe. In many ways, this analysis enables an examination of developments up until the time period of the livelihood case studies covered in this book.

The debate involves fundamentally different conceptions of the Zimbabwean crisis. On the one hand, there is a radical nationalist analytical discourse that speaks of a land crisis and that stresses national sovereignty and re-distributive policies. In terms of this discourse, Raftopoulos (2005) says that land "became the sole central signifier of national redress, constructed through a series of discursive exclusions" (Raftopoulos 2005:9–10). This process of exclusion entails sidelining and undercutting sub-national counter-narratives found in what the state would label as the more 'marginal' spaces of Zimbabwean society, including rural Matabeleland and the urban trade union movement (Raftopoulos 2001). On the other hand, there is a liberal democratic analytical discourse that refers to a governance crisis and that emphasises human rights and political democratisation (Hammar and Raftopoulos 2003, Sachikonye 2002), and that involves a "managerial, modernising nationalism" (Rutherford 2002:1).

The first discourse focuses on the external (imperialist) determinants of the crisis and the latter on its internal (nation-state) determinants (Freeman 2005). However, both discourses seem to have roots in the notion of the National Democratic Revolution, with the former prioritising the 'national' (in struggling against imperialism) and the latter the 'democratic' (in struggling against an authoritarian state) (Moore 2004). For example, Mandaza (with historical links to the ruling party) says that during the late 1990s post-nationalist forces in alliance with foreign elements were engaged in a subterranean "social crisis strategy" that sought to make Zimbabwe ungovernable, and that the (supposedly radical) intellectual representatives of these forces sought to prioritise issues of governance and democracy "at the expense of addressing the National Question" (The 'Scrutator' in *The Zimbabwe Mirror*, 28 April to 4 May 2000). Thus, the civic nationalism propagated by these theorists (such as Raftopoulos) is portrayed as 'progressive' in urban civil groups warring against the state, and this entails seeking to undermine economic (re-distributive) nationalism rightly articulated (according to Mandaza) by a beleaguered nation-state under the onslaught of imperialism in the capitalist periphery.

Clearly, this theoretical debate captures the contradictory tendencies embedded in post-2000 restructuring in Zimbabwe, including both an economic nationalism (such as fast track land reform and, more broadly, the state's indigenisation policies) and an authoritarian nationalism (an inclusive nationalism as well which defines opposition groups as falling outside the Zimbabwean nation). These tendencies, representing the underlying structures and processes of the Zimbabwean political economy, continue to work themselves out in complex, fluid and multiple ways within specific historically- and spatially-delimited sites such as those forming the basis of the case studies in the chapters that follow. In the end, the very character of the Zimbabwean nation and state, as unfinished products, remain highly contested as Zimbabweans continue to search for a future unbounded from the colonial past (Ndlovu-Gatsheni 2015).

Livelihoods studies in Zimbabwe

Research on livelihoods in Zimbabwe highlights the variegated nature of livelihoods in both urban and rural spaces. Bird and Shepherd (2003) for example
show how location influences and affects the character of livelihood options,
such that "persistent poverty was strongly associated with the structural poverty
of Zimbabwe's semi-arid communal areas" while, at the same time, "relative
urban proximity assisted income diversification and improvement" for some
communal communities (Bird and Shepherd 2003:591). While agriculture
remains the most important livelihood activity in communal areas (Moyo and
Binswanger 2011), including crop farming and livestock, there have been notice-
able shifts in livelihood strategies due to droughts and difficult macro-economic
conditions. Rural communities have over the years adopted off-farm activities
such as selling firewood, poaching and cross-border trading to South Africa
(Chiweshe 2012, Scoones *et al.* 1996). Other studies show how rural livelihoods
are also heavily dependent upon natural resources (SAFIRE 2004, Shackleton
et al. 2000). These include the use of baobab, marula, palm and other forestry
products. Gold panning is also evident along with digging for diamonds, for
instance, in the Chiadzwa area. In urban spaces, livelihoods are also very diverse
with studies dating back to the 1990s (Gibbon 1995) focusing on the increasing
significance of informal economic activities notably trading.

Zimbabwean livelihoods studies can be categorised into five thematic areas.
First, there are theoretical and conceptual studies but these are quite limited in
number. In the context of environmental and agrarian issues, Scoones (2015) for
example explores the role of social institutions and the politics of identity in
highlighting the dynamic complexities that affect and influence livelihoods in
Zimbabwe. Another work is a collection edited by Mamukwa, Lessem and Schieffer (2014) that utilises Schieffer and Lessem's Integral Worlds Model, such
that livelihoods are seen as emerging from everyday micro-practices of communities using local resources to develop. Second, there are political economy
studies that tend to focus on macro-economic challenges facing livelihoods
(Murisa and Chikweche 2015). For instance, Chirisa *et al.* (2016) analyse the
political economy of peri-urban areas in Zimbabwe. Their focus on actual livelihood patterns is however clouded because of the concentrated focus on challenges facing urban dwellers such as land tenure insecurity, poor infrastructure
and services, land use conflicts, stringent planning law and land use planning
regulations. Post-2000 studies using (loosely) a political economy perspective
have tended to focus on farms redistributed under the fast track programme, with
many studies existing in relation to specifically A1 farmers (Chiweshe 2012,
Mutopo 2014). Third, there are studies highlighting agency and which emphasise
survivalist strategies employed by Zimbabweans to make ends meet. Such
studies focus on multiple strategies involving livelihood diversification such as
migration, which has been adopted by people of all ages and classes to earn a
living (Gaidzanwa 1999, Polzer 2008). Studies have shown that households with
migrants are better off than those who do not have migrants (Anich *et al.* 2014,

Crush and Tevera 2010). Bracking and Sachikonye (2006) also highlight the importance of informal networks of trust as mechanisms to channel remittances back to Zimbabwe.

A fourth theme is that of gender, with some studies speaking to how livelihoods intersect with women's life-worlds in Zimbabwe and the ways in which women are carving out livelihood spaces. For example, Mutopo (2014) shows how women's livelihoods intersect with negotiations and bargaining within the family, and the way interventions by traditional authorities facilitate access to land specifically in Mwenezi District. Mudimu (1997) demonstrates women's domination of urban agriculture in Harare, and Chiweshe and Muzanago (2016) examine how women in informal settlements in Harare become involved in sack potato production as a form of urban agriculture with varied success. As well, Goebel (2007) traces the evolution of changing livelihoods amongst smallholder farmers in Wedza, noting how marriage, sexuality and culture are important determinants of women's livelihood spaces. Fifth, there is scholarly work which adopts a narrative method by articulating the voices of ordinary Zimbabweans (especially within the post-2000 era) and their everyday concerns in pursuing livelihoods. Orner and Holmes (2011) thus recount the experiences of Zimbabweans, including politically-charged experiences, and the disruption of their livelihoods through loss of land, home and property arising from political violence, including stories of detention, torture and rape. Additionally, Chiweshe (2015) provides narratives of women in Harare outlining their experiences with livelihoods and space in Harare, including involvement in sex work, noting how livelihood options are framed culturally and spiritually by those involved. The women's attempts to occupy spaces for livelihoods are simultaneously a quest for identity and belonging.

Conclusion and policy insights

The following chapters in this volume are thematically arranged according to space and place: urban spaces, and then communal areas, informal settlements and fast track farms in rural areas. The first four chapters (chapters 2, 3, 4 and 5) speak to the urban crisis in Zimbabwe and the ways in which different groups of individuals have sought to pursue livelihoods in the face of everyday challenges. Chapter 2, Takunda Chirau, examines the livelihood strategies of urban women, particularly women traders at the Magaba market in central Harare. In detailing the vulnerability context of the Magaba traders and the institutional interventions of the state which regularly complicate the lives of the women traders, the chapter identifies their diverse livelihood activities as well as the assets they deploy in constructing urban livelihoods. Their livelihood activities undoubtedly complement any earnings from formal employment by male household members. But these women face a number of daily challenges in their trading activities (such as police harassment, intense competition and inflationary pressures), which they seek to counteract by way of often ingenious coping mechanisms.

In Chapter 3, Tafadzwa Chevo examines the construction of livelihood strategies in Budiriro, a high-density area in Harare. In doing so, he considers the ways in which urban livelihood activities emerge as incremental outcomes as embedded in a historical repertoire of possibilities. In Budiriro, households engage and mobilise different types of resources and capabilities in making a living. Households obtain income from employment locally or even from other countries, directly or indirectly, within both the formal and informal sectors of the economy, including the manufacturing of goods and offering services for sale. At the same time, wider social, cultural and political structures combined with factors such as household characteristics, values, norms and beliefs; influence household resources and the choice of livelihood activities.

For Chapter 4, Wadzanai Takawira and Kirk Helliker look at sex work as a livelihood strategy amongst women in the border town of Beitbridge along the South African border. In understanding sex work as a livelihood activity in Beitbridge, the chapter provides key insights into the daily lives of sex workers including the context of vulnerability in which they live and work as well as the challenges they face constantly. Diverse and interrelated themes are covered, including sex worker income and expenditure, the motivations underpinning entry into sex work, the home origins of sex workers and their ongoing linkages with their areas of sometimes rural origin, occupational hazards such as client violence and health risks, stigma and discrimination of sex workers, and sex worker solidarity.

In the case of Chapter 5, Manase Chiweshe considers the breadth and depth of migration as a form of economic survival in post-2000 Zimbabwe. Instead of focusing on internal migration, as Chapter 4 does, this chapter examines migration beyond the borders of Zimbabwe. The chapter thus explores various types of migration, notably cyclic, short-, medium- and long-term migration mainly to South Africa, Botswana, Great Britain, the United States of America, Canada, Namibia and Australia. Undoubtedly, international migration through legal and illegal means has become an important part of the Zimbabwean socio-economic fabric, but the characteristics of outward migration vary considerably depending upon the intended destination and the ongoing relationships, which may exist with households back in Zimbabwe. Because of this, the complexities of migration patterns are unravelled in this chapter.

Chapters 6 to 11 analyse livelihoods in communal areas based on a range of themes, with the first three considering the question of participatory development and livelihoods. For Chapter 6, Innocent Mahiya analyses agricultural production systems of small-scale farmers in Hwedza communal areas in the context of innovation platforms introduced by non-governmental organisations. An agricultural innovation platform involves bringing on board a diverse range of actors which function together to generate agricultural knowledge and practices suitable to the needs of a particular small-scale farming community, with the small-scale farmers expected to be key actors in the platform. This chapter critically analyses the platforms in Hwedza with reference to the multi-faceted social relationships embodied in the innovation platform process. The platforms in Hwedza challenge top-down approaches to agricultural interventions by unlocking the possibilities for inclusion of farmers, but they also involve processes marked by exclusions and conflicts that may undermine the platforms.

Kayla Knight Waghorn, in Chapter 7, seeks to understand the participatory methods, accountability and effectiveness of World Vision in Umzingwane District, a deep rural area in southern Matabeleland. The chapter shows that, in manoeuvring through a complex set of donor and state pressures, World Vision Zimbabwe tries to build local government capacity in order to maintain the longevity and measureable outputs of its projects. In doing so, it redefines unintentionally the concept of participation in pursuing practical approaches to 'getting things done'. The chapter concludes that this compromises the deep participatory forms that may heighten the legitimacy of World Vision's role amongst communities, in order for it to maintain its own organisational sustainability in Zimbabwe. Hence, like Chapter 7, a critical analysis is offered of the participatory methodologies of non-governmental organisations.

In Chapter 8, Rachel Gondo provides a critical analysis of community participation at the primary level of the health system in Goromonzi District. The government's primary health care approach frames community participation as central to the design and implementation of responsive health systems. This chapter analyses the existing mechanisms for community participation in the health system in Zimbabwe and brings out multiple perspectives on the underlying contradictions, tensions and processes at play between policy and practice. A case study of Mwanza ward in Goromonzi District is used to illustrate how rural communities have organised themselves to occupy platforms and spaces within and outside of national health policy parameters in order to be responsible and take ownership for their own health in line with what is expected by the primary care approach. How community participation takes place in the health system in Zimbabwe though is influenced by a number of factors, including power differentials.

The next three chapters are more directly concerned with small-scale farmers and the challenges they face under diverse circumstances, but particularly when land and water are scarce. Chapter 9, by Sandra Bhatasara, thus considers narratives and ambivalences around climate variability and livelihoods in a communal area in Mutoko District. The concern is to comprehend how farmers problematise circumstances arising from climatic changes. This is imperative because there exists a lucid discrepancy between the conclusions of macro-assessments of climate change and the experiences of local societies. People in local contexts possess complex cultural ways of reading the climate and their concerns are highly variegated. The chapter not only exposes the apparent and persistent prejudices in climate change knowledge production but more importantly contributes data derived empirically about the meanings of climatic changes occurring in rural spaces in the country.

With regard to Chapter 10, Felix Tombindo offers an analysis of livelihoods vulnerability among Tonga riverbed farmers in Negande, NyamiNyami District in the 'forgotten' northwestern part of the country. The chapter examines a unique seasonal agricultural strategy which involves cultivating the riverbed of the local Mawena River during winter, which is a coping strategy against recurrent droughts; and hence, like Chapter 9, it examines livelihoods in the context of climate. The genesis of the farming strategy is rooted in the semi-arid agroecological conditions that characterise the Zambezi Valley in general and NyamiNyami district in particular. While riverbed farmers are concerned about the sustainability of Mawena River and engage in some measures to prevent uncontrolled siltation, no common understanding exists between these farmers and the local government in terms of the legitimacy of riverbed farming.

In Chapter 11, Jonathan Mafukidze examines differing perspectives on land occupations and livelihoods at Mushandike smallholder irrigation scheme in Masvingo District. From 1999, black producers at the scheme experienced an unprecedented invasion of their land by thousands of land-seekers. The landseekers occupied grazing land across the entire irrigation scheme, built homes, opened up crop fields and grazed their animals at will. This entry altered the social space, imposed new relations and provoked a delicate negotiated coexistence between irrigators and occupiers. This chapter examines the challenges experienced and the understanding of issues by local people as well as by politicians. Politics, power, greed, maladministration, corruption, land hunger, and lack of education dominate as explanations of the causes of invasions and their deferred resolution. To this day, livelihoods continue to deteriorate due to acute land shortage.

The rest of the chapters look at informal rural settlements and fast track farms (chapters 12 to 14). In Chapter 12, Loveness Makonese examines the role of kinship and social capital in providing care and support for the HIV infected and AIDS affected in Chivanhu informal settlement in Masvingo Province. The chapter focuses on how HIV and AIDS affected people negotiate and mobilise resources for dealing with the health impacts of their condition. HIV and AIDS affect all facets of people's livelihoods, including through chronic illness, death and the subsequent care of orphans. Not all households and individuals are affected by the loss of livelihood security and not all HIV and AIDS affected households dissolve or discontinue. Some households survive and continue, and are able for instance to maintain key livelihood assets. But the challenge in most HIV and AIDS studies has been to show which households dissolve and which households continue, and to offer a full account of the processes leading to dissolution or continuity. Through a longitudinal study, this chapter is able to address this challenge.

Takunda Chabata, in Chapter 13, analyses the relationship between insecure land tenure, natural resource use and community-led development in Sovelele resettlement area on an A1 fast track farm. The chapter demonstrates that insecure land tenure does not incentivise A1 settlers to conserve the environment and to invest in the resettlement area. Though having small agricultural plots of their own, the farmers continue to be hesitant in investing in land over which they feel they do not have complete control, as they only have rights of possession to their plots. Further, the character of the settlement, involving villagisation or the presence of homesteads in a centralised area, has tended to lead to an open access system in terms of natural resources, and this has exposed biodiversity to a depletion risk. It has also at times led to tensions between different A1 households.

Finally, in Chapter 14, Loveness Chakona and Manase Chiweshe examine the position of women on an A1 fast track farm in Goromonzi District. Colonial and post-colonial Zimbabwe had instigated, propagated and reproduced land ownership, control and access along a distinctively patriarchal basis which left women either totally excluded or incorporated in an oppressive manner. Although a burgeoning number of studies have been undertaken on fast track, few have had a distinctively gender focus. In examining the A1 farm, the chapter identifies, examines and assesses the effect of fast track on patriarchal relations and the socio-economic livelihoods of rural women. It shows the ongoing patriarchal burdens carried by women but also some of the livelihood activities pursued by them in seeking to acquire some form of autonomy from their husbands. In doing so, the chapter also provides a comparative analysis of the lives and livelihoods of women in a nearby communal area.

References

Anich, R., Crush, J., Melde, S. and Ouchu, D. 2014. *A New Perspective on Human Mobility in the South*. London: Springer.

Archer, M. 1995. *Realist Social Theory: the Morphogenetic Approach*. Cambridge: Cambridge University Press.

Archer, M. 2003. *Structure, Agency and the Internal Conversation*. Cambridge: Cambridge University Press.

Ashley, C. and Carney, D. 1999. *Sustainable Livelihoods: Lessons from Early Experience*. London: DFID.

Banks, N. 2015. Livelihoods Limitations: The Political Economy of Urban Poverty in Dhaka, Bangladesh. *Development and Change* 47 (2): 266–292.

Batterbury, S.P.J. 2008. *Sustainable Livelihoods: Still Being Sought, Ten Years On, African Environments Programme*. Oxford University Centre for the Environment (OUCE).

Bhatasara, S. 2015. Understanding Corruption in Social Service Delivery in Zimbabwe: Case Studies from the Local Government Sector. In Mungai N. Lenneiye (ed.) *Political Economy of Corruption and the Battle for Accountability in Zimbabwe 2000–2015*, (pp. 55–68). Harare: Transparency International Zimbabwe, Chapter 4.

Bebbington, A. 1999. Capitals and Capabilities: A Framework for Analysing Peasant Viability, Rural Livelihoods and Poverty. *World Development* 27 (12): 2021–2044.

Bebbington, A. and Batterbury, S. 2001. Transnational livelihoods and landscapes: political ecologies of globalisation. *Ecumene* 8 (4): 369–464.

Bebbington, A., Hickey, S. and Mitlin, D. 2007. *Can NGOs Make a Difference? The Challenge of Development Alternatives*. Chicago: University of Chicago Press.

Bhaskar, R. 1978. *A Realist Theory of Science*. London: Routledge.

Bird, K. and Shepherd, A. 2003. Livelihoods and Chronic Poverty in Semi-Arid Zimbabwe. *World Development* 31 (3): 591–610.

Biti, T. 2009. *The 2009 Mid-Year Fiscal Policy Review Statement: STERP in Motion*. Presented to the Parliament of Zimbabwe by the Honourable Biti (Minister of Finance). Harare: Government of Zimbabwe, 16 July 2009.

Bourdieu, P. 1977. *Outline of a Theory of Practice*. Cambridge: Cambridge University Press.

Bourdieu, P. 1990. *In Other Words: Essays towards a Reflexive Sociology*. Stanford: Stanford University Press.

Bracking, S. and Sachikonye, L. 2006. *Remittances, Poverty Reduction and the Informalisation of the Household Well-being in Zimbabwe*, Working Paper, No 45, Global Poverty Research Group, Oxford.

Bratton, M. 2016. *Power Politics in Zimbabwe*. Pietermaritzburg: University of KwaZulu-Natal Press.

Brown, D., Chanakira, R., Chatiza, K., Dhliwayo, M., Dodman, D., Masiiwa, M., Muchadenyika, D., Mugabe, P. and Zvigadza, S. 2012. Climate Change Impacts, Vulnerability and Adaptation in Zimbabwe. *International Institute for Environment and Development (IIED) Climate Change Working Paper 3*.

Carney, D. (ed.) 1998. *Sustainable Rural Livelihoods: What Contribution Can we Make?* Nottingham: Russell Press Ltd., for Department for International Development.

Carney, D. 2002. *Sustainable Livelihoods Approaches: Progress and Possibilities for Change*. London: DFID.

Chagutah, T. 2010. *Climate Change Vulnerability and Preparedness in Southern Africa: Zimbabwe Country Report*. Cape Town: Heinrich Boell Stiftung.

Chambers, R. and Conway, G. 1992. *Sustainable Rural Livelihoods: Practical Concepts for the 21st Century*. IDS Discussion Paper 296. Brighton: Institute of Development Studies.

Chene, M. 2015. *Zimbabwe: Overview of Corruption in the Health and Education Sectors and in Local Governments*, Transparency International.

Chikozho, C. 2010. Applied Social Research and Action Priorities for Adaptation to Climate Change and Rainfall Variability in the Rain-fed Agricultural Sector of Zimbabwe. *Physics and Chemistry of the Earth* 35: 780–790.

Chirisa, I., Mazhindu, E. and Bandauko, E. 2016. *Peri-Urban Developments and Processes in Africa with Special Reference to Zimbabwe*. London: Springer Briefs in Geography.

Chitambara, P. 2015. Evidence on the Economic Costs of Corruption in Zimbabwe. In Mungai N. Lenneiye (ed.) *Political Economy of Corruption and the Battle for Accountability in Zimbabwe 2000–2015*, (pp. 17–34), Harare: Transparency International Zimbabwe.

Chiweshe, M.K. 2012. *Farm Level Institutions in Emergent Communities in Post Fast Track Zimbabwe: Case of Mazowe District*. Unpublished PhD thesis, Rhodes University.

Chiweshe, M.K. 2015. Negotiating and Creating Urban Spaces in Everyday Practices: Experiences of Women in Harare, Zimbabwe. In A. Allen, A. Lampis and M. Swilling (eds), *Untamed Urbanisms*, (pp. 219–231). London: Routledge.

Chiweshe, M.K. and Muzanago, K. 2016. Livelihoods in a Sack: Gendered Dimensions of Sack Potato Farming Among Poor Households in Urban Zimbabwe. In A. Fletcher and W. Kubik (eds), *Women in Agriculture Worldwide: Key Issues and Practical Approaches*, (pp. 91–102). London: Routledge.

Cowen, M. and Shenton, R. 1998. Agrarian Doctrines of Development: Part 1. *Journal of Peasant Studies* 25 (2): 49–76.

Crush, J. and Tevera, D. 2010. Exiting Zimbabwe. In J. Crush and D. Tevera (eds), *Zimbabwe's Exodus, Crisis, Migration and Survival*, Southern African Migration Programme, Cape Town.

de Haan, L. and Zoomers, A. 2003. Development Geography at the Crossroads of Livelihood and Globalisation. *Tijdschrift voor Economische en Sociale Geografie* (94): 350–362.

Ellis, F. 1998. Survey Article: Household Strategies and Rural Livelihood Diversification. *Journal of Development Studies* 35 (1): 1–38.

Fairbairn, M., Fox, J., Ryan Isakson, S., Levien, M., Peluso, N., Razavi, S., Scoones, I. and Sivaramakrishnan, K. 2014. Introduction: New Directions in Agrarian Political Economy. *The Journal of Peasant Studies* 41 (5): 653–666.

Freeman, L. 2005. Contradictory Constructions of the Crisis in Zimbabwe. *Historia Journal of the South African Historical Association* 50 (2): 287–310.

Fuchs, C. 2017. Critical Social Theory and Sustainable Development: The Role of Class, Capitalism and Domination in a Dialectical Analysis of Un/sustainability. *Sustainable Development*, published online 10.1002/sd.1673.

Gaidzanwa, R. 1999. *Voting with their Feet: Migrant Zimbabwean Nurses and Doctors in the Era of Structural Adjustment*. Uppsala: Nordiska Afrikainstitutet.

Gasana, J.K., Bell, L., Kajume, J., Mupindu, S. and Smith-Jon, M. 2011. *Evaluation of FAO Cooperation in Zimbabwe (2006–2010)*. Rome: The Office of Evaluation, Food, and Agriculture Organisation.

Government of Zimbabwe. 2010. *Medium Term Plan, January 2010–December 2015*. Harare: Government of Zimbabwe, Ministry of Economic Planning and Investment Promotion.

Gibbon, P. 1995. *Structural Adjustment and the Working Poor in Zimbabwe*. Uppsala: Nordic African Institute.

Goebel, A. 2007. We Are Working for Nothing: Livelihoods and Gender Relations in Rural Zimbabwe, 2000–06. *Canadian Journal of African Studies* 41 (2): 226–257.

Gwimbi, P. 2009. Cotton Farmers' Vulnerability to Climate Change in Gokwe District (Zimbabwe): Impact and Influencing Factors. *JÀMBÁ Journal of Disaster Risk Studies* 2 (2): 81–92.

Hammar, A. and Raftopoulos, B. 2003. Introduction. In A. Hammar, B. Raftopoulos and S. Jensen (eds), *Zimbabwe's Unfinished Business: Rethinking Land, State and Nation in the Context of Crisis*. Harare: Weaver Press.

Harriss, J. 1997. Policy Arena: 'Missing Link' or Analytically Missing? The Concept of Social Capital. *Journal of International Development* 9 (7): 919–971.

Kanyenze, G., Kondo, T., Chitambara, P. and Martens, J. 2011. *Beyond the Enclave: Towards Pro-poor and Inclusive Development Strategy for Zimbabwe*. Harare: Weaver Press.

Laakso, L. 2003. Research Debates in Zimbabwe: From Analysis to Practice. In Staffan, D and Laakso, L. *Twenty Years of Independence in Zimbabwe: From Liberation to Authoritarianism*. Basingstoke, (pp. 1–14). New York: Palgrave MacMillan.

Leach, M., Mearns, R. and Scoones, I. 1999. Environmental Entitlements: Dynamics and Institutions in Community-based Natural Resource Management. *World Development* 27 (2): 225–247.

Levine, S. 2014. *How to Study Livelihoods: Bringing a Sustainable Livelihoods Framework to Life*, Secure Livelihoods Research Consortium, Working Paper 22.

Long, N. 1984. *Family and Work in Rural Societies*. London: Tavistock Publications.

Lyon, C. and Parkins, J. 2013. Toward a Social Theory of Resilience: Social Systems, Cultural Systems, and Collective Action in Transitioning Forest-based Communities. *Rural Sociology* 78 (4): 528–549.

Mandaza, I. 2016. *The Political Economy of the State: The Rise and Fall of the Securocrat State*. Harare: SAPES.

Manjengwa, J.M., Karsiye, I. and Matema, C. 2012. *Understanding Poverty in Zimbabwe: A Sample of 16 Districts.* Paper Prepared for Presentation at the Centre for the Study of Africa Economies Conference 2012, Oxford, United Kingdom, 18–20 March 2012.

Mamukwa, E., Lessem, R. and Schieffer, A. 2014. *Integral green Zimbabwe: An African Phoenix Rising.* Surrey: Gower Publishing Limited.

Mawere, M. 2011. *Moral Degeneration in Contemporary Zimbabwean Business Practices.* Bamenda: Langaa.

Moore, D. 2004. Marxism and Marxist Intellectuals in Schizophrenic Zimbabwe: How Many Rights for Zimbabwe's Left? A Comment. *Historical Materialism* 12 (4): 405–425.

Morse, S. and McNamara, N. 2013. *Sustainable Livelihood Approach: A Critique of Theory and Practice.* New York: Springer.

Moyo, S. 2014. *Corruption in Zimbabwe: An Examination of the Roles of the State and Civil Society in Combating Corruption.* Lancashire: University of Central Lancashire.

Moyo, S. and Binswanger, H. 2011. *Agricultural growth trends.* Draft paper commissioned by and prepared for the World Bank. Harare: World Bank.

Moyo, S. and Yeros, P. 2011. Introduction. In S. Moyo and P. Yeros (eds), *Reclaiming the Nation: The Return of the National Question in Africa, Asia and Latin America.* London: Pluto Press.

Mukherjee, S. 2002. Blame the Rulers not the Rain: Democracy and Food Security in Zambia and Zimbabwe. *South African Institute of International Affairs (SAIIA) Reports, Report 32.*

Muzondidya, J. 2009. From Buoyancy to Crisis. In B. Raftopoulos and A. Mlambo. *Becoming Zimbabwe: A History from Pre-colonial Period to 2008,* (pp. 167–200). Harare: Weaver Press.

Mudimu, G. 1997. Urban Agricultural Activities and Women's Strategies in Sustaining Family Livelihoods in Harare, Zimbabwe. *Singapore Journal of Tropical Geography* 17 (2): 179–194.

Murisa, T. and Chikweche, T. 2015. *Beyond the Crises: Zimbabwe's Prospects for Transformation.* Harare: Weaver Press.

Mutopo, P. 2014. *Women, Mobility and Rural Livelihoods in Zimbabwe: Experiences of Fast Track Land Reform.* Leiden: Brill and African Studies Centre.

Mwonzora, G. 2016. *A Critical Analysis of the Role of the Movement for Democratic Change (MDC) in the Democratisation Process in Zimbabwe from 2000 to 2016.* PhD Thesis, Department of Sociology, Rhodes University, Grahamstown.

Ndlovu-Gatsheni, S. 2011. *The Construction and Decline of Chimurenga Monologue in Zimbabwe: A Study in Resilience of Ideology and Limits of Alternatives.* Pretoria, University of South Africa; Department of Development Studies.

Ndlovu-Gatsheni, S. (ed.). 2015. *Mugabeism?: History, Politics, and Power in Zimbabwe.* New York: Palgrave-Macmillan.

Nyamwanza, A.M. 2012. *Resiliency and Livelihoods Inquiry in Dynamic Vulnerability Contexts: Insights from Northern Zimbabwe.* Unpublished Thesis. University of Manchester.

Nyathi, P.T. 2004. Re-integration of Ex-combatants into Zimbabwean Society: A Lost Opportunity. In B. Raftopoulous, and T. Savage (eds), *Zimbabwe Injustice and Political Reconciliation,* (pp. 63–78). Cape Town: Institute for Justice and Reconciliation.

Nyazema, N.Z. 2010. The Zimbabwe Crisis and the Provision of Social Services: Health and Education. *Journal of Developing Societies* 26 (2): 233–261.

Orner, P. and Holmes, A. 2011. *Hope Deferred: Narratives of Zimbabwean Lives.* San Francisco: McSweeney.

Parliament of Zimbabwe. 2010. *Parliamentary Portfolio Committee Report on Health Delivery in Zimbabwe.* Harare: Parliament of Zimbabwe.

Polzer, Tara. 2008. *South African Government and Civil Society Responses to Zimbabwean Migration.* Southern African Migration Project (SAMP) Policy Brief No. 22. /brief22.pdf

Prowse, M. 2010. Integrating Reflexivity into Livelihoods Research. *Progress in Development Studies* 10 (3): 211–231.

Raftopoulos, B. 2001. The Labour Movement and the Emergence of Opposition Politics in Zimbabwe. Striking Back. In B. Raftopoulos and L. Sachikonye. *The Labour Movement and the Post-Colonial State in Zimbabwe 1980–2000*, (pp. 1–24). Harare: Weaver Press.

Raftopoulos, B. 2005. The Zimbabwean Crisis and the Challenges for the Left. Public Lecture Delivered at the University of Kwa-Zulu Natal. 23 June 2005.

Rutherford, B. 2002. Zimbabwe: The Politics of Land and the Political Landscape. *Green Left Weekly*, 487. www.greenleft.org.au

Sachikonye, L. 2002. Whither Zimbabwe? Crisis and Democratisation. *Review of African Political Economy* 29 (91): 13–20.

Sachikonye, L. 2015. Corruption and the Political Landscape in Zimbabwe. In Mungai N. Lenneiye (ed.), *Political Economy of Corruption and the Battle for Accountability in Zimbabwe 2000–2015*, (pp. 35–53). Harare: Transparency International Zimbabwe.

Sachikonye, L. 2011. *When a State Turns on its Citizens: 60 years of Institutionalized Violence in Zimbabwe.* Harare: Weaver Press.

SAFIRE. 2004. *Annual Report 2003.* Harare: SAFIRE.

Sakdapolrak, P. 2014. Livelihoods as Ocial Practices: Re-energising Livelihoods Research with Bourdieu's Theory of Practice. *Geographica Helvetica* 69: 19–28.

Scoones, I. 1998. *Sustainable Rural Livelihoods: A Framework for Analysis.* IDS Working Paper. Brighton: Institute of Development Studies.

Scoones, I. 2009. Livelihoods Perspectives and Rural Development. *Journal of Peasant Studies* 36 (1): 171–196.

Scoones, I. 2015. *Sustainable Livelihoods and Rural Development.* Rugby: Practical Action Publishing.

Scoones, I. and Wolmer, W. 2002. *Pathways of Change in Africa: Crops, Livestock and Livelihoods in Mali, Ethiopia and Zimbabwe.* Oxford: James Currey.

Scoones, I., Chibudu, C., Chikura, S., Jeranyama, P., Machanja, W., Mavedzenge, B., Mombeshora, B., Mudhara, M., Mudziwo, C., Murimbarimba, F., and Zirereza, B. 1996. *Hazards and Opportunities. Farming Livelihoods in Dryland Africa: Lessons from Zimbabwe.* London: Zed Books.

Sen, A. 1981. *Poverty and Famines. An Essay on Entitlement and Deprivation.* Oxford: Oxford University Press.

Serrat, O. 2008. *The Sustainable Livelihoods Approach.* Washington, DC: Asian Development Bank.

Shackleton, S., Shackleton, C. and Cousins, B. 2000. Re-valuing the Communal Lands of Southern Africa: New Understanding of Rural Livelihoods. *Natural Resource Perspectives*, No. 62 (November). London: ODI.

Shana, G. 2006. *The State of Corruption in Zimbabwe*, Mass Public Opinion Institute Seminar.

Solesbury, W. 2003. *Sustainable Livelihoods: A Case Study of the Evolution of DFID Policy.* London: ODI Working Paper 217.

Southall, R. 2011. Too Soon to Tell? Land Reform in Zimbabwe. *Africa Spectrum* 46 (3): 83–97.

Speranza, C., Wiesmann, U. and Rist, S. 2014. An Indicator Framework for Assessing Livelihood Resilience in the Context of Social-ecological Dynamics. *Global Environmental Change* 28: 109–119.

Sutcliffe, J. 2012. "Shinga Mushandi Shinga! Qina Msebenzi Qina!" (Workers Be Resolute! Fight On!): The Labour Movement in Zimbabwe. *Journal of International Studies* 8: 1–42.

Tevera, D. 2008. Perspective on the Brain Drain. *Migration from Zimbabwe: Numbers, Needs and Policy Options, 19–22.* Centre for Development and Enterprise.

Thieme, S. 2008. Sustaining Livelihoods in Multi-local Settings: Possible Theoretical Linkages Between Transnational Migration and Livelihood Studies. *Mobilities* 3 (1): 51–71.

Vambe, M.T. 2008. *Hidden Dimensions of Operation Murambatsvina.* Harare: Weaver Press.

van Dijk, T. 2011. Livelihoods, Capitals and Livelihood Trajectories: A More Sociological Conceptualisation. *Progress in Development Studies* 11 (2): 101–117.

WCED, 1987, *Our Common Future. The Report of the World Commission on Environment and Development.* Oxford, Oxford University Press.

Wilshusen, P.R. 2012. Capitalizing Conservation/Development: Misrecognition and the Erasure of Power. In B. Büscher, Fletcher, R. and W. Dressler (eds), *Questioning the Market Panacea in Environmental Policy and Conservation.* Tuscon: University of Arizona Press.

White, S. and Ellison, M. 2006. Wellbeing, Livelihoods and Resources in Social Practice. In I. Gough and J.A. McGregor (eds), *Wellbeing in Developing Countries: From Theory to Research,* (pp. 157–175). Gough Cambridge: Cambridge University Press.

Wood, G. 2003. Staying Secure, Staying Poor: The "Faustian Bargain". *World Development* 31: 455–471.

Zoomers, A. and van Westen, G. 2011. Introduction: Translocal development, development corridors and development chains. *International Development Planning Review* 33: 377–388.

2 Livelihood strategies of urban women

Emerging evidence from Magaba, Harare

Takunda Chirau

Introduction

The notion of livelihoods is predominant in academic literature on Africa, where many of the world's underdeveloped and poorest countries lie and are continuously facing ongoing economic and political crises. In sub-Saharan countries, urban livelihoods are often tenuous with employment and income generation possibilities mainly in the informal sector. Poor black women in many cases dominate the informal sector and they show acts of ingenuity and courage in thorny circumstances in contributing to household income generation. At the same time, they in the main are 'managers' of a significant proportion of urban households. In this sense, they carry a dual responsibility and burden. This chapter explores, examines and analyses the livelihood strategies and challenges of poor urban women in contemporary Zimbabwe in the context of harsh socio-economic and political conditions. The focus is Harare and specifically an area called Magaba that is located in Mbare, a (low-income) high-density area in the capital city of Zimbabwe.

Background to the study area

This section provides a background to the study site, namely Magaba in Mbare, Harare. Mbare is a high-density suburb (or township) in Harare Urban that was established in 1907 as an Urban Native Location located southeast of the city centre. It was built as a dormitory location for domestic servants and industrial workers. Mbare is known to have the country's biggest market (known simply as *musika*) where people from the countryside and nearby farms bring their produce for sale. Magaba is approximately 3.9 kilometres from Harare's central business district. Magaba (meaning 'empty tins') is a geographical area within Mbare. It was unofficially established in the 1950s by a small group of tinsmiths who produced tin cans and other steel products to generate income.

Two informal sector sites of importance developed in the 1960s in Magaba as the surrounding population increased. First, there was the establishment of Mupedzanhamo market. Mupedzanhamo (meaning 'ending all problems') is renowned for selling diverse products such as second-hand clothes, traditional medicine and plumbing materials. With the advent of the Zimbabwean crisis in recent years, it stocked goods that were scarce within the formal market. Second, SiyaSo market was formed, selling steel products including window frames, door frames and tin cans, and engaging in motor repairs. In addition to these two informal sites, Magaba Shopping Centre was opened in 1967 with vendors informally trading in open spaces there. These three sites are not contiguous and together they constitute what is referred to as the Magaba market (in the Magaba area).This chapter covers all these sites. Magaba is one of the areas demolished by Operation Murambatsvina (also known as 'Operation Restore Order') in July 2005. Magaba remains as a heterogeneous hub of petty traders, both men and women.

Research methods

Methodologically, this study was mainly qualitative in nature. However, my research utilised both qualitative and quantitative methods of data collection in order to complement each other and, in the end, to derive 'thick descriptions' of livelihood activities. Three techniques were used to pursue the objectives of this research: a closed-ended survey questionnaire was administered, in-depth interviews with women vendors were conducted and participant observation was pursued. Purposive non-random sampling was employed to identify women participants for survey questionnaires and in-depth interviews. A survey questionnaire, as a quantitative research technique, was administered to 49 women vendors. The central purpose of the survey questionnaire was to provide a broad extensive profile of the Magaba women traders. With respect to qualitative data, in-depth interviews with 24 women at Magaba were conducted. In-depth informal interviews allow for greater flexibility in asking questions; therefore, the researcher is able to investigate issues in greater detail (compared to survey questionnaires). While the survey provides breadth to the data, the interviews provide depth; hence, they complemented each other. The fieldwork was conducted from February to April 2012.

Trading activities and income generation at Magaba

In recent years, vending has emerged in Zimbabwe as 'the employer' of last resort (and increasingly of first resort) in providing livelihoods and income for low-income urban Zimbabweans, especially women. In this context, Magaba women traders engage in a number of activities in a bid to survive and to manage the shocks and stresses of urban life in times of crisis. The nature of these activities is myriad. In the past, women traders in Harare tended to focus their vending activities on fruits and vegetables, whether in the streets, at a bus terminus or elsewhere (MacPherson 1998). However, this study brings to the fore that the majority of wares sold at Magaba are now mainly durable commodities. This change in the nature of trading activities, namely a broadening of the product-base in informal trading, is a reflection of the emergence of a range of parallel markets during the crisis in Zimbabwe. It marks informal vending as an altern-ative commodity-source to formal supermarkets and retail outlets (as the official sources suffered from intermittent commodity shortages). Magaba market occu-pies a very spacious area and is packed with vendors of all kinds. The main types of products found at Magaba include fruits, vegetables, mobile phone credits (juice cards or airtime), cigarettes, cosmetics and fast foods. Because of the heterogeneous character of the items sold at the market, I categorised vending operations into three broad categories: perishables, durables and services.

Dube and Chirisa (2012) categorise vendors in Harare's central business dis-trict as falling into two broad units (white collar vendors and green collar vendors). This study also adopts this categorisation, classifying women selling perishable goods (often vegetables) as green collar vendors and those selling durables and offering services as white collar vendors. Specific traders at Magaba often altered their product or service line (and hence their source of income) in response to supply and demand. It was during the peak of the crisis in Zimbabwe in 2008 – with the seemingly near collapse of the local mainstream manufacturing and retail industries – that women started to hoard durable goods from outside Zimbabwean borders and offer them for sale at Magaba. Because large numbers of Magaba traders engaged in this, competition was very stiff which consequently led to the lowering of profit margins. Thus, women traders regularly engage in more than one activity simultaneously.

Out of the 49 individuals interviewed through a survey questionnaire, results indicate that 8 respondents (16.3%) were selling foodstuffs such as sandwiches, cooked rice and boiled eggs (other than fruits and vegetables). Foodstuffs were seen as important because they attract workers who pass through town on a daily basis. The traders also claimed that foodstuffs entail low investments, quick turnover and constant cash earnings compared to other commodities; this cash met consumption needs (mainly food security in the household) as well as being converted into capital for investing in the next day's vending activity.

A significant 22.5% of traders (11 respondents) reported selling second-hand clothes (commonly known as *mazitye/mabhero*) and this activity has prospered because retail clothing stores are very expensive given the fall in real wages (particularly for residents living in high-density areas such as Mbare). As a result, many urban poor have resorted to buying second-hand clothes, as exem-plified by the numerous flea markets (along main roads and in the high density suburbs in Harare) selling clothes and shoes. The decline of the Zimbabwean clothing industry has also contributed to the rise in the importance of second-hand clothes. Foreign currency trading was another popular trading activity at Magaba (14.3%). This is mainly because a large number of Magaba traders fre-quently travelled across the borders of Zimbabwe (for example, to South Africa) to source different commodities.

Over 10% of respondents (6 respondents or 12.2%) sold 'juice cards' (airtime for cellular phones) or cellular phone lines. This was popular as a vending activ-ity because urban Zimbabweans are highly dependent upon mobile phones as a means of communication. Cell phone lines at one time became very expensive;

between 2005 and 2008, they sold for up to 700 South African rand. They are now abundantly available in telecommunication outlets and sold for less than US$5 (or about 40 South African rand at the time of this fieldwork). Other activities of less significance included selling roasted mealies (or maize cobs) (2%), carrier bags (2%) and books (2%). Mealies are not popular for vendors because of the time consumed in preparing them for sale. Books are a low priority because of the location of Magaba (a short distance from schools).

Magaba women traders tend to be quite ingenious and astute in terms of monitoring market forces (notably supply and demand imbalances), such that they shift between specific trading activities depending on market signals. This is evident in the case of movements away from what are now lower profile vending activities (such as cellular phone lines). Movement between trading activities was also affected by seasonality. Specific goods are only available during particular times of the year (notably perishables) and some goods (such as specific lines of clothing) are more viable as sellable commodities during particular times of the year. In this regard, the women traders are highly sensitive to questions around their cash flow, rate of turnover and profit margins.

Many of the vendors claimed that selling durable goods has high returns compared to selling perishable goods. This was because the sheer amount of profit from durable products is more than the comparable amount for perishables; the amount for the latter is considered as mere petty cash or pocket money. Furthermore, white-collar vendors assert that durables do not lose value or deteriorate, such that they can stock them until the demand is high (especially at the end of the month). One divorced respondent aged 28 reported the following:

> It's different when you are selling profitable goods, I get more dollars when I sell aluminium pots, clothes and shoes … I can get more than US$20 per day compared to selling biscuits for US$1 for two packets … that money is for transport only, you can just sell biscuits at home.

On the other hand, green collar vendors argued that quick cash through selling perishables was viable as compared to durables. The main argument was that the Mbare public, which is generally living in poverty, cannot afford to procure food from supermarkets.

The expenditure level varies considerably between traders. In examining the expenditures, I discovered that 37.5% of the traders used US$100 or less a month to purchase goods for resale; while 62.5% used more than US$100 a month to purchase goods for resale. It is difficult to slot green and white-collar expenditures into these expenditure levels. However, as a general tendency, purchasing of durables for resale by white collars vendors is more expensive than it is for green collar vendors who specialise in perishables.

The profit margin varies considerably between traders. In examining income or earnings generated, I distinguished between low, medium and high-income traders. Overall, 57.1% of traders generate medium to high returns (over US$150 per month) while 42.9% generate low returns (up to $150 per month). It is difficult to slot white and green collar vending and the selling of services into specific income levels; however, as a general tendency (and as noted above), selling perishable goods has lower returns in terms of income and slots into the lowest income category. Selling durables (including second-hand clothes and cosmetics) and services (such as money changers) can be classified as medium to high returns in terms of income. Income earned on a particular day (even earnings derived from sales of durables) is mainly used to meet immediate consumption needs, rather than for building an asset base for future economic prosperity. Given the rising cost of living, the income earned by the vendors per month is not adequate. This is reflected by the following comment from one trader aged 35 who specialised in perishables:

> I will tell you this, vending is just making money for consumption of one day and tomorrow. I have to come and do the same thing [every day] ... normally I get [US] $10–15 ... it's too little but I have no option; where would I get money for water, electricity, school fees and all other things that require cash?

Vendors spend their entire earnings covering basic daily consumption costs within their households; there is nothing to spare. Insofar as the earnings by the woman trader is the main source of household income, or the only source, then the livelihood of the household on a longer-term basis becomes hugely problematic.

The Magaba study indicates that there are clear linkages between the informal and formal sectors of the Zimbabwean economy, including in relation to the source of goods sold through informal vending. The majority (51.1%) of the women petty traders at Magaba sourced products mainly from the formal sector in Zimbabwe. Only 10.6% sourced their products from other informal traders; for instance, those selling human hair (braids) sourced this from a nearby supplier at a wholesale price. Even less, a mere 2.1%, spoke about goods as being self-provided. A considerable number of women (36.2%) reported travelling across the Zimbabwean border to purchase goods in another country and then reselling these goods at Magaba. There were various reasons for sourcing goods from outside Zimbabwe. First of all, there was exorbitant pricing by retail shops and companies in Zimbabwe, which produced the same products sourced outside Zimbabwe. Second, traders sometimes sought to acquire brand name goods, which customers preferred over the many Chinese products, sold in Zimbabwe (these products are locally known as '*zhing zhong*', meaning 'products below standard'). Finally, the manufacturing sector in Zimbabwe had not yet regained its productive capacity such that certain products remain scarce on the local market. South Africa was the main country from which durable goods were sourced, but other countries included Zambia, Mozambique and Botswana.

Goods that were sourced from these countries included new clothes, shoes, electrical gadgets and basic commodities such as sugar, cooking oil and washing powder. Two important and popular markets in Johannesburg were mentioned, namely China City and Dragon City. Buying durable goods in bulk was preferable as it lessened the number of journeys and hence traders saved on transport costs. Bus operators though demanded exorbitant fares between Harare and Johannesburg, to the extent that sometimes the extra-luggage charge was higher than the bus fare for the passenger. These cross-border traders also faced a number of challenges and extra fees, including customs tariff duty and long delays at the border post. Corrupt tendencies by some custom officials also reduced eventual profits. The women vendors spoke very critically of course of Operation Murambatsvina (in 2005), a state-driven operation that destroyed illegal houses and informal sector structures in urban areas. Though most of the Magaba traders had set up their vending activities at Magaba subsequent to this government operation (and had no prior history of vending elsewhere), some current traders had engaged in trading activities previously (and elsewhere) and these activities were disrupted by the operation. They therefore claim that the operation seriously undermined the livelihoods of many traders (and their households) and led to less diversification of product and service lines. Prior to Murambatsvina, they note that women pursued a wider range of activities, including running tuck shops, salons and flea markets at home and making use (for vending purposes) of available space at shopping centres and roadsides in their residential suburbs.

Other women were not directly affected by the cleanup campaign at Magaba but (like the Magaba traders whose involvement at Magaba pre-dates the operation) their vending activities were undermined because of the pervasiveness of the operation nation-wide. When respondents were asked about their feelings about the operation, one married respondent aged 33 argued:

> It is very unacceptable we lost our property, tuck shops and flea markets, and from then on we can't even afford to buy property and we are really still affected ... I cannot watch TV (it was destroyed) and I think in future such operations should be avoided. I can hardly think of the benefits of such an operation ... It eroded our rights to human dignity, to shelter, to employment and the right to freely engage in business activities.

Besides Operation Murambatsvina, harassment by municipal police is a constant threat to Magaba traders (as discussed later). This is a broader problem for urban traders in Zimbabwe and it has occurred both before (Mombeshora 2004) and after Murambatsvina. Despite Murambatsvina and subsequent police operations, Magaba women traders argue that vending activities (as a livelihood strategy) has been normalised compared to previous years. In part, this is because the dollarisation of the economy had contributed towards stabilising the trading environment and allowing for more regular, and therefore less erratic, earnings. The empirical evidence presented clearly underlines the significance of vending for Magaba women traders in the context of urban poverty. In this regard, a significant number of women vendors (49%) purported that their household's livelihood condition had improved since they started operating as vendors. The balance indicated that there had not been any significant improvement. The following section considers 'off-market' activities.

Off-market livelihood activities

Urban women do not rely exclusively on vending as a livelihood strategy. Instead, beyond formal employment, they (and their households) pursue diversified livelihood activities for purposes of household income and food security, or rely on alternative cash and commodity streams.

Remittances: cash and commodities

Remittances are increasingly important. Zimbabwean nationals have left the country in their hundreds of thousands over the past decade, mainly as economic refugees, and they have remitted cash and commodities to Zimbabwe through a variety of channels (Bracking and Sachikonye 2006, Mupedziswa 2009). Urban women at Magaba have at times been recipients of these remittances. From the study it emerges that 14.2% of the sampled respondents received remittances from elsewhere in the country or from outside Zimbabwe, and from different people including family members. The main source of outside remittances for Magaba women traders was South Africa and primarily in the form of commodities (both perishable and durable); cash though is also remitted and used, for example, for educational expenses. Though some of the commodities remitted are readily available in Zimbabwe, they may be very expensive. Earnings by Magaba vendors may be as low as US$50 per month. In this regard, the testimony by one unmarried woman is very revealing:

> I always come here [Magaba] at 9 am in the morning and spend the whole day until the sunset ... but sometimes it's not worth it when I get less than [US] $10, at times I can even go home with $7; if I subtract transport I am left with $6 this is not enough. With this little I cannot afford most of the basic foods had it been not for my sister who works in South Africa. I always receive groceries every month; without her I could be struggling more.

Such sentiments clearly show that, despite their significance, earnings from vending activities are not necessarily able to sustain urban households. Remittances from further afield in the diaspora were reported to be mostly cash remittances, considering the expenses incurred in trying to send commodities from afar; however, goods are also sent. Cash transferred from far afield normally goes through the formal channels (like Western Union) regulated by the Zimbabwe Reserve Bank, while cash coming in from South Africa is done unofficially. In terms of usages of cash remittances by Magaba households, the primary focus is monthly household sustenance such as accommodation, food consumption and security, education and health, and electricity and water bills (see also Sander and Maimbo 2003). However, some cash becomes an investment by being channelled directly into informal vending activities through the purchase of commodities for resale. Remittances do make a contribution to household sustainability by mitigating the effects of the crisis in Zimbabwe;

however, they may be an unstable form of household sustenance because their ongoing transference is beyond the control of Magaba households and thus the latter depend quite heavily on the choices made by friends and family living, studying or working elsewhere.

Urban agriculture

A significant number of urban households in Zimbabwe practice urban farming for food security purposes, despite the scarcity of land as natural capital in urban centres. This is done throughout the year, but it is intensified during the rainy season from late November. This is manifested specifically amongst Magaba households. The survey indicates that the vast majority (84.1%) of women vendors practice urban agriculture. The site for farming varies considerably. Only 21.1% of households undertook farming at the place of residence. Others practice it elsewhere, in part because there is often limited space available in high-density areas like Mbare for a plot and also because of the fear of local municipal authorities and police who at times intimidate urban farmers and destroy their crops. In this context, 23.7% of households engaged in agricultural practice alongside roads, 23.7% along railway lines, 18.4% on utilised residential stands, 7.9% on land allocated for urban agriculture and 5.3% on hillsides.

Magaba women traders grow a variety of crops. Women themselves provided the labour and are sometimes helped by household members. Of particular significance is the staple crop of maize (73.5% of households), but also important are onions (6.2%), tomatoes (8.2%), sweet potatoes (10.2%) and sugar cane (2%). These are similar findings to the study by Kutiwa *et al.* (2010) of urban Zimbabwe. A factor that contributed to the focus on the growing of maize is the high cost of mealie meal in the supermarkets. In addition to the crops listed above, a majority of households seemed to grow leafy vegetables (such as *covo*, *tsunga* and *rugare*) for purposes of eating with sadza (cooked mealie meal); these vegetables were treated as a substitute for meat which is far too expensive in the butcheries for Magaba vendors to afford (with one kilogramme costing about US$4.50 at the time of fieldwork). Sweet potatoes (locally known as *mbambaira*) were also substituted for bread that costs US$1 a loaf.

Urban farming is mainly for household consumption but there is also some income generation through agriculture. A slight majority (53.1%) of households indicated that they sold crops that they grew. A majority of the crops grown were sold in the places of residence while smaller quantities of the grown crops were sold at Magaba. Data from the survey shows that a reasonable amount of income was being generated through the marketing of produce. Half of the households (50%) indicated that they earned US$21–40 per month while 31.3% earned less than US$20; 14.6% earned US$41–60 and 4.2% earned US$61–80. The income generated was used for urgent household needs, such as school fees and the purchase of school uniforms for children in the household.

Urban farming is not without problems. For example, 37.1% of households reported conflicts with neighbours or nearby residents mainly due to boundary demarcation disputes and theft. As well, crop slashing by local police as a deter-rent measure has taken place, and interviewed women cried foul about this dis-heartening practice because it led to reductions in crop yields and often undercut any prospects for surplus sales. Although these and other challenges existed, the Magaba women vendors spoke out strongly about the importance of urban agri-culture. In this respect, Magaba women vendors highlighted the significance of urban farming in facilitating access to basic foodstuffs (26.5%), in supplement-ing income through market sales (30.6%) and in improving food supply and nutrition. Also, by reducing expenditure on foodstuffs that are 'home-grown', income can be released and channelled into other household expenses such as rent and transport.

Renting out rooms

Interviewees (particularly those who owned a house) derive some income from renting extra rooms to lodgers. In Harare high-density areas, the majority of people do not own houses and they depend upon landlords for accommodation. Shortages in accommodation have in fact influenced some house owners to make extensions to their houses in order to provide rental accommodation. Interview-ees who owned houses exclaimed that, prior to Operation Murambatsvina, back-yard accommodation (known as '*boy-sky*') generated significant income for them, but that this was dramatically stopped because the operation entailed the destruction of all illegal dwellings. Lodging though is still pervasive in Mbare and other high-density areas in Harare.

Six vendors, based on in-depth interviews, disclosed that their main source of income was derived from renting out rooms; hence, they 'convert' physical capital into a direct source of income. One married respondent indicated:

> I am proud to own a house; this is very important to me; if I do not get any-thing from selling second hand clothes I always find that I get money at the end of the month. Five of my rooms are rented out and each room costs [US] $65] a month.

Unlike vending, renting out rooms provides a stable and reliable income per month, and this income is used for educating children, paying monthly bills and food consumption; but it is also sometimes used to purchase goods sold by the house-owning vendor at Magaba. However, most of the Magaba vendors do not own houses and they rely upon rental accommodation. With one room costing around US$70 per month (and with most households including a number of dependents) this becomes a major monthly expense for Magaba traders.

Urban–rural linkages

Urban women at Magaba also utilise urban–rural linkages as a supporting mech-anism for their households, and to cushion themselves against shocks and crises.

This is more prevalent in the case of older women (who tend to uphold rural values) and with those who prioritise their historical and cultural roots. This result is consistent with the study by Muzvidziwa (1997:108) who noted that "continued utilisation of rural-urban networks as a survival option was a pragmatic response to scarcity of resources, including jobs". Without keeping the urban–rural linkages alive, the Magaba women openly proclaimed that decent livelihoods in Harare would be a mission impossible. Some respondents have access to land in rural areas. One woman inherited rural land and she claims that land forms a crucial basis for constructing livelihood strategies in Harare. She grew crops there, including maize and groundnuts (to make peanut butter after processing).

Maintaining urban–rural linkages also contributed to barter trade within the village of origin. This was promoted through bringing into the village basic commodities such as cooking oil, bathing and washing soup, sugar and second-hand clothes. Most of these commodities were not available in rural supermarkets and retail outlets because of the bad roads and transport costs, which hindered delivery. These commodities were exchanged for agricultural products (mainly maize), which were for household consumption or reselling at Magaba. In addition to bartering, Magaba vendors also used rural areas as alternative markets for their goods. In doing so, they demanded exorbitant prices because of the scarcity of basic commodities in rural areas. At times they sold goods on credit and this attracted rural buyers. The findings of this study therefore go contrary to the conclusion by Schlyter (1990:188) that "it seemed impossible for women to maintain two places simultaneously as a survival mechanism, they were urban or they left and resided for a longer period in rural areas".

Cross-border activity

As raised previously, the continuity (and indeed the very existence) of the informal trading activities of Magaba and indeed other vendors relies quite extensively on the ongoing importation of goods by informal cross-border traders. This is because of the scarcity of many commodities within Zimbabwe, the lack of diversity within product ranges and their comparatively high local prices when available (Banda 2010), compared to primarily South Africa. It is therefore important to reiterate the significance of cross-border trading. This informal importation is done either by the Magaba traders themselves or by others (mainly women) who specialise in cross-border trading. Cross-border traders often travel on a weekly basis (over weekends) to ensure a regular supply of commodities at markets such as Magaba. Because of long border delays, new duty tariffs and corrupt officials, traders often feel compelled to bribe customs and immigration officers in order to proceed on their travels without excessive hindrance and to reduce expenses (for example, paying the duty tariffs would likely lessen profit levels on the commodities once sold). The majority of urban women traders who traded in durable goods relied on crossing the border to stock (and sometimes hoard) commodities for resale at Magaba; these commodities included clothing, electrical appliances, pots and linen.

In feeding directly into Magaba vending, cross-border trading contributes significantly to household sustenance (Peberdy 2002). In undertaking cross-border trading, Magaba women sometimes use the opportunity to engage in casual domestic work (including laundry and ironing) outside the country. This is commonly referred to as piece work (or *mabasa emaoko* in Shona). At times, some Magaba traders organise themselves as a group, based on trust and reciprocity (or social capital broadly), to engage in the collective purchasing of goods in South Africa, Mozambique, Botswana and Zambia. New clothes and shoes are sourced from South Africa, caterpillars or mopane worms (locally known as *madora*) from Botswana (this is sometimes substituted for meat or leafy vegetables) and second-hand clothes packed in large bags (locally known as *mabhero*) from Mozambique. However, this collective spirit is eroded and dissipates when it comes to the day-to-day practicalities of vending at Magaba, which is based on stiff competition even between traders who form part of the same group involved in collective purchasing.

Livelihood challenges of women traders

Informal livelihood activities play an important role in providing safety nets for millions of unemployed people in Zimbabwe. However, livelihood activities are not without challenges. These challenges are economic in character but also involve the politicisation of urban space.

Credit loans

The bulk of people in urban areas acknowledge the significance of access to credit in either cash or kind. Credit acts as a means of increasing household incomes through allowing for investments in income-generating activities and small business ventures. Despite this, the majority of poor households do not have access to credit from banks and other moneylenders. Credit loan facilities are not new in Zimbabwe but, historically, most of these have been aimed at small to medium enterprises and not petty traders like women at Magaba (Mupedziswa and Gumbo 2001). The majority of women who participate in petty trading do not benefit because they do not meet loan requirements, such as collateral security set by banks and other moneylenders (Mhone 1993). Women traders at Magaba therefore face this credit obstacle due to limited or no collateral. Further, they normally lack a guarantor with long-term and sufficient income to act as security for them, and their informal activities generate low and irregular returns deemed unacceptable to moneylenders.

The Government of Zimbabwe, through state and statutory bodies such as the Small Enterprises Development Corporation, the Ministry of Youth and the Ministry of Gender and Women Affairs, provide credit facilities. However, few traders at Magaba knew anything of significance with regard to these credit opportunities, and none had in fact benefited. In any case, due to the economy performing under a necessary threshold, these bodies had exceedingly limited funds for credit disbursement. Given the inadequacy of finances, livelihoods are threatened and compromised. The majority of traders knew of the existence of informal money lenders. But Magaba traders were afraid of borrowing money from these lenders. Interest rates on these loans are very high, and paying a loan back to these lenders was like tying a rope around one's neck.

Competition

A significant challenge for the women traders is the question of competition. Even after the formation of the Government of National Unity formed in 2008, there was no meaningful improvement in the Zimbabwean economy and new and old entrants swamped the informal trading sector. Most of the informal trading places in Harare are characterised, it seems quite literally at times, by the law of the jungle. Women traders at Magaba expressed, in one way or another, the emergence of market saturation – in fact of over-saturation – that has contributed to the lowering of profits and profit margins. Competition at Magaba was marked by constant fluctuation as, during my field work, I noticed changes to the number of traders on-site on a daily basis; and this also leads to significant irregularity and variation in daily sales. As well, competition comes about because of the existence of weekend and month-end traders who do not vend on an ongoing basis at Magaba. These traders, who are often employed in the formal economy, trade at Magaba to supplement their regular income; in doing so, they impact negatively on the sales of the permanent traders.

Generally, prices for traders lower goods at Magaba when demand decreases, which in turn lowers profit margins during the expected slower days of the month. The ever-increasing competition has also contributed to increased working hours by traders to maximise sales; according to the Magaba survey, 63.3% of traders have increased their working time for this reason. Despite this intense competition, and the stress that it invariably put on women traders given the livelihoods demands of their households, women traders regularly shared information with other traders about where they sourced their goods for resale and at what cost price. This was mainly done among traders with well-established and high levels of trust between them. Competition does not only emanate from within the informal trading sector. In recent years there has been some recovery of the formal retail sector in terms of availability and cost of basic commodities in Zimbabwe. Prices in supermarkets and shops are still high compared to the informal sector; high and medium income urbanites frequent these retail outlets while lower income groups still purchase commodities in the informal sector.

Seasonality

Beyond the many economic challenges noted already (including the fluctuations in sales within a particular month), Magaba traders face seasonal peaks and troughs in sales and this leads to ebb and flows in livelihood activities.

Seasonality affects traders differently (or possibly not at all), depending on the wares in which they are trading, as the sales of certain products dropped or rose during different seasons. Some of the traders revealed that they are not directly affected by seasonality because they have a number of income sources besides the one at Magaba, including traders who also relied on remittances and renting-out of rooms. Traders who lack diversification, either within their trading activities in terms of commodity inflexibility or outside trading completely, are mostly affected by seasonality. Furthermore, vendors selling durables (such as clothes and braids) expressed different opinions with regard to the existence and effects of seasonality. But most claimed that, during the festive seasons (for instance Easter and Christmas holidays), they experienced high demands while other parts of the year were off-season in this regard.

Harassment by police

The Zimbabwean police and the municipal police are involved in joint or solo operations in urban areas against traders and others, despite the fact that officially the municipal police are responsible for enforcing municipal by-laws. Some urban residents believe that these operations are politically motivated in seeking to regain power over an urban populace that tends to support the opposition Movement for Democratic Change (MDC). Others believe that the informal sector has congested the city and hence police operations are genuinely motivated to enforce law and order. In this context, the pros and cons of Operation Murambatsvina was the subject of intense debate in urban Zimbabwe. The MDC critique of this and other smaller operations is that they are "designed to destroy the party's urban support base, relocate the people to the rural areas where they would be under the sway of ruling party-aligned chiefs, and forestall popular protests by the poor as the food crisis deepened" (Maroleng 2005:3). Related to this, a local newspaper, *The Zimbabwe Independent* (29 September 2006), reported that vendors from opposition strongholds in Mbare and Highfields were threatened with withdrawal of vending permits if they missed President Mugabe's homecoming at the Harare International Airport after one of his foreign visits. Some writers on Zimbabwe argue that harassment (and even the threat of harassment) by police is a critical obstacle to the realisation of fruitful livelihood strategies (Mombeshora 2004, Chirisa 2007). In the case of Magaba, some interviewees indicated that they can be raided up to four times during one day by different police officers. Women traders at Magaba experienced the loss of their goods, payment of fines and of course loss of business and income. Many traders highlighted that the goods confiscated by the police, especially clothes and foodstuffs, were not surrendered at the police station by the officers concerned as they took the goods straight to their houses.

Besides trading operations directly, the local police in Harare threaten urban-based farmers under the slogan 'NO CULTIVATION'. It is believed that the majority of people living in high-density areas in Harare engage in urban agriculture (including women traders at Magaba, as highlighted earlier), and they often do so illegally on un-used pieces of land. Harare regulatory instruments do not allow cultivation on open urban spaces and, towards the start of the rainy season in October, banners reading 'NO CULTIVATION' are placed in all areas which are known to be prone to urban cultivation. Nevertheless, these signs are regularly ignored and municipal by-laws resisted out of sheer economic necessity with full knowledge of the risks involved including crop slashing by the police.

Militia terrorising vendors

Besides the police and their attacks on informal traders and urban farming, militia groups linked to the ruling ZANU-PF party have been actively involved in politicising urban spaces by disciplining the supposedly unruly populace. I focus specifically on a group called *Chipangano*. Members of ZANU-PF's youth wing (under the banner of *Chipangano*) have been terrorising urbanites including informal sector workers. These youths are renowned for violence, intimidation, looting and disrupting livelihoods of the urban people who earn a living through their ingenuity and creativity (albeit often illegally). Markets such as Magaba, Mupedzanhamo and Mbare Musika have been the sites for *Chipangano* activity. In the case of Magaba, these activities are of great importance as they impede the livelihood activities of vendors.

The majority of Magaba vendors spoke openly about this group, saying that the group is a law unto itself; traders are in constant fear of the group especially during and after elections. When the group visits the general area, trading comes to a complete halt not only at Magaba but also at nearby markets and formal trading enterprises. Everyone is forced to attend rallies at the open grounds close to Rufaro Stadium in Mbare. In-depth discussions with vendors also brought to the fore current anxieties and fears because of the impending national elections including for the state presidency. Aside from election times, vendors also mentioned that when a national hero dies they are forced by *Chipangano* to attend the funeral service at Stodart Hall in Mbare and the burial too at the national shrine or Hero's Acre. Such activities posed a challenge to livelihood strategies for the traders due to the fact that income is lost during the time when vendors are forced to discontinue trading. The group has committed many acts of violence against traders without any repercussions.

Conclusion and policy insights

The importance of the livelihood strategies of urban women at Magaba cannot be underestimated as they provide for household economic well being. Trading activities and some off-market activities dominate the livelihoods of urban women. Despite the socio-economic and political situation that animates contemporary Zimbabwe, the trading activities and off-market activities have contributed to household sustenance. Both livelihoods are counteracted by challenges; however, Magaba women traders continue to display significant agency and ingenuity in seeking to defend and pursue their livelihood strategies. This study provides knowledge and insights useful for policy makers and development practitioners. The findings indicate, first, that policy makers need to acknowledge the significance of urban women livelihoods, such that policy makers need to reformulate urban policies so as to facilitate women's informal trading activities. Second, there is also a need for urban policy makers to integrate urban agriculture into urban system design and planning to optimise agriculture outcomes for Harare high-density residents.

References

Banda, I. 2010. Zimbabwe: Informal Sector Lures University Graduates. www.ips.org/TV/beijing15/zimbabwe-informal-sector-lures-universitygraduates/ [Accessed: 18 August 2012].

Bracking, S. and Sachikonye, L. 2006. *Remittances, Poverty and the Informalisation of Household Wellbeing in Zimbabwe.* Global Poverty Research Group, Working Paper Series No 045. Manchester: Global Poverty Research Group.

Chirisa, I. 2007. Post-2005 Harare: A Case of the Informal Sector and Street Vending Resilience. What Options Do Key Players Have? *Local Governance and Development Journal* 1 (1): 53–64.

Dube, D. and Chirisa, I. 2012. The Informal City: Assessing its Scope, Variants and Direction in Harare, Zimbabwe. *Journal of Geography and Regional Planning* 1 (1): 016–025.

Kutiwa, S., Boon, E. and Devuyst, D. 2010. Urban Agriculture in Low Income Households of Harare: An Adaptive Response to Economic Crisis. *Journal of Human Ecology* 2 (2): 85–96.

Maroleng, C. 2005. *Zimbabwe: Increased Securitization of the State.* A Report of Institute of Security Studies. Issued 7 September 2005.

McPherson, M.A. 1998. *Zimbabwe: A Third Nationwide Survey of Micro and Small Enterprises, Growth and Equity through Microenterprise Investments and Institutions.* USAID.

Mhone, G. 1993. *The Impact of Structural Adjustment on the Urban Informal Sector in Zimbabwe.* ILO: Geneva.

Mombeshora, S. 2004. *Philanthropy of Community in Zimbabwe. Past, Present and Future.* A Paper Prepared for the Building Community Philanthropy Project at the Centre for Leadership and Public Values, Graduate School of Business. University of Cape Town: South Africa.

Mupedziswa, R. 2009. Diaspora Dollars and Social Development: Remittance Patterns of Zimbabwe Nationals based in South Africa. *Global Development Studies* 5 (3–4): 229–272.

Mupedziswa, R. and Gumbo, P. 2001. *Women Informal Traders in Harare and the Struggle for Survival in an Environment of Economic Reforms.* Research Report 117. Uppsala: Nordiska Afrikainstitutet.

Muzvidziwa, V.N. 1997. Rural–Urban Linkages: Masvingo's Double-Rooted Female Heads of Households. *Zambezia* 24 (2): 97–123.

Peberdy, S. 2002. *Hurdles to Trade? South Africa's Immigration Policy and Informal Sector Cross-Border Traders in SADC.* Presented at SAMP/LHR/HSRC Workshop on Regional Integration, Poverty and South Africa's Proposed Migration Policy, Pretoria.

Sander, C. and Maimbo, S.M. 2003. *Migrant Labor Remittances in Africa: Reducing Obstacles to Developmental Contributions Africa Region*, Working Paper Series No. 64, World Bank: Washington DC.

Schlyter, A. 1990. Women in Harare: Gender Aspects of Urban–Rural Interaction. In J. Baker (ed.). *Small Town Africa: Studies in Rural-Urban Interaction*. Uppsala: Scandinavian Institute of African Studies.

3 Livelihood strategies in Harare

The case of low-income households in Budiriro

Tafadzwa Chevo

Introduction

Sub-Saharan Africa is urbanising rapidly and UN-HABITAT predicts that by 2025 most of the continent's population will be residing in urban areas rather than in rural areas (UN-Habitat 2010). Additionally, the rate of urbanisation is higher in southern Africa than any other region on the continent. Broadly, the urban growth rates within southern Africa range from 3% to 5% per annum (UN-Habitat 2010). UN-Habitat also reports that Botswana and South Africa are already over 60% urbanised and that by 2030 the two countries will be over 70% urban. By 2030, the UN agency also expects Mozambique, Zimbabwe, Namibia, Mauritius and the Seychelles to have reached over 50% urbanisation. With such projections, it is clear that sub-Saharan Africa is moving towards becoming a largely urbanised space (Chen *et al.* 2016).

In Zimbabwe however, this urbanisation is not accompanied by industrialisation due to the failure by central and local governments to formulate and implement the social, economic and political policies that generate employment and are inclusive and pro-poor. This problem is combined with recent declines in agricultural production, shortages and the high cost of electrical power and water supplies, the near collapse of the country's infrastructure, unregulated competition from South African and Chinese imports, and sanctions on Zimbabwe by Western countries (Mlambo 2017).

In recent years, a significant amount of literature has emerged studying the character and extent of livelihood strategies of households and individuals in both urban and rural areas of Zimbabwe from various perspectives, disciplines and backgrounds, and using a variety of methodological and conceptual tools (Chirau 2012, Chagonda 2012, Jones 2010, Magure 2014, Tamukamoyo 2009). For example, using participant observation, Magure (2014) highlights the agency of urban residents in Chegutu in constructing their livelihoods within an urban space characterised by a scarcity of formal employment and a local and central government that does not perceive the informal sector as a key feature of national development. In another study, Shand *et al.* (2016) found that the informal sector in Harare is an important space for street youth and children when it comes to earning an income.

This chapter seeks to contribute to this discussion on urban livelihoods by describing, examining and analysing the livelihood strategies and activities of households situated in Budiriro. This high-density area islocated in Harare – the capital city of Zimbabwe. It is important to note that even though there are a significant number of studies focusing on the livelihood activities of urban households in Harare (Tevera and Chikanda 2000, Mukwedeya 2012, Chirau 2012, Manjengwa *et al.* 2016), there are no studies to date that have focused on the livelihood strategies of residents and households in Budiriro. This is despite the fact that Budiriro is marked by extreme poverty and poor service delivery which led in fact to a cholera outbreak in 2008: Budiriro was the epicentre of this epidemic (Musemwa 2010, Kone-Coulibaly *et al.*, 2010). This chapter first discusses the methods used to collect data in Budiriro and the characteristics of the Budiriro households sampled for the study. It then examines the activities and strategies of these low-income Budiriro households in making a living and the challenges they face in doing so. Finally, the chapter concludes and provides policy implications arising from the study.

Methodology

To address the research objective, this study utilised a mixed methods approach that combined qualitative and quantitative methodologies to collect data on the livelihood strategies and activities of households in Budiriro. This involved a multiple sampling strategy. For the quantitative aspect of the research, I employed a random sampling strategy that minimised bias in neighbourhood and household selection. For the qualitative sample, I sought to ensure maximum variation. The first level of sampling (for the quantitative dimension) was at ward level. The study demarcated Budiriro neighbourhoods on a map, identified their names and gave each neighbourhood a unique number. After this, I proceeded to generate random numbers to select two neighbourhoods from each ward. For example, if ward 43 (one of the wards in Budiriro) had ten neighbourhoods, these neighbourhoods were named and numbered one up to ten. A website (www.random.org/integers/) was used to generate two random numbers between one and the maximum number of neighbourhoods in the ward (in this case, ten). After determining the two neighbourhoods to be studied in each ward, I selected the houses or properties that would participate in the study in each neighbourhood, up to a maximum of 50 households per neighbourhood. In total, the quantitative survey had a sample of 300 households, randomly selected through the generation of random numbers. In Budiriro, as in many high-density areas in Harare, properties are clearly numbered in a consecutive fashion. Therefore the study used the pre-existing property numbers to generate random numbers for the selection of households.

In addition, I developed a protocol for replacement of households where a particular household refused to participate or was not available at the time of the study. In instances where there were multiple households occupying one property, one household would be chosen randomly for inclusion into the study. For the qualitative data, the study utilised maximum variation sampling. This strategy was advantageous because it allowed the researcher to select different kinds of people with different characteristics for the qualitative study particularly covering different forms of livelihood strategies and outcomes.

The fieldwork was carried out between 1 June 2015 and 31 October 2015 and involved three data collection methods, namely a small scale household survey, focus group discussions and life history interviews. In gathering quantitative data, the household survey questionnaire identified, amongst other things, household composition, income and expenditure as well as household survival strategies. Households with either male or female heads were included, and the economic activities of all members of the head's family (whether present within the household or not) and their contribution to household income were examined. As a result of the sampling strategy for the household survey, 81% of the household heads interviewed were male with 19% of the sample being female heads of households. In addition, 24 life history interview were conducted which enabled me to understand the individual life courses of household heads and how their livelihood strategies had possibly changed over time given the fluctuating political economy of Zimbabwe. Five focus group discussions with six household heads were also conducted in different parts of Budiriro. These discussions enabled the researcher to understand in more depth the meanings and interpretations given by household heads to their livelihood context and activities. The quantitative evidence was analysed using the computer-based statistical package for social scientists (SPSS). In the case of the qualitative evidence, common themes were extrapolated, coded and examined in an iterative manner (Aronson 1995).

Characteristics of Budiriro households

Households in Budiriro are not homogeneous and therefore can be described as heterogeneous. To cater for this heterogeneity and differentiate the households into wealth-status categories, the study computed the expenditure of households as a basis for measuring the wealth of the sampled households. Expenditure was considered to be a suitable measure in categorising the households in Budiriro because it is less vulnerable to under-reporting, it captures permanent income, and it accommodates income from illegal activities as well as private and government transfers (Meyer and Sullivan 2003). As a result, three categories of households emerged, labeled simply as households that are the better off, average and poor based on their expenditure and household wealth. With regard to expenditure, the better-off households have an average monthly expenditure of above US$700. The average households spend between US$300–700 per month while the poor households have an expenditure that does not exceed US$300 per month. Overall, 74.8% of the households have a monthly expenditure that does not exceed US$700 per month. It is worth pointing out that 51.2% of the surveyed households lived below the poverty datum line of US$485 per month in 2015 (Zimstats 2015).

In order to validate the existence of the three categories, the study also measured the assets that households have access to and own, using a wealth index measurement. The wealth index measurement is considered to be an effective indicator of long-term socio-economic position, living standard or material well being of households (Filmer and Pritchett 1999, Sahn and Stifel 2000, 2003, Howe *et al.* 2009). For this study, the assets that were measured were agricultural equipment, general assets, house furnishings and livestock. Table 3.1 shows the summarised wealth indices constructed based on the data collected from fieldwork on the different types of assets households own and to which they have access. The summarised indices correspond with the expenditure patterns of the households within this study. Thus, the information presented in Table 3.1 validates the existence of the three categories of households, given that the levels of asset access and ownership follow the pattern of poor, average and better off, as derived from household expenditure patterns. There are also significant differences with regard to the levels of ownership and access to assets according to the expenditure categorisation. Thus, the overall wealth index for the better off is 5.93 compared to 3.44 for the average and 2.49 for the poor.

With regard to household headship, the data from the survey demonstrates that men largely head households in Budiriro, given that the selection of the participants within the study was purely random as discussed within the methodology. As indicated earlier, men headed 81% of households while women headed 19% of the households. These results are typical of urban household headship data from other studies such as by Rakodi (1995) and Chirau (2012). For example, the evidence from the study by Rakodi (1995) in Gweru shows that 80% of the household heads were men in the year 1991. This reflects not only the patriarchal nature of household headship but also is consistent with the trends of household headship in Zimbabwe as a whole (Rakodi 1995, Zimstat 2012). There were no significant differences between the poor, average and the better off with regard to household headship and gender.

The study also shows that average age of the household heads is 42.9 years and the majority of households (mode age) headed by 35 year olds. In addition, poor households had heads that are on average 41.8 years old, while 40.9 year olds and 47.6 year olds headed the average and the better off respectively, as averages. What is apparent is that household heads that were better off were older than household heads that were poor and average with a P-Value of 0.006.

Table 3.1 Wealth index of Budiriro households

	Overall	Poor	Average	Better off	χ^2/p
Agricultural equipment index	0.34	0.08	0.23	0.88	0.000
General assets index	2.78	2.00	2.68	4.18	0.000
Household furnishings index	0.47	0.38	0.44	0.65	0.000
Livestock index	0.09	0.03	0.07	0.22	0.000
Total index	3.68	2.49	3.44	5.93	0.000

The majority of households had members of between 3 and 5 in number. However, close to 23% of the households were composed of members numbering between 6 and 13. The average household size was 4.3, which is almost similar to the country's average household size of 4.2 (Zimstats 2012) but higher than Harare average of 3.9 (Zimstats 2012). I now turn to consider the livelihood strategies of households in Budiriro, particularly amongst the household heads.

Employment status of household heads

The household survey shows that 58.1% of the household heads indicated that they were employed within paid permanent employment and/or paid casual/contract/seasonal employment. Most of these employed household heads (45.6%) were engaged in paid permanent employment, while 12.5% were employed in casual or temporary employment. Table 3.2 provides details on the types of employment in which household heads in the different wealth quintiles are engaged.

Table 3.2 clearly shows that paid permanent employment is more prominent amongst the better off and average (51.6% and 49.4% respectively) compared to the poor – with the latter just less than 35%. The fact that only 12.5% of the sample is engaged in paid casual/contract/seasonal employment means that such work was not readily available, popular or accessible to household heads in Budiriro at the time of the survey. Again, though, this kind of employment was found more amongst both the better off and average households, with only 4.5% of household heads in the poor quintile involved in this employment category. Amongst those employed (permanent or otherwise), most (78.4%) of the household heads were employed in private and household business enterprises while 21.6% of the employed household heads indicated that they were employed within the central, local and or state owned enterprises.

Household heads engaged in paid permanent employment or paid casual employment take home an average income of US$337.70 per month, a figure below the poverty datum line of US$485 (Zimstats 2015) by US$147.30. The better off take home on average US$372; while the average and the poor employed household heads take home US$334 and US$305 respectively. With respect to contribution to household income, 83% of the employed household heads claimed that this employment-based income greatly contributes to the household's livelihood, while 13% said that its contribution was moderate and

Table 3.2 Types of employment for household heads

Type of employment	Overall	Poor	Average	Better off	χ^2/p
					0.003
Paid permanent employment	45.6	34.8	49.4	51.6	
Paid employee – casual/contract/seasonal	12.5	4.5	16.9	12.9	

4% stated that paid employment did not contribute at all to household income. The remainder of the household heads describe themselves as unemployed, students, homemakers and retired.

Household business enterprises (HBEs)

In addition to employment, household heads in Budiriro engage in a range of business enterprises to improve household livelihoods, within what is normally called 'the informal economy'. These are usually businesses owned and operated by households and tend to be of low-cost entry, home-based or mobile, and operate without a regular or fixed workplace (Fox and Sohnesen 2012). These enterprises are also seen as survivalist because of their limited potential for growth though they may provide a stable livelihood when compared to alternatives such as a day labourer.

From the household survey data, 49.8% of the households noted that they operated household business enterprises (HBEs), with 46.4% of the poor, 42.9% of the average and 64.5% of the better off indicating that they were involved in running a household business enterprise. Of these running a household business enterprise, just under one-half (49.8%) had been running their businesses for a maximum of 11 months. The poorer households had run their business for 9.24 months, while the average and better off households had been operating their businesses for longer, that is, 11.80 months and 11.14 months respectively. Overall, 86% of the HBEs were owned and run by the household head. Both male and female heads of households are engaged in informal economic activities, with – proportionally speaking – only slightly more female heads involved. Table 3.3 highlights some of the key kinds of informal economic activities.

The 'others' category includes businesses such as knitting, crocheting, weaving mats and baskets, gathering natural resources, beer brewing, operating a shebeen, watch repairs, shoe repairs, wood sculpturing, spiritual healing, and the cutting and selling of firewood.

The household businesses of Budiriro residents did not require huge start-up capital and were also not high profit-earning businesses. The average start-up capital for businesses was US$100 and households received an average of

Table 3.3 Types of household business enterprises (HBEs)

Type of household business enterprise	% of HHs engaged in HBEs
Vending/tuck-shop/cross-border trading	52.2
Artisanal work (mechanic, welder, carpenter)	21.4
Food/vegetable vending	8.9
Sewing	8.1
Poultry and rabbit rearing	4.4
Hairdressing	3.7
Others	1.3

US$162 per month in terms of profit from the small businesses. In the year preceding the study (2014), households operating HBEs received an average monthly income as profit of US$129, US$159 and US$146 respectively for poor, average and better-off households. In spite of the low incomes generated from household enterprises, of those who operate household business enterprises 78% of respondents indicated that income from these businesses greatly contributed to household well being, with only 2.6% saying that the business did not make any significant contribution.

Participants from the qualitative study spoke about the increasing importance of household businesses as a livelihood strategy in Budiriro and, in particular, the dramatic rise in vending over the past ten or so years. One Budiriro head, in a focus group discussion, elaborated upon this:

> Some people have vending stalls in front of their houses and others have tuck-shops, some are into mobile vending whilst some are involved in selling groceries. For example some can go door to door with say cooking oil and sell the bottle at [US] $4 on credit. The customer will pay back $1 a day for that cooking oil. This is also done for other commodities such as Cremora and sugar. Those days when one could raise huge profits quickly are a thing of the past because when you get the $1 installments from your customers, you will also have to pay back to your own creditors who you owe; for example money for the chickens you borrowed and you also need to buy a loaf of bread for the children. In most cases its either you remain afloat or you sink financially; there is no more growing. As long as you are just surviving. This is why the money you get from such kind of business cannot be taken to the bank as savings because it is too little.

Vending has become a way of life for many household heads and their household members. However, Budiriro residents do not see it as a way out of poverty, with any profit earned normally being allocated for the purchase of basic foodstuffs.

The data show that the average age of household heads in households operating a business was 43 and with an average household size of 4.5 members. The household expenditure and wealth index of those who had a business income was higher than those who did not have a business income. Those with less education were more likely to have business income than those who have a higher level of education, although there was no significant difference between the two groups. Table 3.4 illustrates the specific differences between those households that had a household business income and those that did not.

Access to land for agriculture

With regard to access to land for practicing agriculture, the survey results show that 27.4% of the households indicated that they had access to land for the purposes of practicing agriculture. While some agricultural activities took place in the urban area, others took place in rural areas. The survey did not differentiate

Table 3.4 Recipients and non-recipients of household business income

Category of livelihood	Household business income	No household business income	p-values
Male heads (%)	49.3	50.7	0.836
Female heads (%)	50.9	49.1	
Age	43.64	41.91	0.298
Household size	4.54	4.15	0.137
Household expenditure	523.26	397.42	0.0036
Wealth index	3.85	3.52	0.322

between proceeds from rural and those from urban agriculture. Regardless of this, access to land is somewhat gendered, in that 19.6% of the male household heads and 8.8% of the female household heads indicated that they had access to land for cultivation. Access to land for agriculture was 11.5%, 18.4% and 33.4% for poor households, average households and better off households respectively. Households practicing agriculture were therefore more likely to be non-poor. The wealth index score for households practicing agriculture was pegged at 5.95, which is close to the overall wealth index for better off households. While better-off households are most likely to participate in urban agriculture, low-income and female-headed households are constrained by lack of access to land and other resources necessary to undertake urban agriculture. High-income male-headed households thus tend to participate and benefit more from agricultural activity given that they are more likely to be better placed when it comes to systems that govern access to land such as political connections and homeownership (if compared to average and poor households).

It is also important to note that household head age and household sizes for those practicing agriculture and those not practicing agriculture were significantly different. The mean age of those practicing agriculture was 50 years while that of those not practicing agriculture was at 41.1 years of age. In addition, those households practicing agriculture had household sizes of 5.5 per household while those not practicing agriculture recorded a 4.1 average. There are, however, no significant differences between those households that practice agriculture and those that do not when it comes to levels of education. What this implies is that education does not necessarily have an influence in a household deciding to practice or not to practice agriculture, or in its ability to do so. Table 3.5 shows the characteristics of those practicing agriculture and those that are not practicing agriculture.

What is inversely clear is that 71.6% of the households in Budiriro do not have access to land to practice any form of agriculture and therefore cannot produce their own food for consumption. This lack of access to land suggests that households in Budiriro primarily rely on purchasing food for daily consumption and that the demand for food is high. This has the potential of driving up the prices of food if supply is outstripped by demand in cases of drought or when

Table 3.5 Practicing and non-practicing agriculture households

Category of livelihood	Practicing agriculture	Non-practicing agriculture	p-values
Male (%)	19.6	80.4	0.055
Female (%)	8.8	91.2	
Age	50.82	41.08	0.000
Household size	5.55	4.09	0.000
Household expenditure	558.55	440.99	0.048
Wealth index	5.95	3.21	0.000
Education	5.55	5.61	0.805

other food security threats emerge. In some cases, some households scavenge: "After those who had finished harvesting ... we would go around the fields to look for left maize cobs and later went to the grinding mill." The poor in Budiriro also tend to engage in informal and illegal agriculture because of problems with access to land.

But access to land should not be conflated with utilisation of the land for agricultural purposes. Of the households that reported access to land for agricultural purposes, only 49.3% of them indicated that they utilised 100% of the parcel of land to which they had access. A small majority (50.7%) thus indicated that they did not utilise all of their land, and due to a range of factors such as the lack of fertiliser, seed, plough implements, draught power and illnesses within the households. As well, insufficient rains had an impact on their ability to utilise land. Nearly all households (86%) with access to land indicated that they did not receive any form of extension services such as crop husbandry, which is an important component of productivity when it comes to agriculture (though it is unusual for urban households to access the services of agricultural extension officers). This indicates that, even with access to land, there are many problems with food security and production for households in urban areas. Caution should thus be placed on assuming that access to land will ultimately result in practicing agriculture.

In terms of crop production, 89.4% of households practicing agriculture grew maize, which is the main staple food crop in Zimbabwe. Groundnuts were grown by only 21.1% of the households and sweet potatoes by 10.5%. In all cases, household heads indicated that their agriculture depended on rain, confirming the fact that drought represents a source of vulnerability among households that practice agriculture in Budiriro. Overall, 71% of the households purchased fertiliser from commercial enterprises while 13% obtained free fertiliser from the government and 8.9% utilised manure to fertilise their crops. The balance of households did not utilise fertiliser because of lack of any access to it.

A total of 69.1% of the households possess livestock with the better off owning or having access to more livestock that the average as highlighted in the Household Wealth Index, in which the better off have an average score of 0.22 with the poor and average having a total score of 0.1 when it comes to the livestock index. Table 3.6 shows the types of livestock owned by the households.

Table 3.6 Livestock ownership

Type of livestock	Percentage that owned livestock
Cattle	30.0
Goats	16.0
Pigs	2.4
Donkeys	0.6
Poultry	18.9
Rabbits	1.2

Importantly, 16.9% of those who owned livestock had recently sold some of their animals, and their combined sales earned a total of US$7,280 in the last year. The main reasons for selling livestock was to use the money to pay for education (40%), to procure food (28%) and for starting a business (20%). Thus, while livestock acts as a stock of wealth and buffer against shocks, the above reasons for selling off livestock differ from those in rural areas since in rural areas livestock is a source of draught power, milk and manure and is essential in social processes such as paying bride price, settling serious conflicts and payment of fines (Nyamwanza 2012).

Cash transfers and/or remittances

This study shows that 37.2% of the households received cash and in-kind transfers within the last 12 months. Within this group, only 31.1% of the male heads of households received transfers or remittances, but 61.4% of the female heads did so. The number of people living in a remittance-receiving household was significantly smaller than those of households that did not receive remittances, indicating that a household member such as a spouse may be the one sending the remittances. For the households that receive remittances, the average household size is 3.95 while the non-receiving households have a 4.5 average with a p-value of 0.021. The higher rate of female heads receiving remittances can be explained by the fact that there is a male household member working outside Budiriro and sending cash or in-kind items home. There were no differences between households receiving remittances in cash or in kind with regard to the age of household head, household expenditure, wealth index score and education.

The sources of cash transfers and remittances were mainly relatives (54%), children (20.4%) and spouses (9.7%). An additional 15.1% of the households received cash transfers from NGOs and other donor organisations. Clearly, though, family and kinship relations are an important determinant in receiving remittances. These senders of remittances have migrated to other urban and rural areas as well as to neighbouring SADC countries and parts of Europe and Asia. Of the 37.2% who receive remittances, 42.5% were from the poor category, 31.6% from the average category and 36.6% where from the better-off category.

However, while the poor were proportionally more likely to receive remittances than other wealth categories, they received the least amount in terms of value of cash remittances. For example, the average for the last transfer received by households involved the following amounts: US$155.10, US$168.80, US$252.50 among poorer, average and better-off households respectively.

The remittances are also transferred irregularly to 53% of the households while 37.2% said they receive cash on a monthly basis and 6.2% indicated that they receive remittances on a quarterly basis. Only 3.1% said they receive cash annually. For the majority of households in the sample, remittances from other areas do not take place at all, as 62.8% indicated that they do not receive remittances. In addition, there are also challenges related to those that receive remittances. In one of the life history interviews, the respondent indicated that remittances represented an extra social and financial burden especially when a shock occurs within the household and extended family. She indicated that relatives expect her to have money for them since she receives money from her brother:

> My brother is the only person who has helped me in everything that I do. He is a very special person to me. He is the only relative who has helped me. I have friends but they only give me business ideas. Due to my special relationship with my brother I find that at times family members do not contribute money when there is a need such as someone is ill or a person has died. I end up funding various family affairs because most of my relatives think that that my brother who is in the United Kingdom always sends me money and therefore I am expected to have money at my disposal all the time. Even my sister thinks our only brother favours me and is one of those family relatives who think I can fund everything in times of family crisis. And so, these are some of my challenges. I am also facing hardships but everyone thinks otherwise.

While remittances from outside the country helped this respondent to start her own businesses and earn a living, her success has not come without cost, namely heightened expectations from close relatives that she had to help or even foot the bill in the event of an extended family crisis.

Rental income supporting livelihoods

Household heads also earn incomes from rentals, including from land, housing, other buildings, draught power and machinery. Proportionally more females heads compared to male heads had access to rental income. Age was a key determinant for earning this income. On average, those aged 49 earned rental income, while those that did not had an average age of 41.5 years. Given that rental income depends largely on a household's asset base, those with a higher score on the wealth index (at 4.53) had greater access to rental income while those with a smaller asset base did not earn rentals. In addition, household heads with rental income tended to be able to cope more adequately when it came to household shocks, as they could draw upon this income. Important to note is that there were no significant differences when the two categories of households were compared with regard to household size, household expenditure, education, shocks experienced and health within the household. Table 3.7 details the differences between the two groups of households.

Livelihood diversification

Like other households in Zimbabwe and low-income countries more broadly, most households in Budiriro rely on more than one source of income or livelihood activity to make a living. Livelihood diversification enables, among other things, to act as self-insurance against risk in a context where there is an absence of insurance and credit markets to stem declining income, to exploit positive interactions between different activities and to allow for aggregation effects when there are returns to assets (Ersado 2006). This study categorised households into three groups, that is, those households that rely on one livelihood activity, those that rely on two livelihood activities and those that rely on three or more livelihood activities. Apparent from this categorisation was that 35.5% of the households relied on one livelihood source while 39.4% and 25.1% relied – respectively – on two and three or more livelihood sources. To compare the three groups, a *Sidak Anova* test was utilised in order to understand the differences, which exist between the three groups of households.

The results of the *Sidak Anova* test indicate that age, gender, wealth index score and household expenditure are all directly associated with livelihood diversification. More specifically, households with older female household heads were more likely to diversify their incomes as compared to younger male household heads. On average, household heads with an age of 42.8 and 45.0 years of age engaged in more than two livelihood activities. The number of livelihood activities that households engage in is also associated with the wealth index score. The fewer the number of livelihood activities engaged in by a household, the lower the score they had within the wealth index; while the higher the number of livelihood activities, the higher the wealth index score for households.

Table 3.7 Recipients and non-recipients of rental income

Category of livelihood	Rent income	No rent income	p-values
Male (%)	16.0	84.0	0.552
Female (%)	19.3	80.7	
Age	49.04	41.51	0.001
Household size	4.79	4.25	0.125
Household expenditure	496.58	452.49	0.455
Wealth index	4.53	3.52	0.027
Education level	5.40	5.63	0.303

The same situation exists with regard to household expenditure. The data also shows that households which engaged in more than one livelihood activity were less likely to be food insecure using the indicator of the number of meals for a household per day.

Conclusion and policy insights

This chapter has provided an in-depth analysis of the ways in which households in Budiriro are making a living within a challenging context dominated by market and state failures. It is evident that households in Budiriro are engaged in various livelihood activities within the realms of, for example, formal and informal employment, agriculture and livestock rearing. To make a living, households in Budiriro also rely on remittances and rental incomes. It would seem that livelihood diversification is a key response for households in Budiriro with only 35.5% of the households relying on one livelihood activity alone. Further, households in Budiriro are not necessarily the same regardless of their location in the same low-income, high-density neighbourhood. Households in Budiriro are thus heterogeneous when classified according to expenditure and household assets. The three household categories (poor, average and better off) are linked to the type of livelihood activities in which households participate. For example, better-off households that are headed by men with household sizes of 5.5 are more likely to engage in agriculture as a livelihood activity than average households headed by women with a household size of 3.95, who are more likely to rely on cash transfers and remittances. This shows that households in Budiriro engage in livelihood activities depending on various factors such as household size, age, gender, intra and extra household relations as well as the level of household wealth and expenditure.

This study demonstrated that a large proportion of households in Budiriro heavily depend on the informal sector for survival. For example, household business enterprises are a key livelihood activity for households in Budiriro. This means that houses are often spatial sites of income generation and production. For purposes of policy-making for enhanced livelihood construction, this entails for example implementing zoning policies that protect and enhance household business enterprises at residential stands. More generally, this indicates the need for the Zimbabwean government to promote policies that favour the informal sector since the majority of urban households are making a living in this sector. Additionally the importance of systematic linkages between rural and urban areas in terms of farming in order to provide food staples in cities should not be underestimated. More specifically, improving the rural sector and particularly the agrarian economy may have positive impacts on urban dwellers in terms of food security; likewise, recognising the importance of urban agriculture and building its capacity through proper city by-laws and support mechanisms would make this livelihood activity less erratic. Any such policy interventions though need to empower women in particular, as they tend to be particularly disadvantaged when it comes to the urban economy and sustainable livelihoods.

References

Aronson, J. 1995. A Pragmatic View of Thematic Analysis. *The Qualitative Report*, 2 (1): 1–3.

Chagonda, T. 2012. Teachers' and Bank Workers' Responses to Zimbabwe's Crisis: Uneven Effects, Different Strategies. *Journal of Contemporary African Studies*, 30 (1): 83–97.

Chen, M., Roever, S. and Skinner, C. 2016. *Urban Livelihoods: Reframing Theory and Policy*. Sage Publications.

Chirau, T.J. 2012. *Understanding Livelihood Strategies of Urban Women Traders: a Case of Magaba, Harare in Zimbabwe*. Unpublished Master of Science Thesis. Sociology Department. Rhodes University. Grahamstown. South Africa.

Ersado, L. 2006. *Income Diversification in Zimbabwe: Welfare Implications From Urban And Rural Areas*. World Bank Publications.

Filmer, D. and Pritchett, L. 1999. The Effect of Household Wealth on Educational Attainment: Evidence from 35 Countries. *Population and Development Review*, 25 (1): 85–120.

Fox, L. and Sohnesen, T.P. 2012. *Household Enterprises In Sub-Saharan Africa: Why They Matter For Growth, Jobs, And Livelihoods*. Policy Research Working Papers, World Bank.

Howe, L.D., Hargreaves, J.R., Gabrysch, S. and Huttly, S.R. 2009. Is the Wealth Index a Proxy for Consumption Expenditure? A Systematic Review. *Journal of Epidemiology and Community Health*, 63 (11): 871–877.

Jones, J.L. 2010. "Nothing is Straight in Zimbabwe": The Rise of the Kukiya-Kiya Economy 2000–2008. *Journal of Southern African Studies*, 36: 285–299.

Kone-Coulibaly, A., Tshimanga, M., Shambira, G., Gombe, N., Chadambuka, A., Chonzi, P. and Mungofa, S. 2010. Risk Factors Associated With Cholera In Harare City, Zimbabwe, 2008. *East African Journal of Public Health*, 7 (4): 311–317.

Magure, B. 2014. Interpreting Urban Informality in Chegutu, Zimbabwe. *Journal Of Asian and African Studies*, 50: 650–666.

Manjengwa, J., Matema, C. and Tirivanhu, D. 2016. Understanding Urban Poverty in Two High-Density Suburbs of Harare, Zimbabwe. *Development Southern Africa*, 33 (1): 23–38.

Meyer, B.D. and Sullivan, J.X. 2003. *Measuring the Well-Being of the Poor Using Income and Consumption* (No. w9760). National Bureau of Economic Research.

Mlambo, A.S. 2017. From an Industrial Powerhouse to a Nation of Vendors: Over Two Decades of Economic Decline and Deindustrialization in Zimbabwe 1990–2015. *Journal of Developing Societies*, 33 (1): 99–125.

Mukwedeya, T. 2012. Enduring the Crisis: Remittances and Household Livelihood Strategies in Glen Norah, Harare. *Crisis*, pp. 42–58.

Musemwa, M. 2010. From "Sunshine City" to A Landscape Of Disaster: The Politics of Water, Sanitation and Disease in Harare, Zimbabwe, 1980–2009. *Journal of Developing Societies*, 26 (2): 165–206.

Nyamwanza, A.M. 2012. *Resiliency and Livelihoods Inquiry in Dynamic Vulnerability Contexts*. Doctoral Dissertation. The University of Manchester.

Rakodi, C. 1995. The Household Strategies of the Urban Poor: Coping with Poverty and Recession in Gweru, Zimbabwe. *Habitat International*, 19 (4): 447–471.

Sahn, D.E. and Stifel, D.C. 2000. Poverty Comparisons over Time and Across Countries in Africa. *World Development*, 28 (12): 2123–2155.

Shand, W., van Blerk, L. and Hunter, J. 2016. Economic Practices of African Street Youth: The Democratic Republic of Congo, Ghana, and Zimbabwe. *Labouring and Learning*, pp. 1–21.

Tamukamoyo, H. 2009. *Survival in a Collapsing Economy: A Case Study of Informal Trading at a Zimbabwean Flea Market*, Doctoral Dissertation, University of Witwatersrand.

UN-Habitat 2010. The State of African Cities 2010: *Governance, Inequality and Urban Land Markets*. United Nations Environment Programme, United Nations.

ZIMSTAT (Zimbabwe National Statistics Agency) 2012. Census National Report 2012. ZIMSTAT, Harare.

ZIMSTAT (Zimbabwe National Statistics Agency) 2015. Poverty Datum Lines-December 2015. ZIMSTAT, Harare.

4 Sex work as a livelihood strategy in the border town of Beitbridge

Wadzanai Takawira and Kirk Helliker

Introduction

This chapter examines the lives and livelihoods of sex workers in the border town of Beitbridge. In the literature on sex work broadly, and on sex work in colonial and post-colonial Zimbabwe more specifically, a range of themes are addressed. In the case of Zimbabwe, key themes include sex worker/client relationships, single mothers and the feminisation of poverty, HIV and sexually-transmitted diseases, sex work and criminality, alcohol and drug abuse, internal migration of sex workers, and underage sex workers (see, for example, Bhunu and Mushayabasa 2012, Hungwe 2006, Barnes 1992, Schmidt 1991, Elmes *et al.* 2014, Wasosa 2011, Muzvidziwa 1997, Magaisa 2001a, Busza 2004, Wilson *et al.* 1990, Ngugi *et al.* 1996). In addressing some of these themes with particular reference to Beitbridge sex workers, it becomes clear that the lives of the sex workers in Beitbridge are marked by precariousness and uncertainty. But they are not mere victims of their historical and social circumstances, of which patriarchal practices and economic crisis are central, as they are actively engaged in constructing their livelihoods.

Research site and sex worker profiles

The research for this chapter took place during a pivotal and crucial time for sex work in Zimbabwe. The Constitutional Court on 27 May 2015 delivered what has been construed as a landmark ruling in that it makes it more difficult now for sex workers to be arrested and prosecuted (without actually legalising sex work). But negative attitudes towards sex work continue to pervade Zimbabwean society, resulting in stigmatisation, discrimination and victimisation by both public and the police.

The town of Beitbridge is situated along the Zimbabwe-South Africa border in Matebeleland South Province. Beitbridge also popularly refers to the border post along the Limpopo River that forms the political border between South Africa and Zimbabwe. As of 2013, the population of Beitbridge was 26459. Beitbridge is reportedly Africa's busiest border post in terms of the volume and value of goods (and human and vehicular traffic) passing through it (Mate 2005).

In 2005, an estimated 7,000 truckers passed through the border post per month, with most of them spending several days to more than a week waiting to clear goods (Mate 2005).

The district of Beitbridge (in which the town is located) lies in an arid, agro-ecological region with low rainfall and a chronic food deficit. Crop production is near impossible without irrigation. Because of the relative absence of formal employment opportunities, town residents often rely on other forms of income, notably within the informal sector (for example street trading). But illegal activities also exist, including those of foreign currency traders and criminal elements such as thieves known as *magumaguma* (meaning 'to grab something violently'), as well as sex workers. Many Beitbridge residents, and mainly males, migrate to South Africa in search of employment prospects due to the proximity of the country (FHI 2003).

Beitbridge town has a history of being crowded in terms of the availability of accommodation. This crowded condition is attributable to the destruction of informal settlements (called *baghdads* locally) by the town council and the influx of migrants from all over Zimbabwe wishing to cross the border illegally into South Africa. Internal migrants who fail to cross into South Africa often end up taking up residency in Beitbridge. The high-density area called Dulibadzimu is where most informal traders reside and operate from. It is also where most of the town's brothels exist, known in Shona as *mabooking*, or simply *booking* in its singular form. The town's bus terminus and main rank are also situated in Duli-badzimu where hundreds of travellers going to or returning from South Africa pass through. The busy nightlife of Beitbridge (and specifically in Dulibadzimu) is ideal for the hundreds of sex workers who swarm the streets as early as 6 pm until dawn looking for clients.

In Zimbabwe, sex work occurs in the main in an illegal context and therefore access to the field is challenging and difficult. The evidence collected for this study took place over a period of two months in July and August of 2015. Three research methods were used, namely, in-depth interviews with sex workers, focus group discussions with sex workers and observation of the lives of sex workers. Random sampling was not possible because there is no well-defined population of sex workers in Beitbridge. As a result, non-random snowballing technique of sampling was employed as a means of recruiting sex worker participants. A drawback of the snowballing sampling technique is the repetition of evidence as referrals may be within a particular category of sex worker, which inhibits diversity. Because of this, the researchers deliberately befriended sex workers practicing in different locations in Beitbridge so as to ensure heterogeneity. The fieldwork was carried out in Shona, the language spoken by the sex workers and therefore communication was easy as one of the researchers is a native Shona speaker. The interviews were conducted mostly in the late afternoon, after the sex workers had rested in the mornings as their work required them being up the whole night. Interviews were conducted in places the participants felt comfortable and safe to disclose information about their personal lives. Therefore, some of these interviews actually took place in the brothels, either in the sex workers' rooms or the rooms of their friends, while some took place outside in the yard or verandas of brothels.

A total of 25 female commercial sex workers were interviewed, with pseudonyms used when quoting from the interviews and focus group discussions. No male clients were interviewed, so their perspectives and experiences are not covered in the discussion. In terms of age, 10 of the sex workers were in the age range of 21–25 years while the second most common age group (nine sex workers) was that of 26–30 years. The youngest age recorded for the sex workers was 21 years old and the oldest 40 years, though the sex workers referred to the existence of teenage sex workers in Beitbridge. None of the sex workers had any significant educational qualifications with the highest educational level recorded being Form 4 (by eight women), which is the Ordinary level in the Zimbabwean educational system. Four women had attended school up to grade 7, thus completing primary school education. None of the women had proceeded to the Advanced level.

Divorced or separated women (18 of them) constituted the highest proportion of the sex workers. Some women were widows (four) while three had never been married but had been impregnated by lovers. Every participant in the study was a single mother (with up to five children) except for two participants who had once given birth but lost their children in death. The sex work industry in Beitbridge is comprised of a large number of migrant women who have moved from other parts of Zimbabwe as sex workers. Some of the sex workers interviewed had practised in towns such as Masvingo (a few hundred kilometres north of Beitbridge) and even other border towns such as Victoria Falls along the Zambia-Zimbabwe border. Nomagugu, aged 26, had travelled all over Zimbabwe working as a sex worker in towns including Harare, Hwange, Gwanda and back to Beitbridge. Some migrant women had intended to become cross-border traders, but ended up living in Beitbridge after being unable to cross the border; in failing to find any form of secure employment, they ended up self-employed as sex workers. Only one of the sex workers reported that she was a Beitbridge local; the rest considered Beitbridge a place of work, but not a home.

'Sex work' and sex work literature

The term 'sex work' is to be used in this chapter, rather than prostitution. The latter term has negative moral connotations as it is used to demonise and stigmatise women who provide sexual services as a way of living (Tekola 2005). The term is also used as a marker to denote any supposedly unrespectable women, particularly those who move into social spaces that are considered to be male-controlled territories (Gaidzanwa 1995). The term 'sex worker' is a more inclusive and richer term than 'prostitute' as it highlights the complex set of social relations involved in sex work, including the provider of sexual services, the buyers of sex and those who in different ways shape the transactions (including the state's regulatory institutions, the tourism industry and direct intermediaries between the sex worker and client) (Truong 1990). In this respect, the sex workers in Beitbridge tended to view themselves from a sex worker and not prostitute perspective.

The global literature on sex work raises a number of themes such as motivations for sex work, conditions of sex work, sex work and AIDS, sex work and patriarchy, and sex work and client relations. A study for instance in the Tarai border town of Nepal revealed how political and socio-economic crises have had a bearing on the increase of not only voluntary but forced sex work (Hausner 2007). Sex work in Ethiopia is also reported as occurring under conditions of abject poverty, police harassment and brutality (Tekola 2005). A project on HIV and AIDS prevention and cure reveals how female sex workers and their clients play an important role in the spread of the AIDS epidemic in Zambia and elsewhere (FHI 2003). In South Africa a study conducted in Hillbrow on migrant sex workers revealed how sex workers flock to South Africa in search of economic empowerment and even sexual freedom Nyangairi 2010). In pursuing the examination of sex work in this chapter, the focus is on sex-worker livelihoods. But it will become evident that any such examination invariably addresses the many themes highlighted here.

In Zimbabwe, sex work is illegal. The history of sex work in Zimbabwe is closely associated with urbanisation and other processes of capitalist development in towns, mines and farming settlements (Magaisa 2001b, Moyo 1991). Rural women often saw towns as places of freedom from restrictive parents or in-laws. The absence of female employment in colonial towns such as Salisbury (now Harare) meant that these women looked for independent sources of income, leading at times to the provision of sexual services termed as *mapoto* arrangements (Hungwe 2006). Sex work continues to thrive in post-colonial Zimbabwe. The literature on sex work in post-colonial Zimbabwe often highlights the causes of, or motivations behind, sex work. In this regard, the possibility of viable livelihoods in Zimbabwe has been severely compromised since the 1990s because of the implementation of a structural adjustment programme and the subsequent fast track land reform programme. This context of vulnerability had led to increasing numbers of women resorting to sex work. One study in Masvingo by Muzvidziwa (1997) thus understands sex work as a hanging-on or survivalist strategy. The crisis in Zimbabwe has been externalised as well, in the sense that it has led to the migration of women to neighbouring countries to engage in sex work (Mate 2005). The relationship between the AIDS pandemic and sex work is also prominent in the Zimbabwean literature, as is the linkage between sex work and the prevalence of patriarchal practices (Magaisa 2001b). Thus sex work by women becomes contested while male promiscuity is considered acceptable.

Character of sex work in Beitbridge

Sex workers in Beitbridge float in and out of different categories of sex work: there are those who are based at truck stops, those who are street-based, bar- or tavern-based or even home-based. Though a few sex workers operated exclusively from one place, most revealed that they solicited for clients in numerous places depending on the availability of clients. One sex worker named Chipo, aged 25, preferred working at the truck stop along the Lutumba road, but on weekends visited bars such as Kalahari and Eland because the bars were busiest on weekends. In contrast, Thuleki, aged 37, was exclusively a home-based sex worker and preferred to have clients make appointments for home visits. This preference for home-based sex work was mostly noted among the older sex workers who preferred to operate in secrecy and feared public discrimination.

Beitbridge sex workers lamented about the lack of accommodation in the town. Because of this, brothels have become a relied upon source of both accommodation and place of work for sex workers. These brothels, mostly located in Dulibadzimu, are a huge source of income for local landlords who have turned their houses into brothels. Most of these brothels are conveniently situated more specifically near Dulibadzimu Bus Terminus in proximity to the large flow of travellers passing through Beitbridge as well as near local bars, clubs and taverns. Sex workers in Beitbridge refer to local brothels as *mabooking* because women book themselves into these brothels, which involve *kumacurtain* (a term derived from how they use curtains to divide a room into many portions where each sex worker has her own mattress for sleeping and working). Most sex workers reported that they lived and worked in *mabooking*. Even some who rented rooms in houses in Dulibadzimu for US$60 per month (where they lived), tended to work from brothels. This arrangement of sleeping at local houses was done in particular by sex workers who lived with their children in Beitbridge.

The sex workers complained about the steep fees charged in the brothels, with the standard rate in brothel rooms being 70 rand per day per sex worker, which was due every morning in advance. Sex workers might share one (curtain-divided) room with as many as eight sex workers. Margaret, aged 30, reveals the severity of the situation: "Imagine how bad it is when we get clients and we all have to sleep with our clients in that one room. At times you can actually see and hear people in the act". Four of the sex workers interviewed prided themselves on being seasonal sex workers outside of the country mostly in Johannesburg, South Africa where they would temporarily live and work for a few months. Others considered themselves international sex workers due to the fact they had passports and would accompany their truck driver clients to different countries providing sexual services.

Sex work motivation

Scholars such as Nyangairi (2010) and Bowen (2013) argue that exploring initial pathways into sex work plays a pivotal role in explaining the sex work phenomenon. The following quotation from a Beitbridge sex worker summarises many of the motivational factors behind entry into sex work, including socio-structural factors (such as poverty and marital problems) as well as individual dispositions and personal choices:

Some women would have been married before and some wouldn't have and would have just left their parents' homes and started going to bars and night clubs. Some would have been orphaned at a young age and are left with no one to take care of them, and then you try to look for a job but because maybe you are not educated or you do not have connections you end up becoming a sex worker.

A number of the participants narrated their childhood and teenage experiences and how the death of one parent or both parents had financially and socially crippled their lives, such that they turned to sex work. Child marriage was also a problem for some of the sex workers. In situations of poverty or economic crisis, the parents of girl-children – and particularly in rural areas – see marriage at times as a source of wealth generation to escape the cycle of poverty and thus the girl-child is married off. As Mildred said:

I got married at 15 years old to a man born in 1970. We had a 21-year-old difference. I had my first child at 17 and the second one at 19 years but we later divorced and I became a sex worker.

A study by Campbell and Kinnell (2000) showed how sex workers had been driven into sex work after running away from home to escape hardships. Catherine, aged 26, described how, after her parents divorced, life became tough for her because she had to live with an abusive grandfather. Catherine never attended a day of school in her life and, driven by the troubles of home, escaped at a young age to Harare and became a sex worker at 13. Early impregnation and the absence of financial support from the family places the financial burden of taking care of the child on the mother, and this is also a reason for sex-work entry in Beitbridge. This is illustrated by the experiences of Thulani: "I was still 14 years in 2003. I gave birth to a son called Wesley. After I gave birth my mother died. That is when I became a prostitute".

None of the participants in the study were married at the time of the study, though most (except for three) were married in the past. The high rate of divorce or separation amongst sex workers is significant in terms of entry into sex work. The number one cause of marital breakdown cited by the sex workers was gender-based domestic violence by their partner, along with infidelity by the partner. Given the loss of male financial support, these women ended up exploring sex work as a survival strategy. Jennifer recalls her marriage ordeals: "My husband was abusive, he would beat me up and cheat, would not give me money whether it was pay day, end of month or not. If you tried asking for the money, you would get a beating". Marital breakdown is also intensified by the patriarchal system of polygamy. Siwinile's account reveals how her marriage fell apart: "My husband found another wife and I returned to my home village where I began my trade as a sex worker. So up to today I am not married and I fend for myself". Infidelity, even within non-polygamous marriages, was also a problem for the Beitbridge sex workers.

The death of a spouse is also significant in that it often leads to financial insecurity and emotional trauma for the widow. Sex workers who had been widowed revealed how their lives had changed for the worse after the death of their spouses, and sometimes because of patriarchal practices. The case of Cynthia, aged 38, shows how due to the death of their partner, women are left financially unstable and may have to resort to sex work:

> I was happily married for 12 years till my husband died and afterwards my husband's father took all my property because we had bought the house from him and we were not legally married, so life was very hard for me and my sons.

Despite the various social, cultural and personal factors behind entry into sex work, the main underlying motivational factor is economic necessity. The study participants seemed to be locked in cyclical and structural poverty both prior to and during their engagement in sex work. The need to obtain some source of financial income (no matter how unpredictable and erratic) in the harsh economic environment of Zimbabwe precipitated becoming sex workers. Margaret's narrative fully encapsulates this:

> I came to Beitbridge to do this work after I left my job as a bar maid at some night club in Nemamwa, Great Zimbabwe. It was the time when there were a lot of hardships in 2008 and my employer could not afford to pay me so he decided to close his bar and that's when I came to Beitbridge.

The low educational attainment levels of women, absence of work experience and limited capital leads to sex work as a livelihood strategy option. This resonates with Margaret's narrative:

> I chose to be a sex worker because there is no other work I can do in my life. I did not continue with my education. I stopped going to school at form two and there is nothing I can do with my form two education.

All of these factors combined (economic, social and cultural) have led to the existence of sex workers in Beitbridge as single mothers and as female household heads. In this context, some sex workers claimed that sex work gave them a form of cultural and sexual freedom to live their lives without the control of men:

> At times a girl can grow up with a single mother or would have seen other sex workers going to the bar living their independent lives, getting into their own houses, exchanging sexual partners and just aspire to be like that and start thinking that I will be in charge of myself; no one else will control me.

Origins and ongoing linkages

Clearly, the previous life and past experiences of sex workers (including their childhood and marital backgrounds) along with the current context of serious economic challenges in Zimbabwe, together played a crucial role in shaping the current lives of the women in Beitbridge. To further examine the lives of these women, I explore their places of rural and urban origin and ongoing linkages with these places. All of the sex workers with the exception of Elizabeth (who is originally from Beitbridge) stated how Beitbridge was only a place of work and they still considered their place of origin (often specific villages in rural areas) as home. As argued by Wolffers and van Beelen (2003) and Nyangairi (2010), sex workers are highly mobile individuals and rarely practice sex work in their places of birth. Sex workers revealed Beitbridge offered a safe haven for them to work freely with relative anonymity (although their friends or relatives occasionally visited the town). Tendai illustrates this:

> This is only a place of work. I saw I could not work from home because of the way they would treat my children and me. I don't want people calling my children *mwanawehure* [the child of a prostitute], so I would rather work far from home.

Discussions of Zimbabwean sex work have long associated sex work with the mass movement of rural women to urbanised towns in search of work and better prospects in life (Magaisa 2001b, Barnes 1992). Beitbridge sex work fits into this broad narrative. Migration from rural areas in particular to Beitbridge remains significant for sex workers and the socio-cultural systems embedded in rural areas continue to govern the lives of sex workers. This trend of migration to Beitbridge in search of work is evident in the evidence collected:

> I come from Mwenezi, Sarahuru. We [her and her sister] are still based there with our parents because we are both divorced; my sister first came here after she left her husband when they fought and she ran away, so she now told me to come here and we started staying here.

The deepening phenomenon of urban poverty, which has particularly emerged in the wake of the economic crisis in Zimbabwe (Potts 2006), has been pivotal in the emergence and presence of a relatively new type of migration, involving movement from towns in the centre of Zimbabwe to border towns where the proximity to neighbouring countries also provided employment prospects for the women migrants. Some of the sex workers studied thus stated they had come to Beitbridge from the capital city, Harare, in search of work due to acute poverty:

> I was impregnated by my employer's son when I worked as a maid in Harare; they chased me away from their house and refused to help me. I could not survive in Harare, I was jobless and Harare is too expensive so I came to Beitbridge.

Beitbridge town is popular in the wider sex work community in Zimbabwe due to the high rate of sex work returns in the town.

Rural origins (and linkages) are a central part of the lives of many Beibridge sex workers and often a bulk of sex work income is remitted back to rural homes. These women stressed that they were the main breadwinners for their families of origin:

> I am the only one working in my family, so I make sure that my siblings, my mother and my children have clothes and food. When I started sex work, I looked for a stand for them there in the rural areas and I built her [the mother] one round hut.

Busza (2004:238) argues that, despite the adherence to moral values in rural areas and a general disapproval of sex work as "bad work", there seems to be a shift in perceptions towards sex work as a taboo and demonised profession to a legitimate profession, or at least as one acceptable as a form of livelihood activity and income generation for rural existence. When asked if their families were aware of the source of the funds they received, some sex workers replied in the affirmative. They stated that, even though their families initially disapproved, they eventually accepted it because the need to survive took precedence over any moral values:

> At times you know that they know what you do, but they don't say anything to us or, if they do, all they say is we cannot control you or stop you; … because if we stop, what will they eat; there will be no food at home.

Contrary then to some studies (Balfour and Allen 2014:3), the sex workers in Beitbridge do not cut ties with their families of origin, though they preferred to visit their families back home than have their families visit them in Beitbridge. This guaranteed them a certain level of anonymity especially for those who kept their work a secret as Sharon noted: "I go back home to Victoria Falls after about three or four months; they don't come here because they don't know the kind of job I do. They think I am a domestic worker." The home of origin is also seen as a place of refuge in times of trouble for the sex workers, as rural kin for instance act as a support system especially in times of sickness or when their children (who live with their rural family) fall sick as Tatenda highlights: "I visit my relatives such as when my child got sick with nhova [a dehydration-related illness affecting the fontanel]. I went back to the rural village with her for three months to get treated".

Sex work income and expenditure

The key purpose of engaging in sex work, like any other form of work, be it formal or informal, is to ensure a source of income. Income from sex work in Beitbridge was inconsistent and variable depending on a number of factors such as type of sexual activity undertaken and length of sexual episode, location of sex, how the sex worker is dressed, type of client, time of month and the economic climate. However, there seemed to be standard rates for sexual charges depending on location. The standard rate for a sexual episode for street-based sex work was different from that charged in bar-based and truck-based sex work. Street-based work yielded the least amount of income with the standard rate for a 'short time' being 20 rand. A 'short time' referred to a single sexual episode, which lasted from about five to ten minutes and ended when a client ejaculated. If a man takes longer to ejaculate, he must pay more. The standard rate for a 'night', which referred to the provision of sexual services for an entire night, ranged from 150 rand to 250 rand for street-based sex workers. Charges were subject to variation depending upon the client, as some clients were generous enough to pay more if they were deeply satisfied with the sexual services. Some clients nonetheless preferred to negotiate for lesser charges, with the rate going down to as little as 15 rand for a short time, especially with Malawian clients who sex workers accused of being frugal with their money. Bar-based and truck-based sex work yielded a higher income with the standard rate for a short time being 50 rand and for a night ranging from 250 to 300 Rand. This difference in charges was based on the expenditures women incurred in travelling to bars and truck stops looking for clients, and with no guarantee of finding a client.

Variation in income was based on the type of clients, with sex workers reporting that they charged truck drivers more than the typical street clients, as truck drivers were known to offer more money. Truck drivers offered as much as US$100 for sex, albeit unsafe (or unprotected) sex. This corroborates with an earlier study on sex work in Beitbridge which discovered that truck drivers were prepared to pay considerable money as a 'risk allowance' to cater for the possible consequences of unsafe sex for the sex worker. This allowance was supposed to cover the sex worker's future sexually transmitted infection treatment or to compensate for any possible HIV infection (IOM, CARE and SIDA 2003).

The income of sex workers tended to increase based on the way they dressed and the sexual skills they had. Provocative dressing is viewed as a form of identification for sex workers and a way of advertising one's 'wares'. Clothing, make up and good hair are viewed as valuable physical assets that, if well coordinated, could attract more clients and higher earnings for the women. As Sharon said:

> It's important because as you know men have always liked beautiful things, they like beautiful women. If you bath well, dress well and smell good you get more clients; men are disgusted by scruffy looking women.

Enhanced sexual skills and reputation were also important and according to Tendai

> a man will leave you [not be a return customer] if he is not satisfied sexually.

Because of the deteriorating economic climate in Zimbabwe, sex workers in Beitbridge were experiencing a reduction in their sex work income as noted in the focus group discussions:

We don't make as much money as we used to when things were better. Now things are hard for everyone so when clients don't have money it means we also don't have money. When they lose their jobs how can someone come to you and pay for sex.

Though the sex workers stated that they preferred to be paid in monetary terms (that is, cash), some acquiesced to the fact that they occasionally received other forms of payment besides money, such as foodstuffs, cell phones and clothes. Thus, some sex workers operated on a strictly cash only basis, but others were more flexible and would negotiate with clients who were short of cash but in need of sex. Sharon highlighted this:

At times a truck driver can say he has no cash but has groceries in his truck so we could exchange that for sex. You could end up with a 5 litre tin of cooking oil, 1 kg of surf and a bar of soap.

On average, the women in Beitbridge made about R4,000 per month, which is more than they would make in low-paying work including as shop assistants or domestic workers.

Broadly speaking, sex workers in Beitbridge highlighted that sex work was their only livelihood strategy and source of income, though some had other less important forms of income. Those who solely relied on sex work income cited factors, which inhibited their capacity to perform other work, such as the absence of any other form of employment in Beitbridge as well as the time consuming and physically strenuous nature of sex work. Other sex workers who had entrepreneurial skills reported that, apart from sex work, they had other sources of income, albeit smaller than their overall sex work income. For example Cynthia noted: "I sell braids, cobra [floor polish] and drinks so roughly in a month I get about R800 or R500 profit from what I sell".

Many of the sex workers, as indicated earlier, have their children living with family in their place of origin. In the focus group discussions they noted that they regularly remit money to their families, as "they are the reason we are here". As such, sex workers in Beitbridge shared a huge sense of moral responsibility in providing for their families. Sex workers like Tafadzwa illustrate this: "When I started sex work I was able to buy my mother a stand in the rural areas and I built her one round hut. I also make sure that my mother, siblings and children have clothes and food". Other sex workers stated how they had become employers in their own right by hiring help for their families in the rural areas to take care of their children. Therefore, they had to send money occasionally to pay their helpers.

The bulk of sex worker income however is spent on accommodation in Beitbridge. The daily rental fee for brothels took up a large portion of their income, such that it left them with insufficient income to pay for their other daily expenses. In the case of certain sex workers who lived with their children, the amount of income consumed by daily expenses was excessive – they paid for their own accommodation, plus the daily rate for the brothel where they worked, as well as a care-giver at night for their children. Sex work income was also spent on operational expenses associated with sex work. These expenses were incurred in the purchase of products that can be regarded as tools of the sex work trade, such as clothes, cosmetics, tissues, cotton and condoms. Though condoms were given out for free at the local clinic and hospital, some clients preferred to use different brands of condoms deemed as better quality than the free protector-plus condoms. Hence, the women occasionally had to buy condoms from super-markets or bottle stores. Due to the absence of cooking facilities in the brothels where they stayed, the sex workers buy food on a daily basis as noted by one participant: "All you have is your mattress and blankets in the booking. We are not allowed to cook so we buy sadza to eat for five rand or a dollar".

Client and sex worker relations

Client and sex worker relations are tenuous and fall along a continuum from women who have undergone varying degrees of violence to those who have had friendships and romance with clients. The clientele of Beitbridge sex workers is a broad and heterogeneous group of men with varying demographic profiles such that there is no typical client. Sex workers, in general, are non-discriminatory in that any male can be a client as long as he can pay for the sexual services pro-vided. The clients of the local sex workers comprise local informal traders (including touts known as *mahwindi* from the nearby Dulibadzimu bus termi-nus); border jumpers; travellers passing through the border to and from South Africa; truck drivers; and businessmen importing cars. Other clients include gov-ernment officials such as the police and border officials (including clearing agents, as well as Zimbabwe Revenue Authority and Immigration officials) who visited sex workers in civilian clothing.

Sex workers seemed to classify their clients into repeat and one-off clients. One-off clients were total strangers who came once for sexual services and never returned, while repeat clients were those who were regulars. Local Zimbabwean men were the most popular in terms of generously paying the sex workers. More specifically, the women reported that local touts and thieves or robbers paid them more money due to the fact that they had large sums of fast cash, which they could spend on sex workers. Despite the generous tips from thieves and robbers, they posed a threat to sex workers. For instance, sex workers end up being accused as accomplices of the thieves by the police, along with other problems such as theft and violence.

In some cases, the sex workers provided domestic services in addition to sexual services to their clients to increase their income. This was only done for a select grouping of clients who were prepared to pay more than, for example, the average 20 Rand for a short time. These better-paying clients thus enjoyed addi-tional (non-sexual) services albeit for a higher price for sex than the other clients. This domestic service provision was, as well, a strategy used by sex workers to induce the clients to stay longer with the sex workers and thereby spend more money on them. In the focus group discussions, it was highlighted that:

We can cook breakfast even for the one-day clients especially if you see there is a lot of money [from the clients]. You have to take advantage so you take their clothes and wash them whilst they are sleeping, then you also sleep with them afterwards. We can make them stay for some days with us cooking and washing for them and sleeping with them. We just don't cook for the 20 Rand clients.

The interviews also revealed the presence of a certain type of client, namely married men who frequented sex workers. Married men were popular amongst sex workers because they paid well. This of course gives an insight into the high level of infidelity in Beitbridge. The 'small house' is a Zimbabwean metaphor used for women who engage in extra-marital affairs with married men. Some of the sex worker participants seemed to double as both sex workers and 'small houses'. As Tafadzwa indicated:

Yes, I do have a boyfriend, but he's someone's husband. We are in love. The wife knows about it, but she doesn't know me or know where I stay. We just know each other over the phone in calling each other and shouting at each other.

However, there were some sex workers who had simple one-off encounters with married men by providing sexual services but not entering into romantic relationships with them. Despite the income they made from married clients, some of the sex workers confessed that they did not enjoy sleeping with married men because, as women (and former wives), they had gone through the painful experience of infidelity with their own former husbands.

Pervasive violence was evident in the current lives of the sex workers in Beitbridge with many narrating horrifying stories of gender-based violence at the hands of clients. This violence usually took the form of physical violence through being beaten up and robbed, but at times it involved rape. As Tafadzwa recounted:

A client had hired me at the bar and said to me "let's get a taxi and go to my house". Since I was still new to Beitbridge, I did not know that he was leading me on a stray path into the bushes near the Limpopo River. He slept with me without protection and afterwards he stabbed me and stole my phone.

Another sex worker narrated a painful experience of her rape ordeal:

I brought a client home from the bar and after we had sex, I asked for my money and he refused to give it to me and then he started forcefully stripping off my trousers again. Then he raped me.

Sex workers sometimes reported violence, rape and robbery to the police but their cases were hardly taken seriously and their perpetrators went free.

The interviews in fact brought to the fore a common pattern of clients refusing to pay for sexual services rendered or demanding their money back after their sexual encounters. This habit commonly termed *kukerechura* by sex workers was cited as one of the major drawbacks of sex work and regularly led to violence. Thus, refusal to comply with the client's demands, which is linked to refusal to pay for services, was cited as one of the causes of client violence. To guard against *kukerechura*, the sex workers devised coping mechanisms so as to guarantee payment for their services. Sex workers had their clients pay for services before they have sex and they would give this money to their fellow sex workers for safekeeping. Further, some mentioned that they asked their clients to pay them through the mobile payment system common in Zimbabwe such as Ecocash whereby the money is transferred through a mobile banking system.

These traumatic and violent relations with clients are juxtaposed to the harmonious and friendly relations that sex workers had with some of their clients. A number of sex workers had forged friendships with their clients based on mutual understanding and respect. These clients even provided financial support to sex workers when they were stranded as Cynthia highlighted:

> I have become friends with some of them. I can call them when I need help because sometimes you fail to get clients for two or three days and you live from hand to mouth and you need money for food. When things are really tough and I do not have money for my child's school fees, I do have friends who are clients who loan me some money and, if they are far, they send me money via eco-cash.

Some sex worker-client relationships have even became romantic and this has led to marriage.

Due to the multi-sexual partner character intrinsic to sex work, sex workers constitute a high risk and vulnerable group to health hazards from clients, such as HIV and sexually transmitted diseases. Despite attempts by local health authorities and non-governmental organisations to reduce the rate of HIV transmission within Beitbridge, the disease continues to affect a large proportion of sex workers in the town. The most obvious reason for this was attributed, by the sex workers, to the constant refusal by clients to engage in protected sex (i.e. using condoms). Though some sex workers did not reveal voluntarily their HIV status, most sex workers in the study openly confessed that they were HIV positive and had been infected by their clients through their work.

In this regard, structural factors such as sexual violence and perpetual poverty play a restrictive role in limiting the options available to sex workers. Sex workers in Beitbridge explained how they could not always refuse the large sums of money offered by clients for unprotected sex because they needed the money:

> Some offer you as much as [US] $100 for unprotected sex and because you need money you will agree and maybe you would not have had a client for

days or that night and you have no money and you need to pay rent to the brothel so you end up taking it.

Sex workers highlighted how clients would implement exceptional and even extreme measures in having unprotected sex, which included going so far as to deliberately tear condoms while having sex. Chipo maintained that, as sex workers, they had to put the condoms on the men because some men tore holes in the condoms. Even when condoms broke during the sexual encounter, clients were known to refuse to stop to put on another one. Jennifer explained the reasons men usually gave for not using a condom:

> Most men don't like condoms as *vanoda nyoro* [they want it raw]. They say that it's not sweet or nice if it's covered in paper, because then they don't feel anything. Others say to us: 'how can you eat an orange with the peels on? It does not taste sweet' so I guess it's the same for them.

As well as being exposed to HIV and other infections, sex workers in Beitbridge are susceptible to unwanted pregnancies and abortions.

Conclusion and policy insights

This chapter has provided a detailed examination of the lives and livelihoods of sex workers in the border town of Beitbridge. Though there is considerable diversity amongst the 25 sex workers studied, it is quite clear that they experience common challenges in seeking to make a living through sex work, including problems pertaining to accommodation, sexually-transmitted diseases and abuse by clients. Sex work is not undertaken voluntarily (as if it were the profession of choice) as structural factors compelled these single women to enter the sex work trade in Beitbridge, as elsewhere. Once in the trade, they constantly seek to negotiate their way through this troubled space in order to minimise risk and maximise benefits, not only for themselves but for their children and families of origin as well. Though the sex workers reject the broad-based stigma of the sex worker status, they see sex work as a temporary aberration to their ideal life course. They desire work beyond sex work but, given the ongoing economic crisis in Zimbabwe, their temporary status tends to be prolonged.

References

Balfour, R. and Allen, J. 2014. *A Review of the Literature on Sex Workers and Social Exclusion.* UCL Institute of Health Equity.

Barnes, T.A. 1992. The Fight for Control of African Women's Mobility in Colonial Zimbabwe, 1900–1939. *Chicago Journals,* 7 (3): 586–608.

Bhunu, C.P. and Mushayabasa, S. 2012. Prostitution and Drug (Alcohol) Misuse: The Menacing Combination. *Journal of Biological Systems,* 20 (2): 177–193.

Bowen, R.R. 2013. *They Walk Among Us: Sex Work Exiting, Re-entry and Duality.* Master's Thesis. Canada: Simon Fraser University.

Busza, J. 2004. Sex Work and Migration: The Dangers of Oversimplification: A Case Study of Vietnamese Women in Cambodia. *Health and Human Rights*, 7 (2): 231–249.

Campbell, R. and Kinnell, H. 2000. We Shouldn't Have to Put Up with This: Street Sex Work and Violence. *Criminal Justice Matters*, 42 (1): 12–13.

Elmes, J., Nhongo, K., Ward, H., Hallett, T., Nyamukapa, C., White, P.J. and Gregson, S. 2014. The Price of Sex: Condom Use and the Determinants of the Price of Sex among Female Sex Workers in Eastern Zimbabwe. *The Journal of Infectious Diseases*, 210 (S2): 569–578.

Family Health International (FHI) 2003. *Behavioural and Biologic Surveillance Survey in Selected Transportation Border Routes, Zambia.* Institute of Economic and Social Research (INESCOR), University of Zambia Tropical Diseases Research Center (TDRC), Ndola.

Gaidzanwa, R.B. 1995. *Women, Democratisation and Violence in Southern African Experience.* Paper presented at a seminar on Women and the Democratisation Process in Africa, University of Pretoria, South Africa, April 7–11.

Hausner, S.L. 2007. Border Towns in the Tarai: Sites of Migration. *Occasional Papers in Sociology and Anthropology*, 10: 107–123.

Hungwe, C. 2006. *Putting Them in their Place: Unrespectable and Respectable Women in Zimbabwean Gender Struggles.* African Gender Institute, University of Cape Town, South Africa.

IOM, CARE and SIDA. 2003. *Mobility and HIV/AIDS in Southern Africa: A Field Study in South Africa, Zimbabwe and Mozambique.* Pretoria: International Organisation for Migration.

Magaisa, I. 2001a. We Came to the Bridge for Money: Prostitution at a Rural Service Centre. In P. Hebinck and M. Bourdillon (eds), *Women, Men and Work: Rural Livelihoods in South-Eastern Zimbabwe*, (pp. 103–116). Harare: Weaver Press.

Magaisa, I. 2001b. Prostitution, Patriarchy and Marriage: A Zimbabwean Case Study. In A. Rwomire (ed.), *African Women and Children: Crisis and Response.* (pp. 127–142). Westport, Connecticut: Praeger.

Mate, R. 2005. *Making Ends Meet at the Margins? Grappling with Economic Crisis and Belonging in Beitbridge Town, Zimbabwe.* Dakar: Council for the Development of Social Sciences Research in Africa.

Moyo, S. 1991. *The Prostitution Question: With Special Reference to Zimbabwe.* Harare: Zimbabwe Institute of Development Studies.

Muzvidziwa, V.N. 1997. Prostitutes: Vendors of Another Type? *Journal of Social Development in Africa*, 2 (2): 75–89.

Ngugi, E.N., Wilson, D., Sebstad, J., Plummer, F.A. and Moses, S. 1996. Focused Peer-mediated Educational Programs Among Female Sex Workers to Reduce Sexually Transmitted Disease and Human Immunodeficiency Virus Transmission in Kenya and Zimbabwe. *The Journal of Infectious Diseases*, 174 (2): 8240–8247.

Nyangairi, B. 2010. *Migrant Women in Sex Work: Trajectories and Perceptions of Zimbabwean Sex workers in Hillbrow, South Africa.* Masters' thesis, University of Witwatersrand.

Potts, D. 2006. Restoring Order? Operation Murambatsvina and the Urban Crisis in Zimbabwe. *Journal of Southern African Studies*, 32 (2): 273–291.

Schmidt, E. 1991. Patriarchy, Capitalism, and the Colonial State in Zimbabwe. *Chicago Journals. Women, Family, State, and Economy in Africa*, 16 (4): 732–756.

Tekola, B. 2005. *Poverty and the Social context of Sex Work in Addis Ababa: An Anthropological Perspective.* Addis Ababa: Forum for Social Studies.

Truong, T. 1990. *Sex, Money and Morality: Prostitution and Tourism in Southeast Asia.* London and New Jersey: Zed Books Ltd.

Wasosa, W. 2011. Prostitution in Selected Colonial and Post-Colonial Shona Novels. *Journal of African Studies and Development*, 3 (2): 25–32.

Wilson, D., Sibanda, B., Mboyi, L., Msimanga, S. and Dube, G. 1990. A Pilot Study for an HIV Prevention Programme Among Commercial Sex Workers in Bulawayo, Zimbabwe. *Social Science and Medicine*, 31 (5): 609–618.

Wolffers, I. and van Beelen, N. 2003. Public Health and the Human Rights of Sex Workers. *Lancet* 36 (9373): 1981.

5   Migration-based livelihoods in post-2000 Zimbabwe

Manase Kudzai Chiweshe

Introduction

Zimbabwe post-2000 descended into socio-political crisis with devastating economic impact. Migration in its various forms emerged as an important survival strategy. This chapter uses interviews and secondary data to highlight how migration was utilised as a way of surviving the crisis. The Zimbabwean crisis was characterised by rapid inflation, food shortages, high formal unemployment and cash shortages. This chapter does not seek to romanticise the role migration played as a survival strategy. It does not seek to overstate the positive aspects of migration without highlighting emerging issues in Zimbabwe such as child and women trafficking, unaccompanied child migration and xenophobia attacks in South Africa. Most livelihoods based on the various types of migration experienced in Zimbabwe are ephemeral and survivalist in nature. What this chapter does is show how migration within the current Zimbabwean context has been used as a survival strategy in various ways. There are so many important avenues to understanding migration in Zimbabwe including social networks of migrant communities, transnational families, macroeconomics of remittances and impact of migration on the economy, trade and skills transfer. This chapter however focuses on providing an overview of the experiences of various people involved in migration-based livelihood options post-2000.

Background

Whilst the post-2000 Zimbabwean crisis has a long historical trajectory, this chapter will concentrate on outlining the precursors such as farm occupations, the Fast Track Land Reform Programme, political violence, sanctions, corruption and continuous economic mismanagement. By early 2000, Zimbabwe was facing an unprecedented social and economic crisis. The deteriorating economic situation adversely impacted on the pace of land reform. The food riots in 1998 were the beginning of open protest against the ZANU-PF establishment in postcolonial Zimbabwe. The economy was severely compromised by the costs of the war in the Democratic Republic of Congo, and war veterans' pay-outs in the late

1990s also took their toll. The Zimbabwe Congress of Trade Unions took the lead as a conglomeration of civil society organisations challenged the ruling party's hegemony; further, the formation of the Movement for Democratic Change (MDC) in 1999 was the first real threat to ZANU-PF's political hegemony in Zimbabwe. The rejection of the draft constitution in February 2000 was a precursor to the land occupations in Zimbabwe in 2000 and 2001, a period popularly known as *jambanja* (chaos) due to the violent nature of the process (Chiweshe 2011).

Gross Domestic Product (GDP) in Zimbabwe declined by about 43% between 2000 and 2007. Coltart (2008:2) notes that agriculture, which historically was the mainstay of the economy, declined dramatically after 2000 due to the land reform programme. For example, annual wheat production plummeted from a high of over 300,000 tons in 1990 to less than 50,000 in 2007. Tobacco, which was Zimbabwe's single largest generator of foreign exchange and accounted for almost one-third of Zimbabwe's foreign exchange earnings in 2000, fell from US$600 million in earnings in 2000 to less than US$125 million in 2007.[1] The manufacturing sector shrunk by more than 47% between 1998 and 2006, which carried output levels back to figures recorded in 1972 (Coltart 2008:2). Government figures indicate that the rate of inflation had been rising since 2000 and had reached its highest at more than 1,500% in 2008.[2] Independent analysts however placed the rate of inflation at 150,000%. At the time, the second highest inflation rate in the world was Iraq at only 58%.

The end result of this was the widespread migration (legal and illegal) of Zimbabweans (skilled and non-skilled) to all parts of the world but mainly South Africa, the United Kingdom, Australia and Botswana.[3] Further, with unemployment hitting the 80%[4] mark in 2008, Robertson (in Coltart 2008) estimated that the proportion of the population living below the official poverty line had more than doubled since the mid-1990s to over 80%. Coltart (2008:7) adds that Zimbabwe's human development indicators ranked 151st of 177 countries surveyed. In 2006, the World Health Organisation (WHO) reported that people living in Zimbabwe had one of the lowest life expectancies in the world.[5] Since 1994, the average life expectancy for women in Zimbabwe has fallen from 57 years to 34 years and for men from 54 years to 37 years.

According to WHO, an estimated 3,500 Zimbabweans die every week through the deadly combination of HIV and AIDS, poverty and malnutrition. The 2005 Zimbabwe Vulnerability Assessment Committee (ZIMVAC) report also estimated that 36% (2.9 million) of the rural population would not be able to meet its household food requirements during the 2005/2006 season (Murisa 2010:72). According to findings released in July 2006 by the Zimbabwe Demographic Health Survey, the health of Zimbabwean children has deteriorated dramatically. For example, in 70% of Zimbabwe's provinces, more children suffer from stunted growth now than ever before. Coupled with HIV and AIDS, the Zimbabwean crisis hence has had serious humanitarian consequences, which was worsened in 2005 by Operation *Murambatsvina*[6] which displaced over a million people in urban areas.

Methodology

This chapter uses a qualitative research paradigm to engage the voices of purposively sampled respondents who engaged in various forms of migration as a survival strategy. The chapter also utilises desk research to complement the in-depth interviews. Desk research uses statistics and written accounts that highlight the importance of migration in how people survived the Zimbabwean crisis post-2000. Qualitative research methods were appropriate for this (exploratory) study which sought thick descriptions of experiences of migrants in Zimbabwe. The sample of 10 men and 10 women was drawn from people in Harare. Whilst the sample is small and limited in terms of geographical coverage, it provides an important exploratory entry point into an under-theorised area of study. This chapter does not seek to generalise the findings of this study. It provides emerging ways of understanding migration as a historical survival strategy that black Zimbabweans adopted under colonial rule. The sample included an equal number of men and women mainly because migration is a gendered process. In post-2000 Zimbabwe, both men and women are involved in migration but the nature and length of stay are influenced by various factors including gender, age, marital status and class. The interviews were conducted between September and November 2016 in Harare.

The study utilised in-depth interviews mainly because they allow the voice of the respondents to emerge. The focus of the research is on understanding the qualitative impact of migration on livelihoods. The respondents ranged in age between 23 and 38 years of age. The study does not seek to generalise the findings or provide a statistical analysis of migration patterns. The sample is thus not meant to be representative of all Zimbabweans involved in migration. The respondents are adequate for this nature of study because it is exploratory in nature. The study also utilised desk research to highlight the historical nature of migration.

Conceptual framing of migration

Within the context of this chapter, migration is understood as a multi-faceted process which defies simple definitions. Migration is a complex and contested concept. Portes (1999) outlines the various levels of migration which include: the origins of migration; the directionality and continuity of migrant flows; the utilisation of immigrant labour; and the socio-cultural adaptation of migrants. National Geographic defines migration as:

> Migration (human) is the movement of people from one place in the world to another for the purpose of taking up permanent or semi permanent residence, usually across a political boundary. An example of "semi permanent residence" would be the seasonal movements of migrant farm laborers. People can either choose to move ("voluntary migration") or be forced to move ("involuntary migration").[7]

This distinction between voluntary and involuntary migration matters in the context of Zimbabwe. Zimbabwean migrants provide a complex mix of voluntary and involuntary migrants who do not fit neatly in this dichotomy. Economic crisis can be viewed as a factor that forced the majority to undertake migration. Migration was however a rational choice amongst many households facing uncertainty. Hunter *et al.* (2015) use the new economics labour migration theory to show that migration is often a household strategy to diversify risk.

Another interesting concept that is important for this specific chapter is the refugee. A refugee is defined by the 1951 Refugee Convention as:

> ... someone who "owing to a well-founded fear of being persecuted for reasons of race, religion, nationality, membership of a particular social group or political opinion, is outside the country of his nationality, and is unable to, or owing to such fear, is unwilling to avail himself of the protection of that country."

This definition provides the basis to question the status of many Zimbabweans living outside the country both legally and illegally. Most Zimbabwean immigrants (long and short term) post-2000 were often responding to the food shortages and economic crisis whilst a few were responding to political violence and persecution. This definition is thus limited when discussing a group of people migrating for economic and not political reasons. Zimbabweans in South Africa have been often referred to as 'economic refugees' because they are presumably escaping from economic persecution. In international law however there is a distinct difference between refugees and migrants (with the emphasis here on economic migrants). As UNHCR (the UN refugee agency) argues:

> Global migration patterns have become increasingly complex in modern times, involving not just refugees, but also millions of economic migrants. But refugees and migrants, even if they often travel in the same way, are fundamentally different, and for that reason are treated very differently under modern international law. Migrants, especially economic migrants, choose to move in order to improve the future prospects of themselves and their families. Refugees have to move if they are to save their lives or preserve their freedom.[8]

The 1969 Convention Governing the Specific Aspects of Refugee Problems in Africa expands the meaning of refugee to include people who left their countries of origin not only because of persecution but also due to acts of external aggression, occupation, domination by foreign powers or serious disturbances of public order. Even within this framework, Zimbabwean economic migrants cannot be defined as refugees.

Evolution of migration in Zimbabwe

Movement of people across southern Africa predates colonially imposed borders. People and communities migrated freely for various reasons including relocation, hunting and war. Migration in Zimbabwe emerged under colonial rule through various processes. Hungwe (2012) outlines three reasons for the emergence of migration in Zimbabwe.

> 1. cyclical recurrence of droughts in the semi-arid regions of Masvingo, Matabeleland South, Matabeleland North and the Midlands which depended mostly on rainfed agriculture. 2. expropriation of land through various legal instruments such as the Land Apportionment Act of 1930, the Land husbandry Act of 1951 and taxation (hut tax, poll tax, dog tax etc.). 3. 'forced labour' under the Rhodesian Native Labour Bureau (RNLB). Most desertions from Rhodesian mines resulted in migration down South. The RNLB wages simply could not compare with the attractive wages offered by the Witwatersrand Native Labour Association.
>
> (Hungwe 2012:132)

Van Onslen (1976) describes this system of stimulation and strangulation to induce labour migration as *chibharo* (loosely translated as forced labour). The loss of land coupled with the introduction of taxes ensured that black people turned to wage labour. South African mines offered better salaries and thus began the great trek to the gold mines.

Zimbabwe and most parts of southern Africa were largely unaffected by the slave trade; thus colonisation fostered migration as we understand it today. The Berlin Conference in 1884 marked the beginning of borders imposed on African communities and geographical space came to define national identities. As national borders emerged across Africa, movement between territories was now governed by bureaucracy and political processes that sought to exclude outsiders. Zimbabwe's migration history is however interesting in that the country acted in three distinct ways. First, the country was a source of labour migrants for the gold mines in South Africa. Second, it acted as a corridor for migrant labourers from other countries such as Zambia and Malawi on their way to South Africa. Third, it was a recipient of migrants from other neighbouring countries; for example, at the time of the 1951 census, there were 246,000 foreign Africans in Zimbabwe (40% of them from Mozambique). Zimbabwe was thus a source, a destination and a corridor.[9]

The types of migration discussed in this chapter thus emerged out of the colonial processes where artificial borders demarcated 'international' versus 'national' migration. Migration has historically been used as a wage earning strategy. Colonisation in the 1960s and 1970s induced multiple types of migration across the world. Some black people left for schooling and military training to other countries – mostly socialist countries including the Soviet Union and Cuba. The 1970s saw the migration of many young men and women to

Mozambique and Zambia to join the armed struggle against colonial rule. These movements are part of an evolutionary pattern of migration in Zimbabwe. They indicate an important epoch in the history of migration whilst showing that migration is not a new phenomenon. There are thus spatial and temporal dimensions to the trajectory of migration in Zimbabwe. Many communities also migrated to neighbouring countries to escape the hardships of the liberation war. This type of migration was largely forced by circumstances of war and not a rational choice of actors.

After independence, the nature of migration evolved as increased opportunities for black people led to massive internal rural to urban migration. As education opportunities increased for Zimbabweans, there were opportunities as well for employment outside the country. Migration to foreign countries thus became more prevalent. Women traders selling various crafts to South Africa also continued during this period, though Gaidzanwa and Cheater (1996) show that migration was mainly a male pursuit. Gaidzanwa (1999) also explores the increased migration of professionals after the adoption of structural adjustment in 1992. What is clear then is how migration is a historical activity which has been used as a livelihood strategy over the years to respond to challenges. The post-2000 migration, which is the focus of this chapter, has thus to be understood as a phase in a historical continuum of migration in Zimbabwe.

Post-2000 migration to South Africa has been extensively researched by the South African Migration Project based at University of the Witwatersrand in South Africa. They have shown the various facets of migration noting the contested nature of conceptualising this process. Their work highlights how the Zimbabwean case post-2000 provides a complex understanding of migration given the multiple motivations driving people to immigrate. One of the debates the project has dealt with is the issue of numbers and volume. Poltzer (2008: p. 6) argues that:

> ... there are no empirically reliable statistics on the number of Zimbabweans who have entered South Africa since 2000 (estimates range from 1 million to 5 million and vary so greatly because of the high percentage of undocumented border crossings ...

What is clear from this literature is that South Africa has been the destination of choice for most Zimbabweans and this has a historical explanation if one provides an analysis of migration in the subregion. Economic motivated migration has historically followed centres of economic production. In colonial times, urban and mining centres attracted migrants looking to earn a wage. Centres such as Johannesburg and Salisbury (now Harare) were some of the economic hubs that attracted a lot of migrants during the colonial period.

In terms of volume, there are contestations over the number of Zimbabweans that have emigrated post-2000. This politics of numbers is affected by various factors within and outside Zimbabwe. One of the key issues is the lack of official records about numbers of emigrants mainly because of those who migrate illegally. This leads to speculative numbers that are based on political considerations and not factual events. One such figure is the one attributed to then president of South Africa, Thabo Mbeki, who in 2003 indicated that there are three million Zimbabweans in his country.[10] Crush and Tevera (2010) argued that this number is highly exaggerated, alarmist and without sound statistical basis. Migration in southern Africa has historically been cyclic, making Scoones argue that

> ... there is no way of knowing the actual facts. No-one on either side of the border keeps proper records, people move back and forward between countries in the region with a high frequency and much movement is illegal in any case.[11]

Kiwanuka (2009:24) calls this circular migration and notes that:

> Apart from Botswana, where males continue to predominate, female migrants constitute an increasingly large proportion of Zimbabwean migrants. Many come as visitors, informal cross-border traders and shoppers. Other Zimbabweans move to find "piece-jobs", especially in the service, construction, and tourism industries. Fieldwork established that Zimbabweans in these four countries [Botswana, Malawi, South Africa and Zambia] usually migrate alone, leaving their families and other dependents behind, and staying for short periods.

The 'type' of migrant has also been an important part of the debate post-2000. Post-independence, migration continued to be mostly an endeavour dominated by low class males, with limited numbers of educated or professional individuals leaving. Professionals tend to shy away from migration in a stable environment. It is only when conflict, economic crisis or a better offer emerges elsewhere that professionals look to migrate. Tevera and Crush (2003) argue that there are international pull and local push-forces that are forcing professionals to migrate from Zimbabwe in high numbers. Pull factors include the increased opportunities for Zimbabwean professionals across the world and local push factors include the economic crisis which erodes savings and earnings. The local push factors are more important in the Zimbabwean case as professionals either migrate illegally or end up doing menial work in the host countries. Professionals were forced to leave by circumstance, without planning or securing employment in the countries they migrated to. What is clear from the research is how migration defies clear class boundaries as people from all economic categories were involved.

Cross-border trading and cyclic migration by Zimbabweans

One of the major livelihood activities to emerge post-2000 is cross-border trading. This type of activity is characterised by short term migration lasting a few days to a few weeks. It includes people focusing on various items of trade which vary from food items to electrical goods, clothing, blankets, kitchenware, household furniture and various other goods for resale. The success of cross-border traders between 2002 and 2008 has to be understood from a context in which formal shops could not trade using foreign currency according to the law. This meant that shops could not make a profit using the Zimbabwean dollar which was depreciating daily.

Cross-border traders on the other hand demanded foreign currency and because of their informality the government could not impose trading in the local currency. There are different types of traders but all seeking to turn a profit from product resale. Mutopo (2014) for example narrates the example of rural women from Mwenezi who farm and sell their produce on the streets of Johannesburg. In my sample, the four cross-border traders are a different type of trader because they only go to South Africa or Botswana to buy supplies. They do not sell any products in the host countries. One elderly woman who has been a cross-border trader for 17 years highlighted how the trade has changed for her over the years:

> When we started, we used to go to South Africa to sell doilies, crafts and various handmade items. There was a market for those things especially amongst white women. These days we are only going to Johannesburg or Musina to buy goods for resale. Most Zimbabweans selling on the streets are semi-permanent residents here. Cross-border traders are only here for one or two days at a time.

Trading is done at different scales with some enterprising individuals involved in supplying cars, building materials and other high-end movable properties. Around 2008, food and fuel shortages provided an opportunity for cross-border traders who went to neighbouring countries and bought the items to resale at higher profits in Zimbabwe.

In border towns and nearby areas, fuel trade is still a lucrative enterprise given the cross country differences in fuel prices. According to one respondent who is involved in 'deals' at the border, there are some individuals still dealing in fuel. He argued:

> Fuel is cheaper in South Africa given the strength of the American dollar we use here in Zimbabwe. There are some people at the Beitbridge border post who use bicycles at a small scale and trucks at a much larger scale who buy cheap fuel at the service stations across the border and come and resale it in Zimbabwe. The profit margins may not be very high but they at least provide an income.

Such practices highlight the unsustainable and ephemeral nature of most cross-border trading enterprises. Cross-border trading is also about ensuring that traders respond to the needs of the people at that particular time. After adoption of a multi-currency system in Zimbabwe, food was readily available in the country and thus traders involved in food had to change to other items. Clothing is proving to be an important part of livelihood activities of cross-border trading. In my sample I had two different women involved in different types of clothes trading. One of the women buys and sales clothes from South Africa and Botswana. The clothes are new and mainly from Chinese run shops in the two countries. She has a flea market table in the city where she sales her wares. She is also involved in supplying clothes for other traders who fail to travel. The other woman is involved in bringing second-hand clothing from Mozambique. This type of clothing is known as *bhero* because it comes in bales. It costs an average of US$200 to bring a bale of clothes, but it can be higher depending on quality, type of clothing, transport costs and money paid at the border to facilitate the entry of the clothes. The woman noted that she sells from a flea market in the commercial business district and the activity is providing food, rentals and school fees for her family of six.

Food stuffs were also an important commodity for cross-border traders. In 2008, Zimbabwean shops were eventually empty and the traders took this opportunity to fill the vacuum and create a market given the shortages of food. One of the traders in my sample narrated her experiences with buying and selling rice from Mozambique:

> There was no rice or maize meal in the shops across the country. Many people started going to neighbouring countries to buy these goods. For rice, Mozambique was particularly favoured because 50 kilogram sacks were cheaper than everywhere else. I also started going to get rice from Beira and at times Matupo and bringing it back to sell. I had many customers who would buy as much as three to four bags of rice. Some were also buying sacks from me and repackaging them for resale. I also started doing the same because the profit was higher. People make money when there is a need and demand for goods.

Beer and fizzy drinks also provided opportunities for traders. According to some respondents, importing these drinks from South Africa or Botswana and selling them for American dollars proved to be profitable for the involved traders.

The experiences above highlight that circular migration was critical to survival in two key ways. First, the food shortages opened up new avenues for both employed and unemployed people especially youths to make a living through cross-border trading. Second, the imported food was essential for many households because there was virtually nothing in the shops. Another characteristic of cross-border trading practicing cyclic migration is the fact that most are involved in day trips. Zanamwe and Dellivard (2010:14) note that, "… post-2000, Zimbabwe witnessed growing numbers of day trippers mainly to South Africa and Botswana. The number of day trippers increased from 651,703 in 2005 to 629,387 in 2006. The figure declined to 431,951 in 2007."

Illegal short- and long-term working migrants

One of the emerging concepts from migration post-2000 in Zimbabwe is the talk of piece jobs. According to Kiwanuka (2009:24), "piece jobs refer to work acquired in part-time 'pieces' to constitute a working week – for instance, a domestic worker might work one day per week for one employer, and two days per week for several others". The respondents in this research expanded this definition to include any short term work in which you are paid instantly after the job is done rather waiting for a weekly or monthly wage. They also highlighted that from 2005 to 2009 professional people such as teachers would use leave days or absent themselves from work to find piece jobs in South Africa and Botswana. One female respondent who is a teacher noted that:

> I am a teacher by profession since 1997. By 2008 our salaries were worthless and because of cash shortages we slept on bank queues. There was nothing else to do but find ways to feed the children. I just decided to follow my sister to South Africa. She was working as a maid and I thought it was better to go and work and send back food and some money to my family. It was worth it at the time. I was lucky that when I came I got my job back. There are some teachers I know who did not get their jobs back.

This is one example of short-term migrants who utilised migration to survive. Respondents noted that most countries in southern Africa allow visa free entry to Zimbabweans for 90 days a year but you are only allowed to stay 30 consecutive days. After 30 days one has to leave and get their passports stamped at the border before coming back. To avoid this, some people would send their passports with friends or family who paid passport officers at the border to stamp the passports.

Other migrants have settled and in many ways assimilated to their new environment. This includes learning the language and even marrying local partners. In countries such as South Africa, there were stories of Zimbabweans changing names and buying citizenship papers from corrupt government officials. Such migrants have accessed the right to stay and work in South Africa through illegal means. According to the respondents, having citizenship was important in accessing better paying employment. Having legal papers is also important if one is to avoid being arrested, detained or deported by the police. One respondent who was an illegal migrant noted the following:

> I was working at a garage owned by a white South African in 2007 earning a very low salary because I was illegal. My major challenge was the police who saw me as a moving ATM [automated teller machine]. They would wait for me every Friday outside the garage without fail. I ended up leaving Tembisa and going to Cape Town because I was basically working for the cops. I was not able to send back anything to people at home.

This highlights the importance of having legal papers for migrants to live and work without police harassment. This story also demonstrates that there are likely many other migrants who due to various reasons did not make profit from their endeavours. Respondents spoke of many migrants who ended up in criminal activities or were in prison, or were killed by thieves or during the recurrent xenophobic attacks in South Africa.

Professionals voting with their feet

The economic crisis in Zimbabwe forced many professionals to migrate out of Zimbabwe. For most, migration was forced by the loss of employment, lack of salaries and continued devaluation of the local currency. Many companies as well as government institutions were at some time in 2008 failing to pay workers, and other companies were closing down or retrenching workers. Migration thus became one of the most viable livelihood alternatives for professionals especially those with technical skills that were in demand in other countries. This section of the paper utilises desk research because it was difficult to get access to professionals who migrated because most of them are still outside the country. In 1999, Gaidzanwa outlined the 'voting with their feet' thesis to explain the increased option of migration for professionals working in the health sector in Zimbabwe. This process has continued post-2000 but there is a general lack of reliable data in Zimbabwe. In this context, Zanamwe and Devillard (2010:35) argue that:

> Although the characteristics of Zimbabwean migration – mainly irregular and circular – impede the gathering of reliable estimates on migration flows and stocks, it is nevertheless useful to look at official data disseminated by ZIMSTAT. Such estimates are based on a definition of the notion of emigrant that includes the following two categories: residents who, on departure, declare on border crossing cards that they are leaving for more than 12 months, and persons who registered themselves as visitors on arrival but stayed for more than 12 months in the country of destination. According to 2005 estimates, 11,620 emigrants left the country, mainly to African countries (6,256) and European countries (3,758).

What is clear even without official statistics is that there has been a general increase in the migration of professionals. The cyclic and irregular nature of migration has meant understated national figures. Many more Zimbabweans are leaving the country as students for universities abroad and the majority do not return to Zimbabwe. This has meant an increased loss of skills and human resources. According to a British Broadcasting Corporation report:

> The Southern African Migration Project (SAMP) did a study on health professionals leaving Zimbabwe in 2002, and found that economic factors were cited by the greatest number of migrants (54% of the interviewees) as

their reason for leaving Zimbabwe. Around 30% pointed to professional reasons such as inadequate working conditions, and a similar number said political considerations had been a factor in prompting them to leave Zimbabwe. Since 2000, a further economically important group of migrants has been white farmers – government policy changes led to the seizure of 4,000 white-owned farms, and many who lost land sought new opportunities elsewhere in Africa or overseas.[12]

There is thus evidence of skilled migrant movement out of Zimbabwe. Migration as a survival strategy is thus not limited to poor people. The nature of migration and livelihood options in the recipient countries however depends upon social class and the skills one possesses.

Remittances: food, cash and property

One of the defining images of the Zimbabwean crisis is the role played by remittances in the survival of families. People who had migrated became an important source of livelihood through money, food, clothes and other items. One respondent highlighted that:

> There was nothing in the shops. People were starving and there was no food anyway. For some reason there was a shortage of everything from maize meal to milk and even eggs. It is as if the chickens were no longer laying eggs or the cattle had refused with their milk. We were sending bread back home from South Africa because there was nothing in the shops.

Many people with access to foreign currency through remittances or trade were also involved in migrating to Musina in South Africa and Francistown in Botswana to buy their groceries and supplies. Through migration, families were able to access basic food stuffs and avert hunger. Enterprising Zimbabweans took the chance to make money from this crisis through various schemes involving foodstuffs. One such enterprise was described by a respondent who noted:

> There were some people in the diaspora [term here is used to describe any place outside Zimbabwe] especially in the UK who started a business. One such business involved paying someone money in the UK and their local agents will deliver food hampers to your relatives in Zimbabwe. This was especially helpful for those with aged parents or who in live in rural areas. The food was delivered to their door and there were no problems such as going to a neighbouring country to buy food.

Remittances were thus in different forms but all geared towards basic survival of households. The remittances in terms of cash also led to the emergence of money sending, receiving and forex exchange businesses for individuals. People were sending money using various formal and informal networks. Before 2009 when the Zimbabwean dollar was still in use, a lot of young people in urban areas became foreign currency dealers popularly called *change monies*. Even post-2009, the *change monies* have continued with foreign currency dealings even within the multi-currency system. Some Zimbabweans actually started a money sending service called Mukuru.com.

Malaicha, bus drivers, border officials and making a living from migrants

In this section, the focus is on those individuals who have inhabited mostly border towns and take advantage of high numbers of people in transit at border points to make money through extra legal and illegal means. Illicit transactions are done through various networks with border officials in the middle. The increased migration of Zimbabweans to neighbouring countries post-2000 led to the emergence of many licit and illicit livelihoods around border towns. One such livelihood is the *malaicha*, which are drivers of hired trucks transporting goods between Zimbabwe and neighbouring countries especially South Africa. They are involved in facilitating the transportation of a variety of goods including moving corpses for burial back in Zimbabwe. One of the respondents narrated that:

> *Malaicha* is capable of doing anything for you. Whatever you want transported, even children or coffins, they can do it if you can pay. They have ways of avoiding border control. They have networks with border officials that ensure that they are able to pass through without problems.

Just like the *Malaicha*, bus drivers and conductors have also carved a livelihood niche out of the increased number of migrants especially at the South African border. They are involved in various illicit deals which include avoiding duty and facilitating passengers without proper papers to cross the border.

Malaichas are synonymous with pickup trucks which are fully loaded. People tend to prefer these transporters for two reasons. First, they are cheaper than all other forms of transport. Second, they are better at ensuring cheaper duty and transportation of illegal contraband. They have become an important face of the cyclic migration post-2000. In an interview, a man who was once a *malaicha* noted that:

> Being a *malaicha* required knowing people working at both the border posts. On the border anything is possible if you have money to pay. The officers at the border on both Zimbabwean and South African sides will allow many things if you pay a bribe. Bribing is part of doing business at the border. There is a whole economy based on bribes and middlemen which have built livelihoods for many of the involved people including tax officials, border officers, police, security people, transporters and business people.

The large volumes of traffic at the border daily have provided livelihood opportunities for multiple groups of people. Migration-based livelihoods have thus become important aspects of the Zimbabwean social architecture. *Malaichas* and bus drivers have become important actors in a network of actors at the borders who through illicit activities facilitate the movement of people into and out of the country.

Child migrants in the context of Zimbabwe

A rather recent phenomenon within the context of migration-based livelihoods is the emergence of child migrants. Migration is often viewed as an adult survival strategy, yet experiences in Zimbabwe are highlighting how children are increasingly becoming active participants in this pursuit. According to a report by Save the Children (2007), 8,631 unaccompanied children were deported from South Africa and were assisted at Beitbridge Reception and Support Centre. Unaccompanied migrant children refer to immigrants who are under the age of 18 and are not under the care of a parent or legal guardian. This includes children fleeing violence or unrest, those seeking work, and those who are victims of trafficking.[13] Hillier (2007) notes that poverty, hunger, lack of educational opportunities, the death of caregivers at home, and the high rate of orphanhood in Zimbabwe (as a consequence of the HIV and AIDS pandemic) are major factors which have contributed to the disintegration of the family unit and has resulted in the movement of children. Children from Zimbabwe are mainly undocumented and often found in hidden and low paying jobs such as house maids, farm workers or beggars.

Conclusion and policy insights

The Zimbabwean case has shown that migration is an important part of strategies employed by households and individuals in crisis contexts. Migration is employed in differing ways and has varying results at individual and household level. Whilst the net national impact of migration post-2000 in Zimbabwe continues to be debated, what is clear is how at localised levels, the activity provided livelihoods and access to food. This exploratory discussion was narrowly focused on showing how migration is utilised as a survival strategy. It outlined the experiences of various actors involved in various migration-based livelihoods. What is clear is how such livelihoods are mostly ephemeral and survivalist in nature. The sustainability of most activities is easily affected by the broader macroeconomic context; for example, when Zimbabwe abandoned its local currency and assumed a multi-currency system, food became readily available in the shops. Cross-border traders concentrating on food trade therefore had to change to other goods. Respondents also highlighted the low profit margins which do not allow for savings but rather focused on everyday survival needs. Migration was shown to include people of all genders and ages. We also have examples of children migrating on their own. The paper has shown how post-2000 migration is another phase in the continued use of migration as a survival strategy in Zimbabwe.

The study poses serious policy questions which require further action from various stakeholders involved in migration. Migration as a survival strategy is not novel but has continued to evolve in response to the ever-changing national and global contexts. The movement of people between Zimbabwe and South Africa has a long history that needs to be reflected in any policy announcements. Facilitating this form of livelihood requires the Zimbabwean government to ensure affordable and easy access to travelling documents which eases movement into foreign countries. The Zimbabwean passport requires US$56 to access and it takes six weeks to process. Such costs are prohibitive especially for those in rural spaces because the process of application remains centralised to urban centres. This unfortunately forces people to migrate illegally, leaving them vulnerable to border officers, army, police and *malaichas*. The governments of Zimbabwe and South Africa also need to further look into the viability of a one-stop border post to ease the traffic at the border. Participants in the research noted how, at its busiest, it takes over six hours to get processed through the two border posts. Child protection issues need serious attention as an increasing number of children are involved in migrating on their own. Most of the children questioned reported abuse. This is especially the case for girls who might be made to exchange sex for transportation by truckers. There have also been reports of children sexually and physically abused by *magumaguma* (guides) at the border crossing points and at destination sites by their employers in the commercial or domestic workplaces (Save the Children 2007). The two countries can ensure protection of children through increasing police patrols, and having social workers and counselling points accessible for children at the border.

Notes

1   It should be noted that tobacco production has increased and small farmers are starting to produce. Tobacco output increased from 58 million kilogrammes in 2009 to 123 million kilogrammes in 2010. www.thecropsite.com/news/7639/more-land-in-crop-production-in-zimbabwe/ [Accessed 3 March 2016].

2   CNN, 19 August 2008, *Zimbabwe inflation hits 11,200,000 percent*, http://edition.cnn.com/2008/BUSINESS/08/19/zimbabwe.inflation/index.html?eref=edition   [Accessed 11 April 2016].

3   Between 3 million and 4.5 million Zimbabweans are estimated to be living abroad. Development Foundation for Zimbabwe, www.dfzim.com/wp-content/downloads/Victoria_Falls_Conference_Concept.pdf [Accessed 23 February 2016].

4   Formal sector urban employment shrunk from 3.6 million in 2003 to 480,000 in 2008 (*Mail and Guardian*, 18 January 2009).

5   Thornycroft, P. 2006. *Life expectancy of Zimbabwean women plunges to just 34*, www.telegraph.co.uk/news/worldnews/africaandindianocean/zimbabwe/1515260/Life-expectancy-of-Zimbabwean-women-plunges-to-just-34.html [Accessed 14 March 2016].

6   92,460 housing structures were demolished directly affecting 133,534 households. 32,538 structures of micro- and medium-size enterprises were demolished. Thus 569,685 people lost their homes and 97,614 lost their primary source of livelihood. United Nations (UN), "*Report of the Fact-Finding Mission to Zimbabwe to Assess the*

Scope and Impact of Operation Murambatsvina by the UN Special Envoy on Human Settlement Issues in Zimbabwe", 18 July 2005, www.unhabitat.org/documents/ ZimbabweReport.pdf [Accessed 3 March 2008].
7 Asare, P. 2012. *Labour Migration in Ghana*, Friedrich Ebert Stiftung, http://library. fes.de/pdf-files/bueros/ghana/10511.pdf [Accessed 4 March 2016].
8 www.unhcr.org/pages/49c3646c125.html [Accessed 3 March 2016].
9 www.queensu.ca/samp/sampresources/samppublications/policyseries/policy25.html [Accessed 3 March 2016].
10 https://zimbabweland.wordpress.com/2012/10/01/migration-myths/ [Accessed 3 March 2016].
11 Ibid.
12 BBC News 8 November 2005, *So where are Zimbabweans going?* http://news.bbc. co.uk/2/hi/africa/4416820.stm [Accessed 23 February 2016].
13 www.migrationpolicy.org/article/unaccompanied-immigrant-children-growing-pheno menon-few-easy-solutions [Accessed 3 March 2016].

References

Chiweshe, M. 2011. *Farm Level Institutions in Emergent Communities in Post Fast Track Zimbabwe: The Case of Mazowe District.* PhD thesis, Rhodes University.
Coltart, D. 2008. A Decade of Suffering in Zimbabwe: Economic Collapse and Political Repression under Robert Mugabe, *Development Policy Analysis* No. 5, CATO Institute. Available from: www.genocidepreventionprogram.org/images/Zimbabwe_24_ Mar_08_A_Decade_of_Suffering_in_Zimbabwe_Economic_Collapse_and_Political_ Repression_Under_Robert_Mugabe.pdf [Accessed 23 November 2015].
Crush, J. and Tevera, D. 2010. *Zimbabwe's Exodus: Crisis, Migration, Survival.* Cape Town: SAMP.
Gaidzanwa, R. 1999. *Voting with their Feet: Migrant Nurses and Doctors in the Era of Structural Adjustment.* Research Report 111, Nordic African Institute.
Gaidzanwa, R. and Cheater, A. 1996. Gender and Mobility in Southern Africa: Citizenship in Neo-patrimonial States. *Journal of Southern African Studies*, 22 (2): 189–200.
Hillier, L. 2007. *Children on the Move: Protecting Unaccompanied Migrant. Children in South Africa and the Region.* London: Save the Children.
Hungwe, C. 2012. The Migration Experience and Multiple Identities of Zimbabwean Migrants in South Africa. *Online Journal of Social Sciences Research*, 1 (5): 132–138.
Hunter, L., Luna, J. and Morton, M. 2015. Environmental Dimensions of Migration. *Annual Review of Sociology*, 41: 377–397.
Kiwanuka, M. 2009. *Zimbabwean Migration into Southern Africa: New Trends and Responses.* Johannesburg: Forced Migration Programme Wits.
Murisa, T. 2010. *An Analysis of Emerging Forms of Social Organisation and Agency in the Aftermath of 'Fast Track' Land Reform in Zimbabwe.* PhD Thesis, Rhodes University.
Mutopo, P. 2014. *Women, Mobility and Rural Livelihoods in Zimbabwe: Experience of Fast Track Land Reform.* Leiden: Koninklijke Brill.
Polzer, T. 2008. South African Government and Civil Society Responses to Zimbabwean Migration, SAMP Policy Brief No. 22. Available from: www.queensu.ca/samp/ sampresources/samppublications/policybriefs/brief22.pdf [Accessed 3 April 2016].
Portes, A. 1999. Immigration Theory for a New Century: Some Problems and Opportunities. In C. Hirschman, J. Dewind and P. Kasinitz (eds), *The Handbook of International Migration.* pp. 21–33, New York: The Russell Sage Foundation.

Save the Children UK. 2007. *Children Crossing Borders: Report on Unaccompanied Minors who have Travelled to South Africa*, Johannesburg: Save the Children UK.

Tevera, D. and Crush, J. 2003. *The New Brain Drain from Zimbabwe*, Southern African Migration Project. Available from: www.queensu.ca/samp/sampresources/samppublications/policyseries/Acrobat29.pdf [Accessed 14 March 2016].

van Onselen, C. 1976. *Chibharo African Mine Labour in Southern Rhodesia 1900–1933*. London: Pluto.

Zanamwe, L. and Devillard, A. 2010. *Migration in Zimbabwe: A Country Profile 2009*, Zimbabwe National Statistics Agency (ZIMSTAT) and International Organization for Migration. Available from: http://publications.iom.int/system/files/pdf/mp_zimbabwe.pdf [Accessed 23 March 2016].

6 Agricultural production systems of small-scale farmers in Hwedza in the context of innovation platforms

Innocent Mahiya

Introduction

This chapter focuses on the organisation of production systems under the auspices of innovation platforms in Hwedza, including the constraints and challenges faced by small-scale farmers. I seek to unpack key dimensions of the production system (including input and output markets, cropping methodologies and post-harvest technologies) and examine the ways in which these are located within – and shaped by – the prevailing agricultural Innovation Platforms (IP). This allows me to consider non-compliance and contestation of farmers around these dimensions, and the ways in which certain aspects of the IP intervention simply reinforces and elaborates upon existing systems of agricultural knowledge and practices amongst the farmers. This chapter presents the interventions that came about through IPs in Hwedza and how the locals embraced these. However, some of the agricultural problems those small-scale farmers encountered before the coming of IPs remained in existence even after the adoption of the IPs.

This study utilises both quantitative evidence (for example, agricultural inputs, crop output and land areas) and qualitative evidence (such as knowledge of technologies, key challenges and social relations). The fieldwork for the study was conducted in three interlinked phases, from March 2013 to October 2014. However, I had conducted prior field visits during the year 2012 to familiarise myself with the research area. Key informant interviews were carried out with the different stakeholders while focus group discussions were done with mainly small-scale farmers. Open-ended semi-structured interviews with small-scale farmers were used as well and these allowed the researcher to collect information on household power dynamics such as who has primary land rights and who controls the harvest. Data collected was analysed using mainly non-statistical tools to provide a coherent outlook of the issues investigated.

Agricultural activities in Hwedza

Hwedza is a rural district in Mashonaland East that is located about 50 kilometres south of the provincial capital of Marondera and 127 kilometres south of the national capital of Harare. Due to its mineral wealth, the district was dominated by the Mbire people (between the ninth and twelfth centuries) who were mining iron in the area. It was only in 1910 that the colonial administration established Hwedza as a rural district. The Zimstat draft census report from 2013 (Zimstat 2013) indicates that Hwedza has a total population of 70,473 inhabitants. Women constitute the majority of the population at 51.3% and the average number of people in a household is 4.1. Tarred roads to Harare connect the district of Hwedza and Marondera hence it has access to markets in these centres for its agricultural produce. In terms of the climatic characteristics of the district, the northern part of Hwedza (that covers areas from St. Barnabas Chisasike to Hwedza centre) falls in climatic (or agro-ecological) region II and is relatively cooler and receives average to high rainfall per annum. The lower Hwedza covers areas from Mukamba through Goneso and Zviyambe East and West. Climatically, the lower Hwedza falls within region III and has relatively warmer to hot temperatures and receives lower rainfall than its upper counterpart.

Hwedza has a unique location in that it offers a vast array of agricultural opportunities. The northern part of Hwedza along Watershed Road leading into Hwedza from Harare is dominated by tobacco, maize and paprika production mainly during the warm wet season from approximately the months of October to March. These areas historically had a mixture of commercial farming areas and small-scale farming areas. The southern part of the district (covering areas of Makarara and Zviyambe and leading into Dorowa) is dominated by sorghum/millet as well as by cotton and cattle ranching. The southern central part of the district has a history of erratic rain hence farming prospects are heavily compromised. The study focuses on communal areas in upper (northern) Hwedza, lower (southern) Hwedza and central Hwedza. Small-scale farmers in Hwedza have always practiced mixed farming involving the production of a variety of crops and the keeping of livestock, with some crops for domestic consumption and others for selling in times of surplus. Crops such as *nyimo* (round nuts), *nyemba* (cowpeas), *zviyo* (sorghum) and *mbambaira* (sweet potatoes) have been primarily produced for domestic consumption. Cash crops included tobacco, sugar beans and paprika and their production has intensified with the coming of innovation platforms to Hwedza.

Crop production is rain-fed, so small-scale farmers in the communal areas of Hwedza constantly face the threat of poor harvest and food shortages due to the unpredictability of rainfall. As such, the precarious nature of agriculture in the communal areas under investigation prompts questions about the need for analyses around initiatives (such as agricultural innovation platforms) that seek to improve the plight of small-scale farmers inhabiting communal spaces.

Undoubtedly food security would be an important issue for the small-scale farmers in Hwedza. Food security in general refers to the availability and accessibility of adequate food at household and community level on an ongoing basis. Household food production systems greatly contribute to the overall food security situation of rural households. This necessitated the need to evaluate how food production at household level influences the overall food security situation of households in Hwedza. The crucial and ultimate goal behind capacitating small-scale farmers through the implementation of IPs in Hwedza was to make them food secure. Selling any surplus or any produced cash crops may be secondary because the main problem that small-scale farmers grapple with is meeting basic subsistence needs. With this in mind, I investigated farming systems in Hwedza, and in particular the prioritising of food and/or cash crops, in terms of their implications for food security as understood by the farmers themselves.

All Hwedza farmers surveyed indicated that their primary crop was maize. This demonstrates that their farming was primarily driven by the desire to produce food for household consumption. The second most popular legume crop was groundnut, also for domestic consumption as it is an important source of protein and fat. Farmers regularly processed groundnuts to make peanut butter which was widely used for cooking and mixing with relish. Cash crops were also important and specifically for generating cash income, notably soya beans, cow peas, sunflowers and sugar beans. One farmer in Wagoneka Village noted that he was producing soya beans mainly to generate income to pay for school fees for his children but also to purchase basic foodstuffs such as cooking oil, sugar and salt. Other farmers argued that they would prefer to grow maize on a larger piece of their land and reduce significant dependency on cash crops citing the high risks and high costs associated with the production of cash crops. It is important to note that there were more successful farmers who enjoyed a large harvest especially of small grains and these farmers would normally call for *humwe* for purposes of community assistance in harvesting (i.e. cooperation of village members to work in one's fields without payment).

The problems faced by small-scale farmers in Hwedza can be understood in relation to the dual agricultural system inherited from the colonial era and which divided Zimbabwe into two sectors: a large-scale commercial sector controlled by white settlers and a small-scale sector controlled by black people. Small-scale black farming was further subdivided into small-scale commercial areas and communal areas. Colonial polices in Rhodesia severely limited land-holdings of black small-scale farmers in communal areas and inhibited their market access. This led to land degradation and declining per capita production (Ministry of Lands, Agriculture and Rural Resettlement 2001). After independence in 1980, the Zimbabwean government began a land redistribution programme for resettling black farmers from communal areas onto former white commercial farms; meanwhile, in communal areas, there was a focus on smallholder irrigation schemes to enhance crop production. Resettlement of any significance only occurred from the year 2000 in the light of nation-wide land occupations and the implementation of fast track land reform – fast track was supposed to decongest communal areas but this has not occurred in all rural areas.

Like fast track farms, communal (sometimes called customary) land is state land but households have held specific plots of land over generations. There are a bundle of rights attached to customary land including right of control, access and usage that are often gender-based. Land allocation remains a source of contestation, with local district councils, political parties and tribal authorities all having varying kinds of control. Agricultural production on fast track farms, including on Model A1 farms where small-scale farmers pursue their liveli-hoods, is higher than in today's communal areas (Moyo 2009). Customary area production continues to involve mixed agriculture and is pursued mainly for sub-sistence purposes. Crop production (maize in particular) provides most of the food for households; and cattle are very important particularly in the lower rain-fall areas (Rukuni 1994, Thirtle 1993). Cattle provide animal draught for tillage, transport, manure, milk and meat. During high-harvest years, farmers produce excess food crops and livestock products for local and national markets. Non-food crops, such as cotton, tobacco and paprika, are also grown specifically for the market (Moyo 2005). Other important crops include sorghum, millets, groundnuts and sunflowers.

Agricultural innovation platforms

The concept of innovation platforms, which is consistent with a range of other participatory methodologies found within the donor-driven international devel-opment system (or industry), has emerged as an alternative framework to guide agricultural research and innovation work in Africa (OECD 2005, Akullo *et al.* 2009, Hawkins *et al.* 2009). The framework entails the incorporation of all stake-holders (small-scale farmers and external agents) – with diverse interests – under a set of operating principles and guidelines which seek to analyse problems per-tinent to agricultural production and to develop appropriate solutions. This approach, when adopted in the generating of agricultural technology, is expected to lead to the emergence of agricultural paradigms that are relevant to local con-ditions and are acceptable to local communities (World Bank 2009). Agricultural innovation platforms, which form part of a broader innovation platform initiative not restricted to agriculture alone, are therefore said to present an opportunity to address the challenges ingrained in bringing on board a whole range of stake-holders within an innovation system methodology, in order to catalyse the trans-formation of agricultural research and crop production amongst small-scale farmers in sub-Saharan Africa (Ejigu and Bayer 2004).

With funding from the United Kingdom's Department for International Devel-opment (DFID), the Forum for Agricultural Research in Africa (FARA) has initi-ated the Sub-Saharan Africa Challenge Programme with Pilot Learning Sites (SSACPPLS) in Nigeria's Kano and Katsina States, Niger's Maradi Province, around Lake Kivu in the Democratic Republic of Congo, and in Kenya, Rwanda, Uganda, Zimbabwe, Malawi and Mozambique (EPZA 2005, FARA 2009, GoK 2004, Dormon *et al.* 2007, Spielman 2006). In Zimbabwe, a NGO called Inter-national Centre for Tropical Agriculture (which has offices in Harare) has been mandated by FARA to implement an Integrated Agricultural Research for Develop-ment (IAR4D) initiative and SSACPPLS more specifically. It has selected innova-tion sites at district level, as well as counterfactual sites where there is no intervention. For Zimbabwe, Hwedza and Murehwa districts were selected in 2008 as intervention districts, with Marondera and Chikomba districts as counterfactuals.

The agricultural innovation systems approach, as it is often called, was thus initiated as an alternative analytical and programmatic framework premised on the principles of conservation farming. The innovation systems approach more broadly focuses on institutional-behavioural change and systemic innovation processes and how these may contribute to economic growth and sustainable development (Edquist and Johnson 1997). Innovation platforms in Hwedza were meant to facilitate the organisation of multi-institutional and multi-disciplinary actors or stakeholders that included researchers, farmers, buyers, financiers, government departments, traditional leaders and agricultural extension workers. This all-embracing organisational arrangement would hopefully innovate more effectively in response to changing (and complex) agricultural and natural resources management contexts. Given the diverse composition of the agricultural platforms, it was sometimes difficult to involve fully all of the mentioned stakeholders. Of particular relevance to the Hwedza agricultural platform was the failure to involve financiers, despite repeated efforts and the critical significance of financing for small-scale agricultural projects and the overall survival of the platform. At the same time, there were village and district level innovation platforms established in Hwedza and these had different stakeholders that sought to meet and plan on a regular basis. The following sections discuss specific interventions that came about through the IPs in Hwedza.

Use of cropping methodologies by farmers

Central to any transformative initiative, which aims at improving agriculture for small-scale farmers, are new agricultural methodologies involving technological improvements to crop production, or cropping methodologies. Any possibility of changes in these methodologies is dependent in part upon past and present social arrangements and world-views (notably of the farmers), as there may be an unwillingness or incapacity to engage with these changes.

In all the five villages where innovation platforms were being implemented, there was significant evidence of water management strategies employed by farmers. On water management technologies, the awareness and practices of the following technologies was assessed: mulching, trenches and terraces, water harvesting, irrigation (bucket, treadle pump and drip) and conservation farming more broadly. The International Centre for Tropical Agriculture (or CIAT) had initiated demonstration plots close to each intervention village to encourage farmers to learn more about conservation farming. Farmers in all the intervention sites had embraced these dimensions of conservation farming, and they spoke about positive results in terms of agricultural yields. Further, they indicated that they would continue practicing it. However, conservation-type technologies were not new to the Hwedza farmers. What they were seemingly lacking was consistent use of such technologies due to only a partial understanding of conservation farming benefits. Thus, IPs brought about a more systematic utilisation of such technologies by small-scale communal farmers in Hwedza.

One of the critical challenges that farmers highlighted, particularly in the context of climate change and variability, was water availability. To illustrate this challenge, I quote the desperation experienced by one farmer:

> I really feel that the government should do more in setting up small-scale irrigation schemes near our village. The rainfall has become highly unreliable and this has been negatively affecting our farming. We might prepare for the farming season but if rainfall is unreliable, then it's likely that we come up with nothing. If only the government could construct some irrigation schemes in our area.

As a result of interactions during regular IP meetings, farmers from Chidora Village adopted water harvesting strategies after receiving training from COMMUTECH, which is a company specialising in irrigation. Other notable stories came from Nyamutsika and Wagoneka villages where IP farmers successfully adopted mulching as a water conservation strategy after receiving appropriate training from IP actors. However, farmers from Chidora Village lamented the inadequacy of the technical support that they were receiving from the technical partners in the IP. Like Hwedza farmers in the other villages, they were prepared to adopt fully-functioning irrigation schemes with new technologies if only the IP process would offer greater support.

The villages involved in the IPs had moderately fertile soils that needed additional application of nutrients for improved yields. Historically, and before the introduction of IPs, the farmers had their own ways of managing the fertility of the soil by adding domestically produced manure such as cow dung to their fields. Interviews with the farmers also showed that they would apply manure that they harvested from the forests to boost soil fertility. One of the farmers had the following to say:

> We have over the years adopted a number of ways to enrich our fields. One of the widely used ways is to dig the soil from an anthill. The soil is naturally fertile. This soil is then spread over the rest of the field to enrich the soil. After the farming season, it will be clear that the portions of the field that has been applied with anthill soil will produce more yields.

However, the coming in of innovation platforms augmented these traditional practices. Conservation farming training that was spearheaded by CIAT and the International Maize and Wheat Improvement Center (CIMMYT) did not only teach farmers about conserving moisture, but also about simultaneously conserving nutrients. All farmers who were part of the IPs were exposed to the practice of conserving soil nutrients as integral to conservation farming. This practice, according to a CIAT officer, involved ensuring minimum disturbances to the soil. Farmers were encouraged to dig a one square metre wide hole, which is also one metre deep. This hole would be filled with fertile soil that is mixed with tree leaves to conserve moisture and nutrients over a number of years. Interviews with Hwedza farmers showed that they appreciated the positive effect this had on their farming activities. Further training from IP actors, including those from the state's agricultural extension officers, brought in other ways to conserve soil fertility such as crop rotation, covering of crops, efficient application of fertilisers, rhizobium inoculation and intercropping.

All of the Hwedza farmers involved in the IP process noted that they had also adopted improved varieties of seeds to optimise their yields, particularly considering that the length and quality of farming seasons were increasingly becoming unreliable. Actors such as CIMMYT trained farmers on improved maize seed varieties, which matured within a relatively short season while producing higher yields. Additionally, such seed varieties were said to be more resilient in relation to moisture strain. Key informant interviews with CIMMYT showed that the organisation had engaged in significant work in intervention villages in Hwedza to train farmers on improved seeds. CIMMYT officers claimed that most farmers had been simply planting the available seed variety without considering the maturity period and yields. However, after their interaction with CIMMYT, there was improved awareness by farmers that they have a choice when it came to seed varieties. CIMMYT was also running demonstration plots in Hwedza to show farmers the merits and demerits of different seed varieties.

Post-harvest crop handling by farmers

A focus on improving the yields of small-scale farmers alone does not necessarily guarantee food security for these farmers let alone the possibility of producing surplus for output markets. The tragedy that many small-scale farmers continue to face is the lack of preparedness in handling any improved yield that they achieve, such that a substantial portion of their harvest may be lost. In this regard, post-harvest technologies, as pursued by the farmers in the IP intervention villages, become important. Hwedza farmers were certainly aware of the traditional method of drying crops using the sun without adopting any new technologies. Drying crops using the sun was indeed preferred by farmers because of the low cost of the method as well as its effectiveness. Farmers would identify an extensive open area (called *ruware*) either at their homesteads or in their fields where they would put their crops for drying (such as sunflowers, soya beans and groundnuts). Many farmers indicated though that, when they are drying their crops, they have to be guarding them in order to chase away birds and livestock. The quality of the crop was determined as well by the way it would be dried. All the Hwedza farmers indicated that they are always careful when drying crops especially maize because if livestock such as cattle and goats eat the dry maize, the animals will die. All this then called for vigilance particularly when drying maize using the sun. It was also evident that there were different ways of drying different crops. Further, some farmers would leave their crop to completely dry in the fields while some would harvest it, shell it and dry it as grains. Threshing was another method which Hwedza farmers used especially for crops such as cowpeas and small grains (for example, sorghum which was produced by a few farmers).

Further, it was evident that all farmers interviewed graded their harvest after drying and threshing or shelling. Grading was done because Hwedza farmers felt that it was important to package their harvest according to quality. For those who were producing cash crops, grading was mandatory because this was a requirement for the market. For soya beans, as an example, buyers would pay for the crop according to its quality. Farmers hence were careful not to mix low quality soya beans with high quality ones as this would generally lower the grade of their crop and minimise farmer earnings. For food crops such as maize, grading was important not only for the market but also for different consumption uses. Normally, low grade maize was not used for domestic consumption by people but rather it was used for small livestock such as chickens. This at least would be the norm during the years of a good harvest but the lower grade maize might be consumed during less bountiful years. Some Hwedza farmers pointed out that they undertake grading because they sometimes use high grade crops as seed in the coming year to supplement hybrid varieties. In this regard, the fieldwork evidence established that, for all the farmers interviewed, none had been buying certified seeds for groundnuts, sorghum and sunflowers though the IP did insisted that they should do so. This underscored the importance of grading for farmers.

The study established the nature of storage facilities that farmers had and any improvements that they were adopting. With the advent of cash crops such as soya beans and cowpeas within Hwedza, small-scale farmers were frantically investing in storage facilities which would minimise the risk of pests and diseases to their crops. Different storage facilities that farmers used were noticed during the fieldwork. The most common one was a pole and fence granary referred to as *ngarani*. Farmers would erect poles which are supported by meshed fence and such a facility was used for maize before it was shelled. The bulk of the farmers also indicated that they stored packed crops in sacks mainly in their houses. A few Hwedza farmers had built pole and dagga structures specifically meant for storing their harvest. What emerged though from the observations of the facilities used by small-scale farmers was the lack of any training meant to improve storage of harvested crops. The stakeholders who provided key informant interviews also indicated that there was no clear training through the IPs which targeted storage of crops after harvesting.

Despite the existence of post-harvest crop facilities and related processes, farmers battled with pests and diseases on their crops before consumption or selling. For a crop to last for more than six months, it needed to be preserved with specifically-designed chemicals. All Hwedza farmers were aware of the different chemicals that they needed to use in order to preserve their crops. Farmers had received training on crop preservation from agricultural extension workers as well as by different stakeholders who were part of the IPs. Furthermore, farmers were aware that pests could cause significant deterioration in the quality of their crops hence affecting what they would receive in sales from the market. Even in terms of domestic consumption, the nutrients diminish from pest attacks. Key informant interviews stressed that extension workers were working with IP-linked researchers to develop and implement organic methods of treating crops. Such methods include the readily-available resources such as cow dung and domestic herbs. Though the methods had not been finalised and fully adopted by farmers, this was the direction in which crop preservation was going. One key respondent from CIAT had the following to say:

> We are currently working with researchers from a local university who are experimenting on the usability and effectiveness of locally available treatments to preserve crops after harvesting. Researches had shown that goat droppings could be used to preserve maize from being affected by pesticides. There are also plans to scale up the dissemination of such knowledge to the farmers who are resource poor. The locally available treatments would be ideal for them because they lack adequate funds to buy pesticides.

It was clear that much of the knowledge that Hwedza farmers had concerning post-harvest handling of their crops had come mainly from their cultural repertoire passed on from one generation to another. And there was notable reluctance by farmers when it came to proactively seeking further information on post-harvest handling of crops. The farmers interviewed indicated that they were content with the methods that they were traditionally using and they implored IP actors to bring about different technologies that would possibly challenge the effectiveness of their time-tested methods. This is not to suggest that farmers were not appreciative of the training that they were receiving from the IP actors on the use of chemicals to preserve their crops. What emerged was that farmers mainly needed long-term preservations of harvests with specific reference to food crops, as they normally sold cash crops immediately after the harvest hence eliminating the need for targeted chemicals. The importance of farmer groups and farmer interactions also emerged as Hwedza farmers indicated that they had learnt different methods of preserving their crops from each other, either on a formal or informal basis.

Marketing of agricultural produce

A central objective of IPs is to link farmers to goods markets in order for them to realise the economic value emanating from their harvests. Lack of knowledge about markets, and failure to access them, on the part of small-scale farmers in Hwedza has led to many of these farmers being unable to add value to their crops through market sales. The competition that Hwedza communal farmers face from their more commercially-orientated counterparts also means that the former are in large part side-lined from mainstream markets. This gap in terms of market access is an issue that IPs are meant to close by mobilising relevant actors to become members of the IP and to work together with the farmers to improve their market capacity. And this is a matter which the Hwedza farmers in the intervention sites constantly highlighted as a major challenge, not only with reference to inaccessibility to viable markets but the consequent exploitation by middlemen in facilitating market access.

Maize was their main crop which they produced for both domestic consumption and selling of any surplus. Farmers expressed disappointment though in the way that the Grain Marketing Board (GMB) was handling its monopoly to buy maize as it was failing to pay for maize delivered on time. Overall, farmers said that they played no role whatsoever in determining prices for the crops they sold, as the buyers set the prices. Farmers felt that this entailed exploitation as it hindered them from making a reasonable profit on their crops or no profit at all. Hwedza farmers also faced transport difficulties to markets and saturation of the market for certain goods at specific times. The latter problem in part related to the absence of long-term storage facilities for cash crops such as soya beans. This absence pressurised farmers into selling their harvest all at the same time and they ended up being affected adversely by the laws of supply and demand. And, because farmers relied exclusively on dry land farming, this meant that they harvested their crops simultaneously and, without storage facilities, entered the market in competition with each other. The transport challenge arose because of the poor state of the rural roads in Hwedza district such that buyers were in the first place very reluctant to come to the villages with their vehicles and have them damaged in the process. For those buyers who made the sacrifice to come and buy the crops in villages, they offered low prices to compensate for any damage to their vehicles and the resultant repair expenses incurred.

Crops such as soya beans and cowpeas in fact had a readily-available market. Farmers who produced these crops did so regularly under contract, or under the auspices of contract farming, such that they were obliged to sell these crops to the relevant contractor. However, it was evident that Hwedza farmers needed new market opportunities so that they could graduate away from contract farming and the relationship of dependency that it created. In fact, despite being informed about the advantages of contract farming (such as guaranteed seeds and output markets), farmers wished to move beyond contract farming. One notable concern raised by the farmers in this respect was that cash crops had no immediate use value to the farmers and they were forced to sell their crops to the contractor even if they were not satisfied with the price. Unlike maize, which forms the staple food in Hwedza households, a cash crop like soya beans was not the preferred food for the farmers. Hence they had no option but to sell it, even below what the farmers considered as a fair market price.

The involvement of IPs in Hwedza with reference to connecting farmers to viable markets was not of great significance to the farmers. The market linkages for farmers remained quite weak. Companies such as National Foods and Olivine were reluctant in committing themselves to provide a market for small-scale farmers and their crops such as sunflower, soya beans and maize. The major reason that was given by the potential buyers was lack of irrigation by farmers which therefore meant that regular and reliable levels of harvests were not guaranteed considering the fluctuations in rainfall.

Besides crops, farmers sold livestock products but they did so mainly to fellow villagers. The levels and forms of livestock marketing were minimal compared to crop marketing, in large part because livestock production (such as cattle, goats, sheep and chickens) did not feature as significantly as crop production in Hwedza. Because of this, the innovation platforms in the villages focused primarily on crops and enhancing crop production and marketing. Since livestock did not take a central role in the deliberations of IPs, including in pursuing access to markets, barter trade dominated livestock marketing. Sometimes, cash was included in the transactions and sometimes farmers, in desperation, would sell livestock to buy crop inputs.

Hwedza farmers also spoke negatively about middlemen 'ripping them off' in relation to their livestock sales. The main market for livestock was between farmers within Hwedza but, when it came specifically to selling cattle which needed a greater cash outlay, farmers would normally turn to the middlemen as they had ready cash. One farmer in Samundera Village noted that particular middlemen specialised in buying and selling of cattle. Such buyers were said to have established linkages with butcheries located in Hwedza and beyond. These middlemen were not part of the IPs. In this regard, I interviewed one cattle middleman who emphasised that he had no interest in being part of the local IP because he felt the IPs were focusing more on crops than on livestock and hence IPs did not serve his business interests. Hence, the IP process in this case failed to incorporate actors who could, at least potentially, add some value to the marketing dimension of Hwedza farmers' agricultural activities.

IP agricultural successes in Hwedza

Despite broad challenges with marketing, there was one success story in Chidora Village. The IP operating in Chidora Village identified a common crop which was sunflowers and the platform managed to incorporate critical actors such as National Foods. National Foods produces a variety of foodstuffs that include animal feeds and it uses sunflowers as a critical raw material for these feeds. Farmers in this village organised themselves into a farming group of 20 farmers who dedicated themselves to produce sunflowers at the request of National Foods. In the farming season of 2012–2013, they obtained a good harvest and they managed to sell as a group to National Foods. It emerged that National Foods has a minimum number of tonnes that it buys and hence Chidora farmers managed to meet this minimum tonnage.

The Chidora group marketing strategy shows that, if farmers come together and agree on a crop and focus all their energies on that agreed crop, then it is possible to access markets. Interviews with representatives of National Foods showed that its membership in the Chidora IP was beneficial because the company was able to obtain reasonably large quantities of sunflowers. At the same time, because National Foods was providing technical support to the farmers and broadly overseeing the production process, the company received sunflowers from the Chidora farmers of good quality. It became clear that potential buyers of any significance for Hwedza farmers were large companies and that access to such a market called on farmers to engage in group marketing (like the Chidora farmers) as large companies operated on the basis of economies of scale. Clearly, involvement in the IP provided the Chidora farmers with market information and ultimately facilitated access, for now at least, to a regular market. Thus networking within the innovation platform was of some significance. At times, with reference to marketing, this also involved interaction between Hwedza farmers across villages and across village IPs. Undoubtedly, though, organisations such as CIAT and CIMMYT played a pivotal role in courting potential buyers for the IPs as well as advising farmers on how best they could market their crops.

The Chidora success story did not take away the fact that Hwedza farmers, in the face of the many marketing constraints, evaluated the marketing support they received from the IPs as inadequate. Though there were a range of marketing actors involved in the IPs, including the GMB, the marketing services in place remained well below farmer expectations. Key informant interviews with a crucial actor in the IPs, namely CIAT, highlighted that all the IPs had not reached what was called the 'maturity stage' in the IP process as they were still in their early years of operation. CIAT claimed that bringing different actors together under innovation platforms takes considerable time and it was not always easy to attract and incorporate all key potential stakeholders at once or over a short duration. With specific reference to marketing, it was further indicated that it takes time for farmers themselves to be organised to such an extent that they can attract reputable buyers. Most buyers only engage with farmers when the latter themselves are organised, as was the case with Chidora. Thus the stage of maturity of an IP determined its attractiveness when it came to luring other serious actors, including buyers as well as financiers, into the IP process.

Farmers who implemented conservation agriculture in their fields benefited from improved productivity and food security, and thus there was a reasonably wide adoption of conservation agriculture by Hwedza farmers. Farmers managed for instance to buy basic amenities such as cell phones and bicycles, as well as pay school fees after their tomato sales. Another story relating to this comes from an inputs supplier. Muvishi is the proprietor of *Nzara Yapera* which supplies inputs to farmers in Hwedza district. During an IP meeting, he narrated the success story of his fellow IP members. According to him, farmers had benefited significantly since the formation of the IP. The increased buying capacity that was evident among farmers involved in IPs demonstrated an improvement of their economic prospects according to Muvishi. This was attributed overall to the improved yields after the adoption of conservation farming through their participation in IPs.

Ongoing production constraints faced by farmers in Hwedza

Despite the efforts made by farmers as well as other IP actors to improve small-scale farming in Hwedza, there are a complex myriad of challenges that were militating against the success of small-scale farmers. Broadly, these challenges acted as constraints and can be categorised into crop-related and livestock-related constraints despite their interwoven and overlapping nature. The major predicament that small-scale farmers faced was ingrained in the colonial legacy that marginalised small-scale farmers despite their important role in making the nation food secure. During the colonial period, communal farmers were subordinated and marginalised and successive white regimes heavily supported white commercial farming. The ignoring of communal farming was also deliberately pursued to incapacitate small-scale farming and effectively coercive rural black people into the labour market, whether on commercial farms or in urban centres and on the mines. There was never any coherent policy on small-scale farmers in then Rhodesia to enhance their agricultural production and productivity. The Zimbabwean government, from the early 1980s, sought to fill this policy vacuum but the challenges to this day remain glaringly clear.

The small-scale farmers who were interviewed corroborated this viewpoint by articulating a range of challenges that they were facing. Chief among these challenges was the sheer lack of state funding and support for their farming activities. Farmers lamented the absence of consistent funding from the central government for making available farming inputs. If such inputs were provided, it was sporadic and the mechanisms of distribution were flawed by favouritism. State institutions that were mandated to rescue small-scale farmers, such as the GMB, were seen by Hwedza farmers as incapacitated in ensuring inputs to farmers. But the absence of support went wider than the state *fiscus*. Hwedza farmers, like all communal farmers in Zimbabwe, do not have title deeds to their land and thus do not have any form of collateral for purposes of accessing loans from banks. Thus, the probability of loans from financial institutions was heavily compromised. Additionally, the introduction of the multi-currency system in Zimbabwe in 2009 meant that financial institutions were prudently exercising high levels of frugality when it came to the disbursements of loans. All this translated of course into the relative lack of for example inputs for small-scale farmers, which diminished their capacity to adequately produce crops and led to an often consequent reliance on government aid support or NGO relief support for food.

The membership of Hwedza farmers in innovation platforms seemed to be of near minimal benefit in alleviating this challenge of lack of funding. Farmers indicated that their IPs had failed to attract committed financiers who were willing to offer loans to support small-scale farming. Key informant interviews with potential financiers, who had been approached to become actors in the IPs in Hwedza, revealed that financiers had their own specific fears when it came to funding small-scale farmers. And, indeed, a key issue was lack of title deeds to the land, hence making it impossible to use the land as collateral. Another reason was the perceived high risk associated with dry land farming which was predominantly practiced by small-scale farmers. This was buttressed by increasing climate change and variability which was making non-irrigated farming ever more uncertain hence increasing the risk of funding such farmers in terms of repayments. The use of livestock as collateral was not acceptable to financiers because all the livestock owned by Hwedza farmers were not insured.

Farmers also lamented the high cost of inputs that was impacting negatively on their farming activities. Self-funded agriculture (by the farmers) was in fact the prevailing pattern of funding in the Hwedza villages, and this related to both crop production and livestock production. All farmers indicated that they were buying, with their own funds, crop inputs such as seeds, fertilisers and chemicals while a few indicated that they were also buying livestock feeds, veterinary services and related drugs. I noted though that companies providing inputs were invited to the IP meetings, resulting in more input supply outlets being made available in close proximity. For instance, NICO ORGO caters for small-scale farmers by providing small 5 kg packs of organic fertiliser that are affordable and easy to carry. It also partnered with MASHCO (an agro-dealer) that has been re-established in Hwedza to make the fertiliser easily accessible.

The lack of funds was given however as a key reason for the minimum use of livestock drugs and livestock feed despite farmers' knowledge of the importance and use of such inputs. As an alternative, the bulk of Hwedza farmers indicated that they relied on indigenous knowledge systems to cure their livestock. To curb livestock losses during droughts, farmers stocked crop residues after harvesting and they would use this to feed their livestock under the strain of diminishing pastures. In relation to such livestock-related problems, farmers expressed concerns about the diminishing quality of pastures in their areas due also to the sheer increase in the livestock population, such that the quality and health of their animals was declining. The lack of grazing land arose as well from the increasing crop farming activities in the villages investigated. Because the primary land rights are possessed by mainly males in all the Hwedza villages, land has continued to be subdivided to cater for young adult men who wish to start their own families, and cropping land for these new families has increasingly encroached onto and taken over grazing land. Farmers believed that their only hope was to embrace skills they gained from their participation in IPs as a way of increasing yield per hectare hence putting a halt on the downsizing of grazing areas.

In bringing to the fore the expansion of the population in the Hwedza villages, farmers highlighted an additional constraint, namely, the deteriorating fertility of the soil that they were farming on. They were facing a situation in which they needed to apply even more fertilisers to realise the same yield. As a result, farmers were now spending more money on inputs because of the declining condition of their land. Additionally, farmers clearly realised that climate change was impacting negatively on the quality of land for crops, with rainfall now unreliable and constantly threatening to bring about lower than expected yields.

Conclusion and policy insights

This chapter has elaborated upon how small scale-farmers in Hwedza organise their production in the context of IPs. It has emerged that farmers are not passive recipients of ideas from external actors as they have their own historically established knowledge systems and agricultural practices when it comes to crop and livestock production. Despite their active participation in IPs, farmers have guarded their knowledge systems of production, which they have refined over a period of time. What this chapter has shown then is an accommodation of knowledge systems between that of farmers and the ideals of conversation farming propagated by the lead NGOs in the innovation platforms. The interface between different actors in Hwedza has created a platform of knowledge sharing between actors, but small-scale farmers still defend their life-world, as shown by examining the different stages in the agricultural cycle, including planting of crops and post-harvest handling of crops. Despite different challenges that were highlighted by the farmers, IPs were said to have improved the yields by the bulk of the farmers who adopted conservation farming. The chapter has given a snapshot of the interface between the small-scale farmers and IP stakeholders in Hwedza. The following are policy recommendations arising from the study:

a   The government should come up with a dedicated policy aimed at address-ing the concerns of small-scale farmers. There is gap in existing agricultural policies that do not address the direct concerns of small-scale farmers.
b   There is a need to revitalise state institutions such as GMB so that they can be more effective when dealing with small-scale farmers. Small-scale farmers heavily rely on state institutions for their farming activities; hence, if these are ineffective, it means inadequate service to the farmers.
c   There is need for the government to incentivise the production of food crops to improve food security. The many private players that are funding agri-culture of small-scale farmers are focusing mainly on cash crops at the expense of food crops.
d   There is need to have a mechanism of subsidising inputs for small-scale farmers because the current input prices are beyond the reach of these com-munal farmers.

References

Akullo, D., Wals, A., Kashaija, I. and Ayo, G. 2009. Building Competences for Innova-tion in Agricultural Research: A Synthesis of Experiences and Lessons from Uganda. In P. Sanginga, A. Waters-Bayer, S. Kaaria, J. Njuki and C. Wettasinha (eds). *Innova-tion Africa; Enriching Farmers' Livelihoods*, (pp. 326–332). Earthscan.

Dormon, E.N.A., Leeuwis, C., Fiadjoe, F.Y., Sakyi-Dawson, O. and van Huis, A. 2007. Creating Space for Innovation: The Case of Cocoa Production in the Suhum-Kraboa-Coalter District of Ghana. *International Journal of Agricultural Sustainability*, 5 (2–3): 232–246.

Ejigu, J. and Bayer, A. 2004. *Towards Co-research: Institutionalizing Farmer Participa-tory Research in southern Ethiopia*. London: FARM-Africa.

Edquist, C. and Johnson, B. 1997. Institutions and Organisations in Systems of Innova-tion. In C. Edquist (ed.), *Systems of Innovation: Technologies, Institutions and Organi-zations*. London and Washington: Pinter/Cassell Academic.

EPZA (Export Processing Zone Authority). 2005. *Horticulture Industry in Kenya*. Export Processing Zone Authority (EPZA), Nairobi, Kenya.

FARA (Forum for Agricultural Research in Africa). 2009. SSA–CP (Sub-Saharan Africa Challenge Programme): Research Plan and Programme for Impact Assessment. Forum for Agricultural Research in Africa (FARA), Accra, Ghana.

GoK (Government of Kenya). 2004. *Strategy for Revitalizing Agriculture 2004–2014.* Government of Kenya, Ministry of Agriculture, Nairobi, Kenya.

Hawkins, R., Booth, R., Chitsike, C., Twinamasiko, E., Tenywa, M., Karanja, G., Ngoobo, T. and Jan Verschoor, A. 2009. In P. Sanginga, A. Waters-Bayer and S. Kaaria (eds), *Strengthening Inter-Institutional Capacity for Rural Innovation: Experience from Uganda, Kenya and South Africa.*

Ministry of Lands, Agriculture, and Rural Resettlement, 2001. *Land Reform and Resettlement Programme: Revised Phase II,* Harare: Government of Zimbabwe.

Moyo, S. 2005. The Politics of Land Distribution and Race Relations in Southern Africa. In Y. Bangura and R. Stavenhagen (eds), *Racism and Public Policy.* Palgrave Press.

Moyo, S. 2009. *Fast Track Land Reform Baseline Survey in Zimbabwe: Trends and Tendencies, 2005/06.* Harare: African Institute for Agrarian Studies (AIAS).

OECD. 2005. *OECD Science, Technology and Industry Scoreboard,* OECD, Paris, France.

Rukuni, M. 1994. *An Analysis of the Economic and Institutional Factors Affecting Irrigation Development in Communal Lands of Zimbabwe.* Unpublished D. Phil. Thesis. University of Zimbabwe, Harare.

Spielman, D.J. 2006. A Critique on Innovation Systems Perspectives on Agricultural Research in Developing Countries. *Innovation Strategy Today,* 2 (1): 41–54.

Thirtle. C. 1993. *Relationship Between Changes in Agricultural Productivity and the Incidence of Poverty in Developing Countries.* Department of Agricultural and Food Economics, University of Reading.

World Bank. 2009. *Enhancing Agricultural Innovation. How to Go Beyond Strengthening of Research Systems.* The World Bank, Washington DC, USA.

ZIMSTAT Draft Report on Zimbabwe Population Census 2013.

7 Development NGOs

Understanding participatory methods, accountability and effectiveness of World Vision in Umzingwane District

Kayla Knight Waghorn

Introduction

Non-Governmental Organisations (NGOs) possess a leading role in both delivering and facilitating development initiatives, particularly in the developing world. Separate from state systems and market systems, they have grown in prominence as the supposed answer to (or substitute for) unequipped states and weak markets that have failed to deliver basic social services and infrastructure (Makoba 2002). The continual rising of their importance and prevalence in the development sector has subsequently led to much debate about the effectiveness and appropriateness of their role. In the case of Zimbabwe, NGOs have occupied a prominent role in the development of rural areas since independence in 1980 (Helliker 2008). NGO work in Zimbabwe currently takes place within a tense and fluid political climate, an economy experiencing contiguous crisis cycles, international skepticism towards long-term donor investment, and global expectations about the methodologies and accountability measures carried out in intervention-based development work.

In light of the participatory methodologies and empowerment-based development frameworks that dominate current global expectations for work within the development sector, this chapter focuses on World Vision in Zimbabwe, with the objective to understand and explain its participatory methods, accountability and effectiveness with reference to enhancing rural livelihoods (using communal areas in Umzingwane District in the south-western part of the country as a case study). In considering such participatory methodologies, this chapter draws on qualitative data, gathered through interviews with World Vision staff, government officials and project beneficiaries. The research finds that in manoeuvring through a complex situation of continuous responses to donor and state pressures, World Vision Zimbabwe acts by building local government capacity in order to maintain the longevity and measureable outputs of its projects. In doing so, it redefines the concept of participation in pursuing practical approaches to 'getting things done'. The chapter concludes that this compromises the deep participatory forms that may heighten the legitimacy of World Vision's role amongst communities, in order for it to maintain its own organisational sustainability in Zimbabwe. The analysis of

World Vision Zimbabwe contributes to a deeper understanding of the role NGOs play in development in Zimbabwe, and in other similar developing countries, as well as of NGOs as a particular organisational form.

Methodology

The research undertaken for this chapter is qualitative, relying on primary sources of data, and was undertaken from 2012 to 2013. It involved gathering information from three groups of stakeholders: World Vision, local government, and project beneficiaries. The main objective of this chapter is considered in terms of participatory methodologies, which are themselves rooted in the deeply qualitative and immeasurable concepts of empowerment and self-reliance. As such, qualitative research is an appropriate approach in attempting to understand the extent and appropriateness of NGOs' (and World Vision's specifically) abilities to carry out their work and achieve their largely un-measurable – as understood in a strict quantitative sense – objectives.

The chosen data collection methods were:

a   Semi-structured interviews with World Vision staff at varying levels, including the national Grants and Human Affairs Director, the regional Food Security and Livelihoods Programme Manager, the Umzingwane District Coordinator and the Umzingwane Field Officer.
b   Interviews with local government officials who have been involved in World Vision projects, including the head of Umzingwane District's Department of Agricultural, Technical, and Extension Services (Agritex), a district-level Agritex field officer and three ward-level Agritex field officers. These interviews helped to understand the role of the state in implementing World Vision projects, and were mandatory for gaining access to project sites.
c   Interviews with seven World Vision project beneficiaries located in communal areas in Umzingwane District. The sample sites were non-randomly selected by the Agritex district-level field officer who was tasked with accompanying me on the site visits. The limitations and potential biases of this sampling are discussed below.
d   Site visits of seven World Vision projects in Umzingwane district's communal areas. This entailed physically visiting current and previous project sites to observe what is still operational and how people are using project resources, thereby gathering details and information on those projects.
e   Collection and review of primary documentation from World Vision, including World Vision's global accountability reports, official policies, a multitude of literature produced as practical guidelines for World Vision employees, and a national-level report from World Vision Zimbabwe. This was necessary for understanding and contextualising World Vision's work in Umzingwane within the organisation's objectives, philosophies, ideologies, values, professed methodologies, and policies.

Data analysis methods included descriptive accounts, theme analysis and critical event analysis as described in the qualitative field research guide by Baily (2007). These techniques allowed thoughtful and careful analysis of the qualitative insights gained throughout the research.

The methods carried out in this study have involved significant limitations, which may involve implications for the research. First, while the semi- to unstructured interviews allowed the collection of vast amounts of personal insights from various stakeholders involved in the projects, they also created a lack of consistency in the information gathered, as particular aspects were prioritised differently by different informants. At the same time, this differing prioritisation does indicate how the different stakeholders give meaning to the World Vision projects. This lack of consistency, however, coupled with the absence of both quantitative and secondary data, does not allow for a comparison against baseline data, nor does it allow for the verification of reliability that could potentially be provided by juxtaposing primary data with secondary data.

Second was the necessity of being accompanied by Agritex officers during the site visits. While this provided an excellent opportunity to gain insight regarding their involvement in the projects, it also created great potential for a biased perspective in these three capacities: Agritex officers selected the sites to be observed; their very presence may have influenced the answers to questions given by the beneficiaries; and the presence of an outsider accompanied by an Agritex officer may have been assumed to be either a donor or an NGO staff member.

NGOs and participatory development

In order to understand the role of NGOs, it is necessary to first understand the term 'development' and the ways in which NGOs are engaged with(in) it. Development can be understood in two ways: as an immanent and unintentional process of structural, political and economic change, or as intentional intervention with the goal of creating change (Bebbington 2004). For the remainder of this chapter, the term 'development' will refer to the latter, unless otherwise specified. NGOs are directly involved in such development, in that they carry out targeted intervention projects and, in doing so, form part of the broader processes of immanent structural, political and economic change (Mitlin *et al.* 2007).

The legitimacy and appropriateness of the prominence of NGOs in development delivery is a complex question. While they are seen by some analysts as alternatives to corrupt or inefficient governments in delivering development and are considered flexible, unburdened with bureaucracy, and more effective at identifying and meeting grassroots needs (Fisher 1997:444), their effectiveness in facilitating long-term sustainable development programmes has been questioned. In addition to being criticised for using development aid to transfer external, Western, donor-driven values of democracy (Brett 2003), NGOs, as external sources of development, are scrutinised for the assumption that local values towards development require modification from external sources. Still, they are generally considered as 'doing good', because they are non-profit, voluntary organisations whose work is charitable in nature, and who operate based on certain frameworks and methodologies that give validity to their existence and legitimacy. They have therefore been often embraced by donor agencies as the preferred method for delivering aid assistance and NGO involvement is often a requirement for international funding for development initiatives.

The use of participatory methods is widely regarded as fundamental and vitally important to implementing development initiatives that promote sustainable livelihoods. The participation of the intended beneficiaries in the planning, implementing and evaluation of these schemes is considered to be both ethically and practically necessary. Ethically, it is deemed necessary to legitimate the actions of donor-funded development agencies (Brett 2003). This is based on the ideological belief that, without local participation and input, an outside agency imposes its own values (namely Western values) and does not understand, or acknowledge, beneficiary values and needs. Such impositions undermine local knowledge, and contribute to a sense of vulnerability rather than empowerment. Participation is also considered practically necessary, as it is believed to build interest and improve the efficiency of development projects by revealing local resources and promoting project sustainability (Kumar 2002). Due to these ethically legitimating and practical aspects associated with participation, it has become not only customary, but a requirement to adhere to participatory policy and practice in the development sector.

Despite the general acceptance of this necessity and the broad adherence to its importance, the concept of 'participation' in development methodology is subject to conceptual slippage and is therefore understood and defined differently in different contexts. This discrepancy between understandings has serious implications on development theory, NGO organisational policy and, most importantly, on the beneficiaries who are 'participating'. Within these varying interpretations of what 'participation' truly means in development, a distinction can be made between top-down participation, or involvement, and bottom-up participation, or popular participation (de Beer and Swanepoel 1998).

Top-down participation is involvement-based, and occurs where a development NGO, already having determined a project plan, consults the local group or community about its plan and mobilises them to take part in carrying out the intended projects. The fundamental focus is on the success and sustainability of the project itself. Alternatively, bottom-up participation is based on the goal of instilling a sense of empowerment. Empowerment is considered to be inherently linked to livelihood sustainability and is therefore the truly meaningful objective of deep participation. This inherent linkage comes from the concept of self-reliance, or people's willingness and capacity to rely on their own abilities and resources (Nikkhah and Redzuan 2010). This self-reliance is the platform for achieving livelihood sustainability and it exists when people are empowered to control and manage their own lives. In carrying out development projects, bottom-up participation contends that empowerment has the potential to grow out of mundane and ordinary development activities (Ndegwa 1996) by transforming the existing state and sense of poverty into self-confidence and self-reliance. The most important aspect of this understanding of participation is the importance of people making their own decisions and controlling the factors that affect their own lives. This deep participation entails much more than mere involvement or consultation.

Questions regarding the legitimacy and effectiveness of NGOs, both in terms of their ability to achieve deep participatory methods and the overall justification for their existence and position in the development sector, ultimately come down to the question of accountability. Accountability defines the relationships between the various stakeholders involved in the NGO development sector. The three primary stakeholder groups are: the local beneficiaries; the donor agencies who provide the funding for NGOs; and the governing powers (both national and local) for the area where the NGO project or programme is located. Ideally, an NGO's actions and its development goals would reflect a high level of accountability to the beneficiaries of their development projects (downward accountability), answering to those whom they aim to help, and thereby legitimating the presence of NGOs in development. The necessity to adhere to the requirements of the other key stakeholders (donors and governing bodies), however, challenges the realisation of this downward accountability. In this way, the notion that legitimises NGOs (that is, downward accountability to beneficiaries) is not necessarily what ensures or defines their existence in practice. Carefully considering the relationships between NGOs and the stakeholders involved in their operations is necessary in order to scrutinise their role in delivering development.

NGOs in Zimbabwe

NGOs operating in Zimbabwe, both national and international, have played a large part in attempting to alleviate poverty and improve livelihood security. The direction and priorities of their involvement have been affected by opposing pressures, including donor priorities and trends, political tensions, government control through legislation and intimidation, and glaring economic and social crises. All of this has contributed at times to an NGO reaction of disengagement from controversial and confrontational aspects of Zimbabwean socio-economic development.

By and large, NGO-state relations in Zimbabwe have been marked historically by a cautious ambivalence on the part of NGOs (Moyo *et al.* 2000). The Zimbabwean government has used several tactics to control NGO activities, including initially an inclusive corporatism (where NGO presence and activities are permitted by government, so long as the direction of such actions remains under state influence and control). This strategy was followed more recently by extreme exclusion, intrusive legislation, slander and bad press, and intimidation. From independence and into the 1990s, the Zimbabwean government employed a corporatist strategy of control through NGO-government partnerships. Some successful desired effects included a variety of groups becoming "almost subservient wings of the ruling party" (Helliker 2008:244). Government tactics towards NGOs turned more intrusive during the late 1990s in response to NGO policy advocacy, as the land question became more sensitive and volatile. Suspicion and accusations by the state of supporting British colonialism were launched at NGOs and donors who were involved in political advocacy. The Zimbabwean government accused NGOs of being imperialist puppets used to further foreign and specifically Western donor interests (Moyo *et al.* 2000). In addition to such accusations, the government subsequently took more legislative measures in order to control the actions of NGOs and other groups. The most directly targeted NGO legislation was the NGO bill of 2004. Despite the fact that it was never signed into law, its broad targeting of all NGOs caused scepticism and apprehension from donors towards committing to medium and long-term funding of NGOs in Zimbabwe (Tsunga and Mugabe 2004).

Throughout the economic crisis following the year 2000, NGO work in communal areas was subjected to suspicion from government over project motivation, particularly in communal areas with historically anti-ZANU-PF sentiment, such as many of those located in Matabeleland (in which my case study falls). During election periods, World Vision, along with other NGOs, was accused of involvement in rural politics (Helliker 2006). Such accusations particularly contribute to the cautious character by which NGOs approach their work. Leading up to and during the most recent election period in July 2013, NGOs working in multiple communal areas were requested to cease their activities and remove themselves from the areas (WVZ Regional Food Security and Livelihoods Programme Manager, personal communication, 4 December 2013). Currently, NGOs working in both development and advocacy carry on the cautious role of avoiding direct confrontation with the state. NGO actions in Zimbabwe must also be understood within the context of donors, donor funding and organisational sustainability, which – as indicated – has been affected by the state's approach to NGOs. In this respect, oppressive and vague legislation, along with a relationship of mutual distrust between some NGOs and the Zimbabwean state, have influenced donors to invest in short-term, specific projects to the detriment of longer-term sustainable investment in development.

NGOs in Zimbabwe are currently precariously located in a tension-riddled field, including responding to a social and economic crisis, the politics of state control over their actions, and international donor interests. Due to such a precarious political and economic context, development NGO action in contemporary Zimbabwe has been directed towards a fluctuating mixture of development and relief work where NGOs seek to manoeuvre their way in accessing whatever donor funding is available, and acting in a way which sometimes amounts to an ambivalent avoidance of politics and an often minimalist engagement with the state. These conflicting interests and pressures affect the motivations, impacts and legitimacy of their work.

World Vision: introduction and history

World Vision International (WVI) is a large-scale, international, Christian NGO which focuses on working against the causes of poverty with a particular focus on children. It works on multiple levels, including global, regional, national, and local, and is present in 97 countries around the world (Gwynne and Miller 2011:25). The ideological framework for the approach of WVI involves the belief in a holistic approach, meaning that the process of livelihood improvement must involve all aspects of life through cross-sectoral development. This emphasis on holism supports a key aspect of World Vision's work: projects cover a wide range of development sectors within whole communities.

World Vision's primary policy framework is called Learning through Evaluation with Accountability and Planning (LEAP). Much can be understood about WVI by studying the LEAP policies, as they present both actual requirements and discursive perspectives regarding World Vision's 'take' on development and participation. By looking within LEAP and comparing its requirements with its recommendations and explanations, it is possible to compare the ideological base of World Vision work with what is prioritised and required on the ground.

LEAP (WVI 2007) outlines a six-step process approach to development projects, where each step includes required standards (what staff *must* do) and advisory guidelines (what WVI *recommends* that staff do whenever it is possible and efficient). The six steps in the LEAP process are: assessment, design, monitoring, evaluation, reflection and transition. The emphasised priorities and values throughout the six steps include: alignment with national strategy; collaboration with major stakeholders about project direction and responsibilities; adherence to WVI organisational tools related to funding, monitoring and evaluation; preparing for sustainability through shared agreements with local stakeholders, namely government; and tangible, measureable outcomes. An additional evident theme throughout the steps is that participation of local partners is suggested as an advisory guideline, rather than a required standard. Further, some of the specific processes outlined within the six steps prioritise the efficient use of resources (namely time and funds) over participation.

The first such process is that secondary (and quantitative) data is the preferred type of data for collection and analysis during assessment. This strategy implies that participatory assessment with general community members may not even take place, as secondary data is preferred. The second process prioritising efficient use of resources over participation is the reliance on local government as the "primary duty-bearer for issues arising in an area" (WVI 2007:42). This removes participatory roles from the beneficiaries and places it with local government. Finally, it is also required within WVI standards that the design process involves participatory approaches with beneficiaries "whenever practical and cost effective" (WVI 2007:38). This provisional statement is revealing, as it specifically places efficiency as a priority over participation.

In addition to its philosophy and approach, the way in which World Vision acquires and maintains funding helps to contextualise its accountability and its ability to carry out participatory methods. WVI has two primary means of acquiring funding: child sponsorship funding and grant-funding from donors. The largest fraction of its income comes from sponsorships (WVI 2011:34), which involve private donations for the support of one particular child. This type of funding is used to fund WVI's Area Development Programmes (ADPs), which involve a variety of long-term interventions across multiple sectors taking place in a specified geographical area. By giving WVI full control of monitoring and reporting requirements, this type of funding helps to guarantee long-term stability for use in a variety of projects within the primary focus area.

Donor funding is less consistent than sponsorship funding, is acquired on a programme- or project-specific basis, and is limited by the parameters set by the donors. In keeping with the WVI ideals of holistic development, individual donor grant-funded projects which are not part of ADPs are still often carried out in groupings within close proximity to each other (both in time and space) and with an overlap of beneficiaries. Such overlap (in time, space and beneficiaries), along with the partnerships that World Vision forms with local stakeholders, seems to allow WVI some flexibility in stretching funding and resources in order to pursue more long term development aims. This is particularly the case in Zimbabwe, as is discussed below.

World Vision Zimbabwe and accountability

World Vision International first entered Zimbabwe in 1973 (Bornstein 2005) and is currently present in each province throughout the country (OCHA 2009), conducting projects and programmes in 28 districts (OCHA 2012). For World Vision Zimbabwe (WVZ) grant-funded projects, the ability to carry out meaningful participation (from assessment through to evaluation) is constrained by funding limitations. In response, it has maintained a close working relationship with the state, which allows it to stretch funding by relying heavily on local state systems for carrying out its development work. This, however, is at the cost of participation.

As discussed earlier, World Vision globally promotes beneficiary participation throughout its publications, but its actual organisational requirements (laid out in LEAP) seem to take a more practical and efficiency-based approach, placing the use of secondary data (thus avoiding more resource-intensive assessment) at a higher value than achieving truly empowerment-based participation. With regard to assessment, WVZ attempts to conduct focus group discussions with community members whenever possible through what the WVZ Grants and Human Affairs Director described in an interview as "quick and dirty consultative processes" (personal communication, 24 May 2012). While at least inclusive of beneficiaries, such methods do not allow for relationship-building, joint understanding, community engagement and a sense of project ownership which is often deemed necessary to bring about empowerment. Additionally, WVZ is not always able to carry out these "quick and dirty" assessments due to lack of funding or time. When that is the case, WVZ bases its funding proposals on the local district government's strategic plan.

Historically, WVZ and its work have involved a cautiously submissive, yet closely tied relationship with the state, marked by both the state's dependence and control over WVZ and, in certain ways, WVZ's dependence on the state. Currently, the nature of this relationship differs depending on the district. At the national level, WVZ is recognised by the state, has regular communication with various government ministries and has developed a presence within the country that allows it some stability in terms of achieving permits and government approval to conduct development assistance.

One aspect of WVZ's work that stood out throughout the research is that great faith and responsibility are placed in local government and its ability to assess, design, carry out, monitor and evaluate projects in partnership with, and sometimes in place of, World Vision. Although this is variable depending on the district, it is WVZ's objective to involve local government in its development projects and to build state institutional capacity in this regard. Additionally, it appears that the practical ability to 'get things done' is more easily achieved in partnership with government, in order to facilitate bureaucratic processes, and maintain positive relationships and good communication.

This relationship of interdependence between WVZ and the state has both positive and negative connotations. In the positive sense, working so closely with government may be the only long-term path to development, as the government is ultimately the long-term institution which is responsible for it. Nevertheless, this close partnership (which allocates both responsibility and credit to the government for work that World Vision is catalysing, funding, and guiding) may unwittingly reinforce faith in unfair or corrupt systems of governance, particularly reinforcing the popularity of political leaders who claim to be the bearers of development.

World Vision in Umzingwane

In order to understand the work of WVZ and its contextual situation with regards to donors, the Zimbabwean state and beneficiary communities, this section examines the work of World Vision in Umzingwane District in Matabeleland South Province. World Vision's work in Umzingwane district focuses primarily on small-scale agricultural development at the household level. There are no Area Development Programmes in the district, which means that there are no sponsored children and all projects are funded through grants from donors. Therefore, programmes are primarily short-term (under three years) and are carried out in close partnership with Umzingwane district-level government. Due to the holistic approach of World Vision's development initiatives, the agricultural projects undertaken involve significant overlap in beneficiaries. The fieldwork and the following discussion cover a range of World Vision projects in Umzingwane and examine the connections and overlap between them.

The World Vision projects include conservation agriculture, rabbit production, guinea fowl production, goat production, layer chickens for egg production, and the rehabilitation of two dam-fed irrigation schemes. All of the projects involved physical inputs, training or both, as provided by WVZ, while implementation was carried out either in conjunction with or through the state department of Agritex. Beneficiaries targeted for physical inputs were selected based on WVZ's 'most vulnerable' criteria. For each of the projects, WVZ was no longer monitoring at the time of research, and monitoring responsibility had been turned over to Agritex. Findings and data gathered from site visits and interviews, about the effectiveness of the projects, are presented in Table 7.1 below.

The Conservation Agriculture (CA) projects targeted large groups of beneficiaries and were carried out through a Trainer of Trainers model in partnership with Agritex, in which World Vision provides training and instructional pamphlets to Agritex, and Agritex in turn conducts training on the ground with beneficiary farmers. All livestock production beneficiaries also received CA training. All such programmes are intended to have a trickledown effect on the entirety of the rural communities in which they occur.

WV methodology in practice in Umzingwane

All of the projects outlined in Table 7.1 have involved great reliance on Agritex.

In accordance with WV's LEAP policy (although LEAP was not mentioned by district level WV staff), the methods used by WVZ in Umzingwane involve a practical and efficient approach with objectives to stretch donor funding through effectively outsourcing responsibilities to local government (Agritex) and to enable long-term project support through building local government capacity. With regard to needs-assessment, there were two different motivations expressed by World Vision staff for WVZ's involvement in the local area. The first motivation entailed WVZ responding to a request for assistance from local government – the Rural District Council (RDC) – in order to implement a development plan, which the council already had in place. The second motivation involved WVZ initiatives to supplement the development projects, which were being requested by the RDC. Information used in needs-assessment for determining project plans was gathered through Agritex as well as directly by WVZ.

Implementation of WVZ projects in Umzingwane is primarily carried out by Agritex. In this context, one World Vision field officer who was interviewed indicated that Agritex officers would be in a stronger position than him to provide details of the multiple projects in Umzingwane, suggesting in effect that World Vision takes a backseat role in guiding and supporting Agritex, rather than taking on a direct role as implementers on the ground (WVZ Umzingwane Field Officer, personal communication, 15 October 2013). When asked about this, the WVZ Regional Food Security and Livelihoods Programme Manager suggested that working through Agritex allows WVZ projects to be more sustainable, as donor funds for WVZ projects have short cycles of time and, therefore, working with and through Agritex (a permanent presence) complements WVZ's efforts (personal communication, 4 December 2013). During the length of WVZ's participation, WVZ ensures that Agritex has or builds the necessary

Table 7.1 Projects in Umzingwane

Project Site	Is the beneficiary maintaining the project?	Results	Further comments
CA Ward 13	Yes	Very positive	
CA Ward 5 – Site 1	Yes	Very positive	
CA Ward 5 – Site 2	Yes	Very positive	
CA Ward 5 – Site 3	Yes	Very positive	
Rabbit Production Ward 5 – Site 1	Yes	Very positive – stock of 7, sold 18	Farmer also benefitted from the CA and rabbit production projects, and was successful in both
Rabbit Production Ward 5 – Site 2	Yes	Very positive – stock of 25, sold 33	Farmer successful in CA
Guinea Fowl Production Ward 5	Yes	Very positive – proceeds from guinea fowl used to invest in turkeys	
Guinea Fowl Production Ward 13	Yes	Birds alive but no profits	
Goat Production Ward 5 – Site 1	Yes	Positive – stock of 5, sold 10, invested in cow, root stock still producing	
Goat Production Ward 5 – Site 2	Yes	Positive – stock of 17, sold 2, able to replace male goat	Farmer very successful with CA – unconcerned with goat project failure; focus on CA
Goat Production Ward 5 – Site 3	No	Both goats died	Farmer had plans to double production with investments
Layer Chickens/Egg Production Ward 8	Yes	Very positive, high egg collection rate; high profits	Contradictory claims from WV employee about funding difficulty
Mzinyathini Irrigation Scheme Rehabilitation	No	Water supply cut off due to local government authority disputes (resolved through a concerned 3rd party)	Difficulty with maintenance (government promised to fix a broken valve, so locals will not contribute to fix it)
Malunika Dam and Irrigation Scheme Rehabilitation	Yes	All 27 farmers are maintaining their plots	

capacity to monitor and sustain the projects. Therefore, World Vision is in effect taking advantage of short-term funding while avoiding its negative implications (namely, lack of resources for long-term monitoring and evaluation). As such, even if funding streams are short-term, projects themselves should not be, in that Agritex remains to see projects through in the long term.

In addition to exhibiting WVZ's organisational values for the significance of local partnership with government and the efficiency of time and monetary investment, WVZ projects in Umzingwane clearly reflect WVZ's value of holistic development. This is evident through the overlap which has been created among project beneficiaries, with many farmers benefitting from multiple and different WVZ projects at the same time. By supporting income diversification through implementing a variety of agricultural projects among the same targeted beneficiaries, World Vision is providing what could be considered a safety net to protect beneficiaries from uncontrollable factors that may lead to project failure. For example, one of the farmers visited had been very successful with her conservation agriculture but had been very unsuccessful with her goats. Therefore, while she had failed at one project, she was still able to sustain herself and improve her livelihood from the other project. Additionally, this diversity of projects, when successful, may inspire confidence that leads to self-initiative among beneficiaries to further expand or diversify their projects. Such success and expansion was seen with the farmer who had been successful in her rabbit, goat and conservation agriculture projects and had therefore invested in a cow, intending to build up a cattle herd over time.

Similar to assessment and implementation, monitoring and evaluation for WVZ projects in Umzingwane are also carried out through Agritex. The trend that is evident among these systems of assessment, implementation, monitoring and evaluation in Umzingwane is that World Vision's approach to participation and capacity-building is very government-focused, centred on empowering and supporting the established systems that exist in local government. This focus on building government capacity has serious implications, some of which came to light during this research.

Local state bodies with the authority to grant permission for WV's development activities include the District Administrator (DA) and RDC. The WVZ programme manager (personal communication, 4 December 2013), district coordinator (personal communication, 5 October 2013) and field officer (personal communication, 15 October 2013) for Umzingwane all expressed a high level of satisfaction with their relationship with both the DA and the RDC. In addition to permitting WVZ to carry out projects, World Vision staff considered the WVZ-local government partnerships to provide WVZ projects and WVZ itself a level of political security. The WVZ district coordinator commented that "the best method to manage political labelling is to plan [site] monitoring with government line ministry departments". He suggested that, because of government's involvement in the projects, World Vision is protected from two possibilities: the first is being blamed for project failure, and the second is being considered as having a political presence or promoting an oppositional political agenda in the area. While protecting WVZ from misconceptions on the part of local government structures, politically-charged struggles appeared to exist with regard to misconceptions about WVZ projects on the part of beneficiaries.

One such struggle arising from the political atmosphere involves the perception among Umzingwane communities that World Vision's funding comes from the ruling ZANU-PF party as a service from the Zimbabwe government. One World Vision staff member indicated that "politicians claim that they can give or take NGO money away, [and make] these claims usually to uninformed or uneducated people when trying to gain political support".

Two types of accountability are evident as the most prominent means of accountability for World Vision in Umzingwane: accountability to government and accountability to World Vision itself. While accountability to donors provides challenges which are accompanied by sacrificing certain priorities, accountability to the government and accountability to World Vision itself stand out as prioritised. That being said, in the view of World Vision staff, they *are* being accountable to beneficiaries *through* being accountable to government and themselves. The dimensions and elements of their accountability to beneficiaries, however, do not directly align with the generally-accepted norms or even concepts of basic participatory development. WVZ meets the basic requirements of participatory development regarding the government and building government capacity, but not at the individual, household and community levels amongst beneficiaries. While wary of politics and careful to avoid political implications of its work, WVZ embraces a close relationship with government in order to achieve both sustainability in its work and to protect itself from the very political implications that it tries to avoid.

Evaluating the work of World Vision

From the discussion in this chapter, the following conclusions can be drawn about World Vision: (1) World Vision has developed its own conceptualisation of 'participation' that allows it to pursue policies and practice approaches which prioritise efficiency and project sustainability while addressing the demands of their donors and authorities of the state; (2) while allowing efficiency and easing constraints from donors and the state, World Vision's heavy reliance on local government, while possibly a recipe for greater sustainability of both development projects and WV's organisational stability, is potentially ethically problematic with regard to supporting existing systems of power that lead to and reproduce vulnerability; and (3) WV's conceptualisation of participation allows WV to pursue its own sustainability and organisational interests and values (prioritising accountability to itself over accountability to beneficiaries) while adhering to the global standards in development assistance that call for participation and organisational learning. These conclusions about World Vision exemplify the inherent conflicts between deep and meaningful empowerment-based participatory aims and other aims of organisational stability and sustainability pursued through efficiency and compliance to donors and the state. I briefly consider these three points below.

In terms of the first point on participation, World Vision is continuously pushing towards two seemingly conflicting aims: stressing the importance of bottom-up approaches to participation and, simultaneously, prioritising the necessity for practicality, efficiency and support of existing local structures of authority. In attempting to achieve these two aims simultaneously, World Vision has questioned at least implicitly the very meaning and application of the concept of participation by questioning the notions of who the true beneficiaries are and how they are reached. By conducting bottom-up participatory methods with local structures of authority (particularly emphasising local government) and top-down participatory methods with direct project beneficiaries, the very role of 'beneficiary' and concept of 'participation' is redefined. As noted earlier, WVZ conducts trainer-of-trainer sessions intended to build the capacity of Agritex to support local farmers. Here, the local government (which World Vision sees as the true means of achieving sustainability in long-term support of the poor and vulnerable) and its employees are treated as the beneficiaries them-selves. The official direct beneficiaries (the poor and vulnerable who receive World Vision's inputs) are benefitting not through their own empowerment-building self-reliance, which should emerge from their own instigation of and leadership in development projects, but through the receipt of long-term support from local state structures, which is intended to generate a sense of stability. That support and stability is intended to create conditions for project success, thereby building confidence in personal achievement that catalyses self-reliance.

This approach to participation allows WVZ to address the demands of its donors and the state. By implementing projects alongside of and through local government systems and structures (Agritex, in the case of Umzingwane), WVZ achieves and maintains positive interactions with the state, while also stretching donor funds. This conceptualisation of 'participation' and its implementation question the foundation of deep participation, which involves the inherent linkage between empowerment and sustainability being driven by self-reliance. WVZ's 'participation' links empowerment and sustainability to long-term stability and support (by way of state structures and project diversification among overlapping beneficiaries) rather than to capacity-building that is merely externally facilitated. Ultimately, WVZ's 'participation' involves flexible and efficient manoeuvring in the face of external pressures (from the state and donors) that allows it to pursue and sustain organisational sustainability while carrying out its projects.

The second point relates to the ethical implications of WVZ's support of state structures. World Vision's reliance on local 'partners', particularly structures of state authority, takes the ethically problematic risk of contributing to factors that lead to vulnerability by supporting existing systems of power which may employ unjust or unethical practices. On the one hand, this conceptualisation of 'parti-cipation' (which rethinks the role of the 'beneficiary' in clear support of state authority and existing structures of power) has the potential to instigate develop-ment and positive change within local government and its approach to respond-ing to local needs and interests. From this perspective, such aims address the long-term complaint made against NGO-driven development that it merely pacifies local frustrations and therefore perpetuates the *status quo*. On the other hand, however, such practices have the risk of reinforcing and providing additional power to potentially unequipped, corrupt or unjust systems of governance that perpetuate vulnerability.

Third, World Vision's approach to participation also allows it to pursue its own stability and sustainability, as well as its organisational interests and values. Through its approach to participation, which both supports local state authority through capacity-building programmes and draws on them for beneficiary support, World Vision has enabled itself to achieve efficiency in the use of donor funds and to maintain an acceptable relationship with government, two elements which significantly contribute to organisational security and sustainability.

Conclusion and policy insights

The NGO objective of catalysing empowerment through pursuing deep participation entails inherent conflicts between achieving such pursuits and achieving the objectives that enable NGOs to exist and carry out development assistance. Ultimately, the legitimacy of the role of NGOs as structures of development, as well as their practices, must be questioned and considered within their specific social contexts. In the context of World Vision in Umzingwane, WVZ has compromised participatory methodology and empowerment for the purpose of enabling continued organisational presence and survival. Additionally, its policies prioritise efficiency in response to the pressures of its domain. That being said, certain recommendations can be drawn from WVZ's work in Umzingwane.

First, the focus on small-scale agricultural development at the household level appears to provide an effective model for achieving self-initiative and confidence in local farmers. This is evident in the success seen with the farmer who had been successful in her rabbit, goat and conservation agriculture projects and had therefore invested in a cow, and planned to further expand her herd. Second, the diversification of projects through a holistic, overlapping approach provided security from project failure and therefore livelihood sustainability. This is seen with the farmer who had failed with her goats, but was still able to achieve a sustainable livelihood through her Conservation Agriculture.

Finally, WVZ's heavy reliance on, and support of, local government structures (Agritex) presents a possible first step in the direction of questioning and restructuring the conventional character and balance of relationships between states, NGOs, and beneficiaries. WVZ has questioned the notion of who the true beneficiaries are, by placing a priority on building the capacity of local state structures rather than the self-reliance of direct beneficiaries. Such roles should be further questioned, and relationships re-examined, but not at the cost of deep participation among direct beneficiaries. Rather, this should be reconsidered in such a way that direct beneficiaries maintain their role as the primary beneficiary through participatory practices; at the same time, the capacity of local state structures to support participatory development of primary beneficiaries should be enhanced. In the end, if progress towards deep empowerment-based development is to be achieved, the existing paradigms that govern the character of relationships between NGOs, states, donors and beneficiaries must be significantly questioned and adjusted. It is only on this basis that NGOs would be able to pursue more deeply-rooted participatory methodologies for purposes of contributing to rural livelihoods in places such as Umzingwane.

References

Baily, C.A. 2007. *A Guide to Qualitative Field Research*. 2nd Edition. Thousand Oaks: Pine Forge Press.

Bebbington, A. 2004. NGOs and Uneven Development: Geographies of Development Intervention. *Progress in Human Geography* [e-journal], 28 (6): 725–745.

Bornstein, E. 2005. *The Spirit of Development: Protestant NGOs, Morality, and Economics in Zimbabwe*. Stanford, CA: Stanford University Press.

Brett, E.A. 2003. Participation and Accountability in Development Management. *The Journal of Development Studies* [e-journal], 40 (2), Available through: Academic Search Premier database [Accessed 24 July 2012].

de Beer, F. and Swanepoel, H. 1998. *Community Development and Beyond*. Pretoria: J.L. van Schaik Publishers.

FAO, 1997. *Annex A-5 Mzinyathini Irrigation Scheme*. S.l.: FAO Corporate Document Repository. [online] Available at: www.fao.org/docrep/X5594E/X5594e11.htm [Accessed 6 March 2012].

Fisher, W.F. 1997. Doing Good? The Politics and Anti-politics of NGO Practices. *Annual Review of Anthropology*, 26 (1): 239–464.

Gwynne, B. and Miller, S. 2011. *World Vision International Accountability Report 2011*. [online] WVI. Available at: www.wvi.org/our-accountability/publication/2011-accountability-report [Accessed 3 August 2013].

Helliker, K. 2006. *A Sociological Analysis of Intermediary Nongovernment Organizations and Land Reform in Contemporary Zimbabwe*. PhD. Sociology Department, Rhodes University.

Helliker, K. 2008. Dancing on the Same Spot: NGOs. In S. Moyo, K. Helliker and T. Murisa (eds), *Contested Terrain: Land Reform and Civil Society in Contemporary Zimbabwe*. (pp. 239–274) Pietermaritzburg: SS Publishers.

Kumar, S. 2002. *Methods for Community Participation*. Warwickshire: Replika Press Pvt. Ltd.

Makoba, J.W. 2002. Nongovernmental Organizations (NGOs) and Third World Development: an Alternative Approach to Development. *Journal of Third World Studies*, 14 (1), Available through: Academic Search Premier database [Accessed 19 August 2012].

Mitlin, D., Hickey, S. and Bebbington, A. 2007. Reclaiming Development? NGOs and the Challenge of Alternatives. *World Development*, 35 (10): 1699–1720.

Moyo, S., Makumbe, J. and Raftopoulos, B. 2000. *NGOs, the State and Politics in Zimbabwe*. Harare: SAPES Books.

Ndegwa, S.N. 1996. *The Two Faces of Civil Society NGOs and Politics in Africa*. West Hartford, CT: Kumarian Press.

Nikkhah, H.A. and Redzuan, M.B. 2010. The Role of NGOs in Promoting Empowerment for Sustainable Community Development. *The Journal of Human Ecology*, 30 (2): 85–92.

OCHA. 2009. *Zimbabwe Who Does What Where by Province.* 1:1,013,859. [online] OCHA. Available at: http://ochaonline.un.org/zimbabwe [Accessed 21 May 2012].

OCHA, 2012. *Zimbabwe: Humanitarian Contact Directory (2012).* [online] OCHA. Available at: https://zw.humanitarianresponse.info/system/files/documents/files/ZHCD %20Donor%20Technical%20Agencies%20(20130719094342).pdf [Accessed 21 May 2012].

Tsunga, A. and Mugabe, T. 2004. *Zim NGO bill: Dangerous for Human Rights Defenders.* [pdf] Available at: www.kubatana.net/docs/hr/zlhr_ngobill_040728.pdf [Accessed 15 March 2012].

WVI, 2007. *LEAP Second Edition.* [online] Washington, DC: WVI. Available at: www. transformational-development.org/ministry/transdev2.nsf/maindocs/34874E1F560858 F088256F1000603B96?opendocument [Accessed 17 June 2013].

WVI, 2011. *World Vision International Accountability Report 2010.* [online] WVI. Available at: www.alnap.org/resource/8772 [Accessed 2 August 2013].

ZimVAC, 2013. *Zimbabwe Vulnerability Assessment Committee (ZimVAC) 2013 Rural Livelihoods Assessment Draft Report.* [online] Harare: ZimVAC. Available at: http:// reliefweb.int/sites/reliefweb.int/files/resources/2013%20ZimVAC%20DRAFT%20 REPORT.pdf [Accessed 19 October 2013].

8 A critical analysis of community participation at the primary level of the health system in Goromonzi District

Rachel Gondo

Introduction

The adoption of the Primary Health Care (PHC) approach by Zimbabwe in 1980 signalled the government's intention to consolidate the gains of the liberation struggle by providing equitable health for all citizens regardless of race and class. The PHC approach frames community participation as central to the design and implementation of responsive health systems. This chapter analyses the existing mechanisms for community participation in the health care system in Zimbabwe, highlighting multiple perspectives on the underlying contradictions, tensions, and processes at play between policy and practice. A case study of Mwanza ward in Goromonzi district is used to illustrate how rural communities have organised themselves to occupy platforms and spaces within and outside of national health policy parameters in order to be responsible and take ownership for their own health in line with what is expected by the PHC approach. The most critical notion presented by the study is that a number of socio-economic, political and societal factors influence community participation that takes place in the health system in Zimbabwe. This in turn has a bearing on how health policy expresses itself in practice. The factors identified – as influencing community participation – are leadership, resource mobilisation, skills and knowledge, communication, legitimacy and organisation within the community health structures. The chapter concludes that in order for the health system in Zimbabwe to better respond to the needs of the most vulnerable through community participation, there is need to recognise the differentials in power and how this influences participation.

Adopted in 1978 by the World Health Organisation (WHO) and the United Nations Children's Fund (UNICEF) through the Alma Ata Declaration (1978), the PHC approach tries to ensure that essential health care be made universally accessible to the poor in communities by means acceptable to them, through their full participation and at a cost that the community and the state can afford (Rifkin 1986). The approach means that community participation would be integral to the functioning of the health system through both the delivery of services and decisions about health and health services. According to Wayland and Crowder (2002), participation is essential to PHC because individual and community action is seen as being more important than medical technology for improving health among the poor.

Community participation in health in Zimbabwe: the last three decades

In the first decade of independence, the health sector was a priority area for the Zimbabwean government in that it was one of the main areas where redress had to occur in favour of the previously racially segregated and economically disadvantaged majority. Adopted in 1980, PHC laid the foundation for, and set standards to which, health policy in Zimbabwe was to be implemented and some significant advances were made in the realm of health (Loewenson 1988). However, serious problems remained and even intensified. For example, life expectancy drastically fell in the 1990s due to the AIDS pandemic.

Overall, the economic and political environment became increasingly volatile from the mid-1990s. Coupled with the onset of the fast track land reform and its wider implications for the political economy of the country, the health status of the nation became vulnerable (see Chapter 1 in this volume for a more detailed analysis of these issues). The crumbling of the economy by 2008 affected the public health sector the most, and made health a hazard for the vast majority of Zimbabweans who use government services, faith-based services and traditional health care, with about a tenth of the population only using the private for profit health sector. The Ministry of Health and Child Care reported in the Zimbabwe Demographic Health Survey of 2011 that the top ten causes of death in the country were HIV and AIDS, influenza and pneumonia, tuberculosis, stroke, coronary heart disease, malaria, diarrhoeal diseases, low birth weight, birth trauma and maternal conditions (ZDHS 2011).

Going back to the 1980s, local government reforms served to decentralise power and authority. In line with these reforms, the health sector decentralised to the primary level through the village health worker (VHW) programme. Frankel and Doggett (1992) provide a comprehensive analysis of the positive and negative features of village health worker programmes: VHW programmes arose from and reinforced more equitable distribution of health resources, enhanced positive relations between communities and health workers, have generated support groups within communities, enhanced appropriate referral patterns and provided community based information within the health system. VHW programmes have also, however, lacked adequate resources and supplies to sustain them as well as adequate technical support and supervision from the health system. With regard to accountability, VHW faced problems in having to be answerable to the health system through health staff and additionally to the community which nominated them. VHWs also have been exposed to personal danger in environments where the state or other powerful interest groups have been threatened by their roles. They have worked for long hours at personal cost, and have faced hostility from formal health workers threatened by their non-professional status (Frankel and Doggett 1992). Overall, the VHW programme in Zimbabwe suffered in the wake of the growing economic and political problems in the period 1998–2008 as the government was unable to sustain the programme.

Along with the village health workers, the health sector had health advisory committees at each local government level (village, ward, district and province). These committees were meant to participate in Local Government development committees representing the health system. Specific health advisory boards were also set up at district hospitals and provincial hospitals in the first decade of independence. According to Loewenson (2000), the committees' initiatives were along self-reliant means such as the development of water supplies and sanitation. These interventions though seemingly increased the distance between the community and the health system as health programmes were more centrally designed.

The 1990s saw the government of Zimbabwe usher in a structural adjustment programme that led to the liberalisation of the health sector. Together with the combined effects of AIDS, drought, poor economic performance and high levels of poverty, the health gains made in the first decade of independence stagnated. This situation saw the disintegration of the health advisory boards and the village health worker programmes as health financing was rapidly decreasing. In 1997 the Ministry of Health published its first draft of a National Health Strategy (MoHCW 1997). This signalled the start of a serious re-assessment of the health sector for Zimbabwe as the system seemed to be failing to meet the needs of the populace. Discontent from the health civil service coupled with a decentralisation policy that was failing to be operationalised due to the dominance of the central level left room for citizens to organise themselves for their own health.

In the period 2000–2008, the economic and political situation contributed to the collapse of the health system especially the community thrust of the programme. As Mlambo highlights,

> the downward economic spiral that followed after 2000, as the Western world either boycotted Zimbabwe or imposed sanctions on its leadership and select businesses saw the country's GDP plummet drastically between 2000 and 2008, while the inflation rate rose to unprecedented heights in modern history.
>
> (Mlambo 2013:367)

These severe political and economic conditions had an impact on public funding for the effective delivery of primary health care in Zimbabwe. With the collapse of the economy and public finance, ordinary citizens were left to fend for themselves against mounting difficulties in order to meet their basic needs (UNICEF 2011). Community participation played an integral role in response to the cholera outbreak in 2008. Organised groups in communities mobilised local communities, conducted health education, and taught health and hygiene practices in support of formal health workers (CWGH 2008).

National health policy in Zimbabwe is implemented through community level (ward and village) that is the primary level, as well as through district, provincial and national level institutions of the Ministry of Health and of the Ministry of Local Government. At the primary care level, community health workers include village health workers, health literacy facilitators and home based carers, and health centre committees (HCCs). Community participation in Zimbabwe has been confined overall to health promotion activities in line with preventative approaches to health management (Loewenson *et al.* 2009). At the base of the health service has been the village health worker (VHW), through whom demo-cratisation of the health system was to be attained. The role of the community was to nominate the VHW who then serves on various health and development committees created to facilitate community participation in the health systems at local level. For Loewenson (2000:17) "these structures played a positive role in more 'self-reliant' health interventions, but did not make services planned and financed at central level more responsive to user demands or inputs". Local gov-ernment mechanisms for participation were weakened by centralised authority and limited capacity. Civil society groups were also excluded (Sanders 1992, TARSC and CWGH 2009). In health, participation was focused on state-driven social mobilisation and compliance with centrally defined programmes, leaving social groups and health officials dissatisfied with the level and forms of com-munity participation (Mutizwa-Mangiza 1997, Loewenson *et al.* 2004).

The unsatisfactory nature in which participation has been taking place in the health sector in Zimbabwe has since 1999 been tracked by a network of civic actors known as Community Working Group on Health. The network has captured the decline of the health system and the continued lack of community presence in health policy in the political and economic landscape that has char-acterised Zimbabwe in the last decade. According to the Ministry of Health (2009), the work of the network has confirmed a view expressed during meetings by civic representatives and health officials that there is a persistent gap in struc-tured communication with communities that acts as an impediment for health promotion (CWGH 1998a, MoHCW 2009). The network together with the Min-istry of Health embarked on a process of restructuring the way communities participate and contribute to national health policy through the Health Centre Committees (HCC). HCCs are a mechanism through which communities can participate at primary care level to support a people-centred health system (CWGH 2015).

The critical analysis of these joint service community mechanisms especially at the village and ward level was the focus for this study. How HCCs occupy legislated spaces for participation is critical to understanding the way participa-tion happens at the primary level in the health system. For the PHC approach, community participation is hailed to be the panacea of health related develop-mental programmes. The intention is to move from centrally defined health inter-ventions to having a health system that is structured to detect and subsequently respond adequately to what the people need the most at that time. There has been extensive research conducted on Zimbabwe's implementation of primary health care in light of health status, accessibility and health services uptake. A few studies have been undertaken to demonstrate that the participation of com-munities in the health system is an important factor in improving the effective-ness of the health system in Zimbabwe.

Mechanisms for community participation in the health system: legislation and regulations governing the health sector in Zimbabwe

The Public Health Act of 1924 (last amended in 1970) is the principal law regulating public health in Zimbabwe. The Ministry of Health and Child Care administer it on behalf of the government. There a number of subsidiary pieces of legislation that frame public health to support the main health act. These include the Health Services Act (Chapter 15:16), Medical Services Act (Chapter 15:13) and the National AIDS Council of Zimbabwe Act (Chapter 15:14).

The legislative framework for health in Zimbabwe provides for community health councils at district level and hospital advisory boards at hospital level and these include community representatives in advising on client care and health management issues. These structures for community participation were weak and had no policy or resource allocation authority. From the viewpoint of Loewenson,

> these structures played a positive role but did not make services planned and financed at central level more responsive to user demands or inputs, particularly given weak district discretion on areas of spending or retention of revenue and lack of meaningful authority in planning.
>
> (Loewenson 2000:17)

It is because of this that these structures disappeared during the troubled economic times the country went through from the mid-1990s. This offered up the opportunity and indeed the necessity for the public to take up spaces in the health system as services were failing against a growing disease backdrop. In the midst of the turmoil, civil society stepped in to rescue the existence of these platforms in the health system.

One such civic actor, as noted, is the Community Working Group on Health (CWGH) formed in 1997. Founder organisations include the Association of Mine Workers in Zimbabwe (AMWZ), Women and Aids Support Network (WASN), Women's Action Group (WAG), Training and Research Support Centre (TARSC), Zimbabwe Farmers Union (ZFU), and the Zimbabwe Congress of Trade Unions (ZCTU) (CWGH 1998b:3). It is a network of civic groups that recognised the need to give and add voice to the health interests of rural peasants, formal and informal sector workers and unemployed people. The group came together to share experiences and information on health, to analyse the health situation and to put forward strategies based on the identified problems (CWGH 1997, Loewenson and Chikumbirike 2000). It identified the existence of public discontent with the manner in which community participation was being expressed in Zimbabwe and the need to strengthen the mechanisms for participation, transparency, consultation and accountability within the health sector from local to national level. The CWGH network thus works to promote and strengthen informed participation in local health planning. The experience of the network in community mobilisation has spanned nearly the last two decades in Zimbabwe. In addition, it has sought to revitalise the community health structures known as Health Centre Committees.

Post-2008, the National Health Strategy (2009–2015) makes a commitment to ensure that communities are empowered to participate actively in the management of their local health services in line with the PHC approach (EQUINET 2015). The predecessor to this current strategy (from 2009 to 2013) emphasised the establishment of and, in some areas, the revitalisation of Health Centre Committees (HCC) as the vehicle through which communities participate in health policy. HCCs were originally proposed by the MoHCW in the 1980s to assist communities in identifying their priority health problems, plan how to raise their own resources, organise and manage community contributions, and tap available resources for community development as health advisory committees. This 'new' community health structure "is a joint community-health service structure linked to the clinic and covering the catchment area of a clinic usually a ward or more" (CWGH 2015). However, it is important to highlight that law does not regulate these HCCs although the Ministry of Health has consistently included the structure in its strategy. This may be attributed to the fact that the Public Health Act has not been reviewed since its last amendment in 1970. This raises a serious problem, as health is an ever-changing concept, which does not remain stagnant over time. It is also critical to note that there is discord between the principal piece of health legislation and current health policy in terms of recognising and acknowledging the existence of a community structure as part of the health system.

HCCs represent a mechanism through which communities at the primary level interact with national health strategy. In terms of composition, the HCCs involve the Ward Councillor, the Nurse in Charge at a clinic, the Environmental Health Technician (EHT), village health workers, health literacy facilitators, home based caregivers, and local civil society or community based organisations representing women, youth, the disabled, children and people living and/or affected by HIV and AIDS. They also include the headmaster or schoolteacher responsible for health, a church leader, a traditional leader, and traditional and faith healers and other health providers. Besides the health workers, the traditional leader and local elected government representative (ward councillor), the local community in the ward is responsible for electing the rest of the HCC members as they are accountable to them (TARSC, CWGH & MOHCW 2011). The Ward Councillor, traditional leader and none of the health workers are allowed to be Chairperson of the committee, and the Chairperson in fact has to be a representative from the community. Formal health workers at the primary care level who are eligible for co-option into the HCC include the nurse, nurse aid, Environmental Health Technician (EHT), general hand and nurse in charge, The Primary Care Nurse (PCN) or Nurse in Charge (NIC) at the clinic is always a member of the HCC and provides secretariat services in the committee. Thus, the HCC has a direct link with the nurse in charge.

In 2011, the Ministry of Health together with the Community Working Group on Health developed guidelines to set out the function and role of the HCC in the community in relation to both the health system as well as the local government framework. Although these guidelines are not regulated as law in Zimbabwe, the Ministry of Health adopted them to the extent that the HCC structure was added to the health system framework formally in 2011 (National Health Strategy 2009–2013). The roles and responsibilities of the HCC, according to the guidelines include:

- Bring community priorities into health plans.
- Ensure that health resources, budgets and fees for service are used in a transparent way.
- Organize community actions for health.
- Promote dialogue with health services on the quality of care issues.
- Make claims on district level funds like the Health Services Fund.
- Advocate for essential resources for their services from the Rural District Council and MOHCW.
- Organise community inputs to health services Monitor quality of care and take up community grievances.

(TARSC, CWGH & MOHCW 2011:23)

In summary, Health Centre Committees are structures through which the health system is meant to engage with patients to elicit information on how best to address the most pressing health needs at the local level. Ideally, in line with the PHC approach, this information flow between the patient and service provider strengthens vertical accountability within the health system thus making it 'people-centred'. The lack of a clear statutory instrument in this instance has not hampered community input into the health system. This is so because there are different laws and policies within the Zimbabwean legal framework, which acknowledge the work and contributions of organised community groups to the health system such as Health Services Act (2005), Public Health Act and National Health Policy 2009–2015.

Methodology

Goromonzi District is one of nine districts in Mashonaland East Province, Zimbabwe. Goromonzi covers an area totalling 2,459 square kilometres or 254,072 hectares. It is a district located 32 kilometres southeast of the country's capital of Harare. A census conducted in 2012 pegs Goromonzi population at 224,987 persons of whom 113,661 (50.5%) are female (CSO 2012). Overall, 96.16% of the population reside in rural areas with the remainder (3.84%) residing in urban areas.

The research took seven months including planning, implementation, and data collection and analysis (from May 2015 to November 2015). Four qualitative research techniques were employed which are focus group discussions with Mwanza HCC, and the District Health Executive; semi-structured in-depth interviews with community members; in-depth interviews with key informants; and simple observation of community health literacy meetings. Sampling of community respondents involved snowball methods. The focus was on community members (male and female of legal consenting age in Zimbabwe, which is 18) who accessed health services on research days as well as attended health literacy meetings at specified times during the fieldwork. Thus, respondents were selected from the available population at the clinic at the given time. Having participated in an interview, a number of respondents recommended others. Semi-structured in-depth interviews were conducted with non-randomly selected community members: 33 community members were interviewed. The questions for this group of respondents was open ended and focused on the existence of the HCC, structures for participation at the village and ward levels and what the community's role was in health in general.

While the focus of the study was community members, it was crucial to gather evidence from the district health executive, rural district council social services officer and CWGH secretariat as well as the health workers at Mwanza rural health centre. For this group of respondents, a combination of semi-structured interviews and key informant interviews were conducted. Questions were more technical for this group and were structured on the history of health policy and strategy in Zimbabwe and the value community participation adds to the health sector. Two focus group discussions were also held, one with Mwanza HCC and the other with the District Health Executive team in Goromonzi. The discussions were important because they provided direct evidence about the similarities and differences in the participants' opinions, experiences and attitudes towards community participation in health.

Direct observation was extensively used throughout the field study. The greatest advantage that this provided was the opportunity to reflect and verify information gathered from other methods used in the study. This included a chance to observe health workers interacting with community members during health literacy campaigns. In addition to the above research techniques, there was an extensive use of primary documentation about health in Zimbabwe from the Ministry of Health and other ministries in the Government of Zimbabwe, such as the Ministry of Finance and the Ministry of Local Government Rural and Urban Development. International and local civic actors have also conducted research on the health sector and health indicators in Zimbabwe, and I consulted their works as well. These include the World Health Organisation (WHO), United Nations Children Education Fund (UNICEF), United Nations Development Programme (UNDP), Community Working Group on Health (CWGH), Women's Action Group (WAG) and Training and Research Support Centre (TARSC).

To analyse information gathered from the various methods employed, standard thematic identification, coding and analysis was used. This mode of analysis provided a more inductive form of interpretation and analysis that allowed space for the evidence (primarily the voices of community members in and outside the HCC) to express their subjective experiences of participation in health. This facilitated room for themes to emerge from these shared experiences rather than being predetermined by the researcher (Denzin and Lincoln 2009, Silverman 2013).

Findings and discussion

A number of pieces of legislation in Zimbabwe on health do highlight channels through which community voice is to be heard in the various stages in national health policy formation and implementation. However, there is no set regulation within the current health legislation that allows for the existence of HCCs in their current form. One key informant from the district health executive felt that, if there was no legal provision that set out and governed HCC operations, it places HCCs in a difficult position. The legislation should be put in place, as this will be the means by which HCCs would be empowered to operate and through which they could receive an allocation from the national budget for their activities and not rely on donor funds and community contributions. What exist are mere guidelines prepared by the Community Working Group on Health, and the Ministry of Health subsequently adopted these in 2011. The adoption of these guidelines by the government through the Ministry was brought on by the weak nature of the health system due to the economic collapse in Zimbabwe. It was more of a survival decision and not so much a 'we have thought this through and this is the clearest and best way forward'. The negative implications of this were highlighted by the HCC itself in a focus group discussion.

Although the health system has undergone various 'facelifts' in three and half decades of independence, there are still remnants of the past present within its operations. The form in which community participation takes place may have shifted from the individual to include that of the group but the following remain:

- A top down approach is still being employed in health policy formulation, as the HCC is not completely involved in health planning. Its role has been confined to identifying and consolidating the most pressing needs of the community of which most have not been addressed. The bottom is still implementing what the top decides.
- There has been a shift in the control over resources especially through a recent (2013) donor led Results Based Financing project. Performance rewards in financial form are handed to clinics through the HCC as custodian of the funds for clinic maintenance and upgrades. The only concern that arises in this scenario is when donor assistance to the health sector has ended. There are no signs especially from what was gathered in interviews with the District Health Executive (DHE) in Goromonzi that point to the government of Zimbabwe being able to sustain this approach as health allocation through the national *fiscus* is decreasing. This model of health financing, though a huge relief to the strained health sector, is not sustainable in the end.
- The lack of clarity between the role of the HCC and Local Government village and ward development committees when it comes to health has bred uncertainty with community members. The status of the HCC once legalised may provide some clarity and address any 'ownership' concerns. These findings also point to weak links between HCCs with local government on local health.

In reviewing the changes that the health system has had to undergo in the last three and a half decades, it is important to note that the health policy has shifted away from a focus mainly on the participation of individuals and viewing health and health interventions from a microscopic perspective through its community health worker programme. The shift in the last five to ten years has been to include the group dimension for harnessing community input in the functioning of the health system through the revitalisation and establishment of HCCs. It is necessary to take note of the levels at which people are participating in terms of the HCC, but it is also crucial to examine the forms in terms of involvement in different activities. Rifkin (1986:12) came up with five forms of participation following an analysis of 100 case studies on community participation in health programmes (Oakley & WHO 1989:10, Rifkin 1986:12). Rifkin (1986:12) states that people can be involved in participation in the following ways:

- Receiving benefits, services and information from experts.
- Participation in programme activities, for example distribution of contraceptives or contributing money to the health programmes.
- Participation in implementing health programmes such as choosing clinic sites or organising child welfare and nutrition clinics.
- Participating in monitoring and evaluation of programmes.
- Participating in decision-making and planning.

When using the Rifkin model to assess the forms in which the Mwanza community operates through the HCC, the findings point to the community fully operating in terms of the first four forms in the model. With respect to the first form, Mwanza HCC receives health literacy training from civic groups within and outside of Goromonzi that it then uses to inform its community meetings and health promotion activities. Health promotion, health education and community mobilisation done by the HCC to complement that of the community health workers in the ward satisfies forms two and three in the above model. The HCC satisfies form four in following up health interventions initiated by council and the Ministry of Health in its ward.

The challenge is in relation to the fifth form, where the HCC itself highlighted a lack of transparency and accountability in planning and budgeting by the DHE coupled with a lack of capacity in terms of knowledge to engage with the system at that level. Information is a missing link in the relationship between the HCC, the government and the wider community. This affects monitoring health service. The health staff from Mwanza clinic noted that while HCC members made input through the renovations and infrastructure maintenance needed to improve the local health centre, the health facility itself was not involved in coming up with a budget. This is the responsibility of the health authorities at the district level, who sometimes did not take account of the priorities set at clinic level. This form of engagement is the core to the community being involved in the framing of future health policy. Even though the HCC facilitates platforms for the community to identify its most pressing health issues, the lack of feedback makes it difficult to assess whether the input has been taken on board or disregarded. The DHE should be in a position to explain and justify decisions taken in coming up with the district plan and budget. It is the role of the government to justify why the chosen course of action is the best option given the array of health issues and the limited nature of resources. Supplying this kind of information would go a long way in addressing some of the challenges raised by the HCC. However, the concept of community participation is a complex one especially when it comes to planning and budgeting. Its complexity lies not only in its many definitions but also in the fact that it has to be acceptable to the community, the service providers and the government.

The Mwanza HCC case study highlights the dynamic nature of the concept of community participation in that in some instances there were nuances where I felt inclined to believe that there seemed to be government complacency and resignation to leave it all to the community. Due to the economic situation in Zimbabwe, communities have had to step in where the government has failed. There seems to be evidence to support the fact that government is 'passing the buck' in terms of service delivery. Communities still find themselves bearing indirect out-of-pocket costs to contribute to health other than through medicines and user fees. These costs are what the HCC collects to pay for security, buy cleaning substances for the clinic and pay for the transportation of patient samples for lab testing. However, it is the role of the government to provide adequate up to standard health services progressively to the maximum of available resources according to Zimbabwe's supreme legislation (Government of Zimbabwe 2013:34).

From observations of community sensitisation meetings in Mwanza ward, there is a high level of health knowledge amongst the community members present at the meetings. For individuals to participate in the HCC and health activities in their communities, there has to be some form of health education that nurtures this behaviour over time. When people are informed, they can then participate and cooperate in health programmes. It is further evident in the case of Mwanza that the communities share the burden of ensuring health care by providing material, financial and human resources, which in many ways fosters a sense of ownership and leads to a sense of control over their self-initiated projects. Without information on how the systems functions, it is hard to have informed active participation, as each stakeholder's role will not be clear. This lack of clarity may negatively influence health practices in the ward if not addressed.

The HCC with a majority of the community members thus identified the major gaps as resources, communications and skills with some calling for training and improved communication. In general, there seemed to be no concerns raised on the representation of vulnerable groups in the committee. Groups represented include those living with HIV and AIDS, orphans, widows and those living with disability (CWGH 2010). There thus appeared to be no gaps in Mwanza HCC's representation of extremely vulnerable groups except for those more distant from the health centre. A concern was however highlighted by the district health executive through the district administrator that the HCC should be wary about distancing itself from the community. He warned that without regular communication, the HCC would lose touch with the social groups that it represents in the HCC and become detached from the community. The HCC in turn indicated that, "members of the district health executive should be included in HCC trainings to raise their awareness on HCC roles and operations so that the relationship is strengthened within the health system itself". The above comment was raised because the HCC generally felt it was held back by lack of knowledge on the managerial roles of key health personnel like the District Nursing Officer and District Medical Officer and lack of direct contact with health authorities besides the Nurse in Charge. The HCC identified a need for direct meetings with the district health authorities.

In terms of identifying factors that enhance community participation with reference to the current character and form that exist in Mwanza ward in Goromonzi, it should be highlighted that political interests have to be objectively balanced although health itself is political in nature. Neutrality has to be maintained as political dynamics may have a destabilising effect on participation. For instance, if members of the HCC are lead political figures in the district, this may be a deterrent to community members attending and participating in health discussions. The government has to be committed to an extent that there is acknowledgement and recognition of HCC functions such that an environment in which organised community groups can realise full potential and flourish in an integrated health system. The government can demonstrate this commitment through the enactment of adequate legislation for HCCs. The local level leadership (such as the traditional and elected leadership) has to buy into the concept of the HCC in a community by being members of the HCC and actively participating in committee roles and activities. For example, the councillor is a member of the HCC as the councillor represents local government on the HCC structure. The role of the councillor is to be a communication conduit between the HCC (and the health system) and the Rural District Council (RDC) in local government. If the councillor is not committed, there can be a duplication of government efforts in the ward due to a lack of synergy in communication channels. For example, local government through district development funds may allocate funds for health facility maintenance and the DHE may plan to do the same in the district health budget. The HCC is the platform through which such irregularities may be avoided or joint interventions identified for effective use of public resources.

Conclusion and policy insights

Within the overall context of reinvestment in primary health care in light of the experiences in the last three decades, the HCC is still to a large extent the most viable way in which the Zimbabwean health sector can fully realise the promise of the primary health care approach. The HCC provides a mechanism for organising community, health literacy, health promotion and social networking on health. The benefits of this are that the community builds itself through the continued interaction and discussion on health issues. There is need for this discussion to be deepened to include aspects of health as a system and how it functions in responding to the needs of those it serves. In general, the HCC in Mwanza would have to improve on the following to better perform its function:

- Clear delineation between all platforms that exist in the community having clarity and a common understanding of each of their roles and function in the ward. Serious consideration must be given to the education of the community on issues such as the decentralisation process and awareness of the structures and programmes in order for people to appreciate and participate meaningfully in health issues.
- Obtain a greater understanding of health planning and budget processes as well as the functioning of the health system. The objective would be to share this information with the community.
- Improve feedback with the wider community to maintain credibility and momentum in the ward and the district to a larger extent.

In order to strengthen the way in which the health system may further integrate community participation and harness it to strengthen the system itself, there needs to be recognition of the differentials in power and how this influences participation. This is most pertinent as primary health care is targeted at the most vulnerable in a society. There is also need for a concerted effort to support and facilitate the sharing of community experiences and use this as hard evidence collated with public health information to identify and plan interventions accordingly with those affected. Lastly, integration of bottom up planning involving community priorities within health planning, with an influence on the allocation and use of local resources and resources from the state and other sources, should be transparent, and done in a manner that seeks to build an integrated health development plan that is multi-sectoral in nature.

References

Central Statistical Office. 2012. *National Census*. Harare: Central Statistics Office.

Community Working Group on Health. 1997. *Health in Zimbabwe: report of a meeting of community based organisations Zimbabwe, January 1998*, supported by OXFAM and TARSC.

Community Working Group on Health. 1998a. *Health in Zimbabwe: Views of Community Based Organisations, Zimbabwe*, supported by Oxfam and TARSC.

Community Working Group on Health. 1998b. *Health Financing in Zimbabwe*. Harare: Penguin Printers.

Community Working Group on Health. 2008. *Annual Report*. Harare: CWGH.

Community Working Group on Health. 2010. *Report of Community Meeting: Chikwaka HCC Meeting May 2010*. CWGH Monograph 5/21.

Community Working Group on Health. 2013. *Annual Report*. Harare: CWGH.

Community Working Group on Health. 2014. *Annual Report*. Harare: CWGH.

Community Working Group on Health. 2015. *Strengthening Health Systems*. Harare: CWGH.

Community Working Group on Health with TARSC and Medico. 2014. *Health Centre Committees as a Vehicle for Social Participation in Health Systems in East and Southern Africa; Policy Brief 37*. Harare: EQUINET.

Community Working Group on Health, TARSC 2015. *Strengthening the Capacities of Health Centre Committees as Health Advocates in Zimbabwe*, EQUINET Case study brief. Harare: EQUINET.

Denzin, N.K. and Lincoln, Y.S. 2009. *Qualitative Research*. London: SAGE Publications.

EQUINET. 2015. *Equity Watch: Assessing Progress Towards Equity in Health: Zimbabwe*. Harare: TARSC, MoHCC, Equinet.

Frankel, S. and Dogget, M.A. 1992. *The Community Health Worker: Effective Programmes for Developing Countries*. Oxford: Oxford University Press.

Government of Zimbabwe. 2013. *Constitution of Zimbabwe*. Harare: Government of Zimbabwe.

Loewenson, R. 1988. Labour Insecurity and Health: an Epidemiological Study in Zimbabwe. *Social Science & Medicine*, 27 (7): 733–741.

Loewenson, R. 2000. Public Participation in Health Systems: Report of a Regional Meeting. *Training and Research Support Centre Southern African Network on Equity in Health* with support from IDRC (Canada) and in collaboration with WHO (AFRO) HSSD Pangolin Lodge, Harare.

Loewenson, R. and Chikumbirike, T. 2000. *Report of the Survey of Health Centre Committee Members Views in Bindura RDC*. TARSC Monograph.

Loewenson, R., Rusike, I. and Zulu, M. 2004. *Assessing the Impact of Health Centre Committees on Health System Performance and Health Resource Allocation*. Equinet Discussion Paper 18, EQUINET, TARSC: Harare.

Loewenson, R., Chikumbirike, T. and Rusike, I. 2009. *Health Where it Matters Most: An Assessment of Primary Health Care in Zimbabwe March 2009*, Report of a Community Based Assessment, Training and Research Support Centre and Community Working Group on Health.

Mlambo, A.S. 2013. From Education and Health for All by 2000 to the Collapse of the Social Services Sector in Zimbabwe, 1980–2008. *Journal of Developing Societies*, 29 (4): 355–378.

Ministry of Health and Child Welfare, 1997. *National Health Strategy for Zimbabwe 1997–2007: Working for Quality and Equity in Health*. Harare: MoHCW.

Ministry of Health and Child Welfare, 2009. *Zimbabwe National Health Strategy, 2009–2013: Equity and Quality in Health-A People's Right*. Harare: MoHCW.

Mutizwa-Mangiza, N.D. 1997. *The Opinions of Health and Water Service Users in Zimbabwe*. Development Administration Group, School of Public Policy, University of Birmingham.

Oakley, P. 1989. *Community Involvement in Health Development: An Examination of the Critical Issues*. World Health Organisation.

Rifkin, S.B. 1986. Lessons from Community Participation in Health Programmes. *Health Policy and Planning*, 1 (3): 240–249.

Sanders, D. 1992. The State of Democratization in Primary Health Care: Community Participation and the Village Health Worker Programme in Zimbabwe. In *The community health worker: effective programs for developing countries* (pp. 178–219). Oxford: Oxford University Press.

Silverman, D. 2013. *Doing Qualitative Research: A Practical Handbook*. 4th ed. London: SAGE Publications Limited.

TARSC; CWGH; MoHCW, 2011. *Supporting the Role of Health Centre Committees. A Training Manual*. Harare: TARSC, CWGH, MoHCW.

UNICEF, 2011. *A Situational Analysis on the Status of Women and Children's Rights in Zimbabwe, 2005–2010: A Call for Reducing Disparities and Improving Equity*. Harare: UNICEF.

Wayland, C. and Crowder, J. 2002. Disparate Views of Community in Primary Health Care: Understanding How Perceptions Influence Success. *Medical Anthropology Quarterly*, 16 (2): 230–247.

Zimbabwe National Statistics Agency and Measures DHS 2011. *Zimbabwe Demographic and Health Survey 2010–11 Preliminary Report. June 2011*, Harare, Zimbabwe National Statistics Agency, and Calverton, Maryland, Measures DHS.

9 Climate variability in local scales

Narratives and ambivalences from Mutoko District

Sandra Bhatasara

Introduction

There is a significant body of literature on climate change in Zimbabwe indicating the trends and nature of changes, and its impacts using systematic observations, quantitative techniques, global and downscaled models, and statistical analyses. Scholarly literature focusing specifically on how people in marginal ecosystems understand, read and interpret the environment is comparatively limited. This chapter examines such narratives in Mutoko District in Mashonaland East Province, based on original fieldwork. The concern is to comprehend how farmers problematise their circumstances – the specific circumstances being climatic changes. This is imperative because there is a lucid discrepancy between the conclusions of macro assessments and the experiences of local societies living with environmental change. At the same time, although there is an argument that the idea of climate change has been somewhat 'universalised', people in local contexts possess complex ways of reading the climate and their concerns are much more variegated. Therefore, there is urgent need for empirical research that moves away from the essentialist discussions and categories developed *a priori* in the macro assessments of climate change, to consider the complex ways in which people in local contexts experience climatic shifts. In doing so, the chapter not only exposes the apparent and persistent prejudices in climate change knowledge production but more importantly contributes data derived empirically to existing knowledge about the nature and meanings of climatic changes occurring in rural spaces in the country.

Methodological reflections

This chapter is derived from broader empirical research on understanding climate variability and livelihood adaptation conducted in Mutoko district. Mutoko is a semi-arid district located in the eastern part of Zimbabwe. A large part of Mutoko falls within natural (or agro-ecological) region IV that receives only 450–600 mm of rainfall per year and is susceptible to regular seasonal droughts (Bhatasara 2015a). Precipitation occurs principally between November and March, followed by a seven-month dry season. Temperatures are fairly high with daily summer averages ranging from 27°C to 32°C while winter temperatures are moderate (14°C minimum). Significant yearly divergences in rainfall or rainfall variability are materialising such as during the 1982–1984 period. Mutoko was severely hit by drought during this period, whilst in 1985 rainfall surpassed the usual yearly average (the total average for 1985 was 900 mm) (Bhatasara 2015a).

Another serious drought affected Mutoko in 1991/1992 season. In fact, rainfall in the district is becoming more erratic and uncertain, as it is marked by the late onset and early cessation of the rainfall season. For example, in the 2012/2013 season, more than 600 mm of rainfall were received in January only, yet the entire season received just slightly more than 850 mm. On 18 January 2013, Mutoko experienced a flash flood with 94 mm of rainfall, surpassing the 74 mm record set in 1963 (Bhatasara 2015a).

The broader study rested on a particular historical timeline of 1992 to 2014. Arguably, it is critical to take temporal dynamics into account given that livelihoods decisions are taken within specific historical, socio-spatial and agroecological conditions. At a more empirical level, the study concentrated on a specific case study where life histories, a small survey, key informant interviews, transect walks, observations and informal group conversations were conducted. The district (Mutoko) was taken as the main case study, ward 3 (Charewa A) as the unit and households in the ward as the embedded sub-units positioned within a multifaceted context including socio-economic, political and ecological processes. The life history interview, which privileges the narration of personal biographies, was the primary data collection method in this study. Such interviews are used to identify key moments in an individual's life (shocks, pivotal moments and transition points) and responses (agency and coping strategies).

Grand narratives on climate change in Zimbabwe

Broadly speaking, climate change in Zimbabwe is projected on a national scale and as a national and quantifiable phenomenon, at least in mainstream academic research and policy documents (Bhatasara 2015b). Others have also noted that it seems there has been trivial focus on the positions and perceptions of smallholder farmers with regard to climate change and variability and the consequences of these for particular agricultural activities (Mutekwa 2009). Based on the existing studies and climate projections employing diverse quantitative models, Zimbabwe is experiencing climate change and increasing climate variability. Indeed, historic and future climate change scenarios have been examined using observed climate data and seven global climate models. Even though the climate in Zimbabwe is regionally distinguishable, studies (see Brown *et al.* 2012) indicate by and large it is getting warmer with numerous erratic rainfall patterns. A coherent conclusion is that the frequency of the country's annual rainfall variations has expanded since the early 1980s, ensuing in iterated droughts and floods. On a similar note, it has been established that annual rainfall will wane by 5 to 18% of the 1961 to 1990 average by the 2080s (Unganai 1996).

Related to the above, the Ministry of Environment and Natural Resources Management Climate Change Office (2008) noted that the decade 1986–1995 has been discovered as 15% drier than average. In a related matter, there have been periods that have been noted to be considerably wetter than average as a result of tropical cyclones. Evidence of increased frequency of floods particularly in the low-lying areas of the Zambezi and Limpopo basins has also been presented. Mutasa (2008) concurs that intense weather events, namely tropical cyclones and drought, have magnified in frequency and intensity. Others agree that Zimbabwe has lately been experiencing regular droughts interchanged with points of very high rainfall; in some cases, floods and mid-season extended dry spells are being experienced in the same season in the same location (see Mutekwa 2009). Simultaneously, the country has an average seven-month dry period yearly but has in recent years experienced frequent droughts (Unganai 2009).

Analyses of temperature changes in Zimbabwe tend to be congruent with the regional and global warming trends. For instance, three models employed to examine climate data anticipate a temperature rise of 2–4°C and an average rainfall decrease of 10–21% by 2100 (Mano and Nhemachena 2006). What is distinctly coming out from studies is that minimum temperatures are gradually increasing as the number of cold days is decreasing. Likewise, Brown *et al.* (2012) reported that daily minimum temperatures have increased by approximately 2.6°C over the last century while daily maximum temperatures have risen by 2°C during the same period. In a similar vein, studies have also envisioned that Zimbabwe will warm more quickly in future than the global average due to its continental interior. Already, annual mean temperatures have increased since 1900, and the 1990s were on record as the warmest and driest decade of the century (Brown *et al.* 2012).

Studies at a sub-national scale report consistent trends. In Masvingo province, analyses of meteorological climate records established that there was an increase in variability of seasonal total rainfall from 1950 to 2007 (Chikodzi *et al.* 2012). Similarly, long term climate scenarios for all seven districts in the same province demonstrate waning rainfall amounts. Downscaled future climate change projections for one district in the above-mentioned province (Chiredzi) also exposed that temperatures have warmed by up to 0.6°C between 1966 and 2005. Specifically, these projections show a rise in surface annual temperatures of between 1.5 and 3.5°C by between 2046 and 2065 across the district (Brown *et al.* 2012). Almost similar approaches reveal consistent trends in other regions of the country. Temperature analysis results from meteorological stations in Beitbridge, Bulawayo and Harare suggest an increase in daily minimum temperatures of around 2.6°C, matched with a rise in daily maximum temperatures of about 2°C, in the last century, and the number of cold days is diminishing at a rate of nearly 15 days per 100 years (Chagutah 2010). In Gokwe, data indicate more dry years with rainfall below the long-term mean of 819 mm and wet years with rainfall above the same long-term average (Gwimbi 2009). For north-eastern Zimbabwe (which includes Chipinge), studies show that predictions from downscaled model simulations indicate that the 2046 to 2065 period will be warmer by between 1 and 2°C and, in the case of rainfall, climate change will produce times of both excess and deficit (see Masanganise 2010).

What is discernible from the above studies is that nearly all of them are founded on systematic disaggregated observation and various quantitative models. They fundamentally dwell on the macro-scale using statistical analysis. While this is illuminating in itself, it is not without challenges. As noted by some scholars, 'such indexes cannot admit the ways in which climate is imagined through cumulative sensory experiences, mental assimilation, social learning and cultural interpretations' (Hulme *et al.* 2009:197). At the same time, Demeritt (2001) argues that even the most advanced climate model is a form of abstract thinking that reduces reality to the terms of its own analytical abstractions. Evidently, the above studies largely disregard how climate and climate change are read and construed by local people in the context of their everyday personal, cultural and social lives.

Yet each scale of climate and climate processes (global, regional and micro) is significant for understanding the biophysical and social contexts that influence how people comprehend changes in climate variability (Bhatasara 2015b). Therefore, local peoples' narratives on change are significant because people dynamically structure and orient multiple possibilities for actions in view of perceived changes in climate and climate variability. From the above discussion, model based studies lack the 'view from below', i.e. the perspective of individuals, households and local societies who are directly experiencing climate change. This view from below is what Foucault (1980) termed 'subjugated knowledge'. This subjugation has to do with the self-acclaimed superiority of the modernist perspective (that includes Western meteorology, sophisticated climate models and highly specialised tools of observation) and the imposition and acceptance of this point of view to the disadvantage of alternative perspectives (Foucault 1980). Therefore, the chapter now discusses the more localised narratives of smallholder farmers in Mutoko district.

Local narratives on climate variability in Charewa

This section presents the climatic changes occurring in Charewa through elaborating on farmers' concerns. To borrow from sociologist Margaret Archer (2003) everyone has concerns in the natural, practical and social order of reality. However, although climate variability is a significant factor constraining farming systems in arid and semi-arid areas of Zimbabwe, one cannot assume that farmers are equally concerned about rainfall and temperature. Invariably, from the survey in the Mutoko study, the majority of farmers (58%) selected rainfall patterns as the current most important issue for them, 29% said it was temperature, 9% indicated that rainfall and temperature were equally important and 4% said none of the two.

Farmers' concerns on rainfall

Rainfall is regarded as the most significant climate parameter affecting human activities. As such, one fundamental factor that cannot be ignored is the rainfall variability both within and between seasons and the underlying uncertainty that it imposes on production (Cooper *et al.* 2008). It is therefore not surprising that 60% of respondents had a high level of concern, 36% moderate, 2% low and 2% were indifferent over the trends in rainfall in the field survey in Charewa. When asked on what best described their feelings regarding general patterns of rainfall since 1992, most farmers (73%) said they were dissatisfied. At the same time, in contrast to other seasons, farmers were generally satisfied with rainfall amounts in the 2012/2013 and 2013/2014 seasons. Nonetheless, even if farmers were satisfied with the amount of rainfall, this is not necessarily sufficient to fully capture the dynamics and characteristics of climate variability. Therefore, within the general phenomena of rainfall variability, rainfall onset, reliability, distribution, quality and cessation as well as extreme rainfall occurrences were primary concerns that intruded into the livelihoods of farmers.

That being the case, one common thread throughout the data was that rainfall patterns have become more unpredictable and unreliable. What differed were the narrative descriptions of these changes. Even so, farmers were overwhelmingly worried about the unpredictability and unreliability because of the complex intricacies between their livelihoods and how the rainfall season behaves. In general, farmers want certainty; therefore, it was important for rainfall patterns to be predictable. Farmers observed that rainfall seasons were distinct but, over the past years, inter-annual rainfall variability has become more unpredictable. Farmers also pointed out that it is becoming more and more difficult to predict rainy season onset, cessation and amounts. In addition, there are certain types of rainfall that farmers use to determine season onset that have become progressively more erratic to the extent that some farmers believe these do not exist anymore. Consequently, farmers cannot predict the onset of rains for planting when these rains do not come.

At the same time, nuances on rainfall reliability revealed that what farmers consider as reliable rainfall is the one that takes their crops to maturity and falls at expected times. Farmers stated that their farming systems are based on *mvura inotembeka* (rainfall that can be trusted). The following statement extracted from the data bears concern that rainfall is growing more unreliable in Charewa: "... During my young years, before I got married in 1997, rain used to come in October but now it comes in November or December. These rains cannot be relied on, they cannot be trusted." Another female respondent expressed her concern as follows:

> ... The problem we have these days is that the rains are not giving us the actual dates we used to know. *Tanga tine madate omvura* [we used to have dates for rainfall]. I would know that rains would come this season and by October we would have planted our seeds already in these fields. We would

know that around 15 October, *mvura inonga yandorova pasi* [it would have rained]. I would know that I would get food. These days I do not have dates. *Mvura yakujambira madate* [rainfall is skipping dates]. It is postponing to November but it used to come in October, which is a difference. I cannot do my farming well.

A point which was reiterated by some farmers was that they had always expected some post-harvest rainfall, usually around June, which they call *mvura yechando* (winter rain), but not heavy rains during harvesting time or at a time when they had harvested but had not yet put crops in *mumatura* (granaries). I had also the chance to witness downpours during my time in the field on 18, 19 and 20 April 2014. From the interactions I had with respondents after the downpours, many farmers were surprised and worried. The rains were coming at a wrong time (time of harvesting) and that is why they were worried. Farmers were surprised because rainfall had ceased early March and most of the crops had wilted, therefore they did not think it would rain again that season. In short, it was too late for wilted crops to recover and it was also inconveniencing their harvesting, particularly of groundnuts. They feared that ripe bambara nuts were going to start germinating. Having said the above, I now elucidate on some of the specific experiences farmers have encountered regarding rainfall onset, season cessation, rainfall distribution, extreme rainfall events, rainfall adequacy and quality.

Pertaining to rainfall onset, it was widely stated that the usual rainfall season should start around 15 October yearly therefore what farmers are experiencing suggests that there is a significant shift in the onset of the rainy season. Whereas farmers' responses were heterogeneous to the extent that one could not establish the exact years when farmers started noticing delayed rainy season onset from their descriptions, what is discernible is that they indicated to have been observing this regularly since the early 2000s. Farmers also made specific reference to the 2011/2012, 2012/2013 and 2013/2014 seasons in which rains sufficient to make seeds germinate were only received in December. The shift in rainfall onset was also almost always recalled and described in conjunction with other meaningful activities, occurrences and life events such as during their childhood years and before they got married.

The problem of early rainfall cessation is becoming more frequent. For these farmers, a normal rainy season occurs between October and March. This period was regarded as *mwaka wakakodzera* (adequate rainfall season) for crops to fully mature and also enable farmers to grow some crops towards the end of the rainy season (around the third week of February) as well as organise their activities such as harvesting. However, whilst it remains very common in literature to characterise a season as normally based on the total amount of rainfall, farmers construe a normal rainy season based on its length, amount received and the implications of received rainfall on crops.

The majority of farmers alluded to a trend towards extreme and intense rainfall events and occurrences. These are extreme events in the sense that these are rainfall conditions that are significantly deviating from the conditions farmers are used to. They are also extremes because farmers perceive them as not desirable for their crops. Rainfall that was either too low or too much thereby having severe impacts on crops qualified as an extreme event. Almost all farmers said they had witnessed increased incidences of droughts, and they pointed to droughts in 1992, 2002 and 2008 as extreme events. However, the 1992 drought was remembered and described as the worst in their lifetime. Those who did not remember this drought in great detail were mostly young at the time. On the same note, when asked to note critical rainfall events other than droughts since 1992, some farmers recalled episodes of heavy rains in the 1998/1999 season and cyclones, especially cyclone Eline as well as incidents of heavy rains between 2012 and 2014.

More so, the seasonal amounts of rainfall are as important as the distribution within the season. As highlighted by Cooper *et al.* (2008), whilst seasonal rainfall totals and their season-to-season variability are in themselves important, the nature of 'within season' variability can also have a major effect on crop productivity. Farmers are therefore anxious over increasing and prolonged dry spells occurring during the rainy season. Farmers also cited sporadic wet spells as occasional menaces. Although respondents mentioned that they have experienced dry spells mostly during drought years, a number of farmers used the 2013/2014 rainy season for reference.

In addition, farmers are finding the changes in the spatial distribution of rainfall problematic. This finding is a significant departure from a number of Zimbabwean studies based on farmers' perceptions that dwell much on seasonal rainfall distribution only, thereby neglecting spatial dimensions. In the study farmers noted how, within the rainy season, there were spatial differences in the distribution of rain, with their area not receiving any rainfall. The general perception among respondents was that *mvura yavakuita zvemana-mana* (rainfall is getting to other areas and skipping some areas). Those who alluded to spatial variability continuously noted how it was raining in the ward compared to other areas such as Chindenga, Danda and Nyamuzuwe. Linked to this, Meze-Hausken (2004:23) found that people in her study in Ethiopia repeatedly alluded to the Afar saying that goes, "while it rains on one horn of the ox, it can be dry on the other". This indicated the importance of localised rainfall, which can benefit one farming area while leaving the neighbouring area completely dry. Similarly, in central Malawi, Simelton *et al.* (2011) found that farmers stated that, during the past few years, rains come on one side of the farm and not the other.

In a related manner, farmers are also grappling with inadequate rainfall and an increasing number of seasons with low rainfall. Interestingly, when one compares farmers' perceptions with results of analysis of meteorological data done for Mutoko district, there are contrary indications of annual precipitation increasing in the district. This was also confirmed by Mudowaya (2014), namely, that there is a positive trend in annual mean precipitation for Mutoko district from 1978–2010 that therefore indicated that precipitation has been increasing during this period. Notwithstanding this, a significant number of farmers were of the view that rainfall has only been substantial since 1992 during two recent consecutive seasons, which are 2012/2013 and 2013/2014.

What the above suggests is that it is not enough to rely only on average annual rainfall to conclude that rainfall is increasing. It may therefore be important to conduct a qualitative inquiry to understand the nuances surrounding the meanings of rainfall amounts, which gives rise to what farmers consider as adequate rainfall. Farmers described adequate rainfall during interviews and informal conversations to mean *mvura yakakodzera kuti mbeswa dzibereke* (rainfall that is appropriate for crops to mature). Therefore, it is possible that there can be increasing rainfall but, when characterised by poor intra-seasonal distribution or if it is of poor quality, it can fail to meet farmers' expectations of adequacy. The majority of farmers highlighted that they had received *mvura zvinji* (a lot of rain) for the past two seasons. They were thrilled for the rains. However, they pointed out that for the 2013/2014 season there is *nzara yemvura* (rainfall induced hunger). This is because incessant rains in January and February 2014 washed away fertilizer and also caused *kundondovera* (leaching) in both gardens and fields. In this case, rainfall was inadequate for farmers. From what the respondents in the study said, *nzara* (hunger) – which many people usually associate with drought – can therefore be induced by little, low or excessive rainfall.

Farmers' concerns on temperatures

In general, respondents in Charewa were worried about trends in temperature. From the survey, 57% of the respondents were dissatisfied with temperature conditions, 31% were satisfied and 12% were indifferent. At the same time, whereas rainfall emerged as the most important concern, respondents established connections between temperature and rainfall. For instance, they indicated that in 1992 *mvura haina kunaya* (it was as if it did not rain at all) because *zuva rakarova* (the sun was too much) and *kunze kwaipisisa* (it was too hot). Further probing revealed that farmers associated the little rainfall they received with high temperatures they experienced. What is also clear from farmers' responses is that they are dissatisfied over rising temperatures, extremes in temperatures, and increasing and intense cold and hot spells.

Farmers generally concurred that temperatures have increased in both rainy and dry seasons. The increasing temperatures were regarded as responsible for problems they were experiencing such as high livestock and crop diseases. In addition, although farmers did not provide actual temperature figures, to clarify that temperatures were rising, they stressed that even if they had received *mvura zhinji* (a lot of rainfall) in some years compared to other years, water sources were drying up rapidly. They expected that in seasons they received a lot of rainfall, water sources would have water for some time, at least up until October. But that was not the case because they were experiencing rising temperatures. On a similar note, scholars have highlighted that there has been a significant increase in daytime and overnight temperatures over the last few years in Mutoko, although actual figures are not readily available (Makonyere 2011).

To further augment the above, other studies, for example by Mudowaya (2014) concluded that annual mean maximum temperature in Mutoko district has been increasing. This increase in annual maximum temperature might be due to an increase in frequency of incidences of hot days (Mudowaya 2014:45). Furthermore, Freeman (1994) concluded that temperatures in the 1980s rose in winter months around Mutoko district by 1°C and precipitation has been fluctuating.

However, although the survey data and other studies show that temperatures are increasing, some farmers were more specific in interviews and perceived temperatures to be particularly higher in years of little rainfall. At the same time, a few farmers were of the view that even in years of normal and excessive rainfalls, high temperatures accompanied the extended dry spells that they have experienced. These findings are also consistent with the opinions in the Intergovernmental Panel on Climate Change, IPCC report. According to the IPCC (2001), in the course of the 1992 drought, which was linked to an El Nino Southern Oscillation, Zimbabwe's temperatures reached maximums of about 47°C, documented along the South Africa and Zimbabwe boarder.

The findings of this study reveal that farmers are experiencing shorter winter seasons. Apart from this, some farmers were of the view that the onset of winter is now difficult to tell while others asserted that winters were getting warmer than before. Farmers' descriptions pointed towards the usual winter season starting in May and ending in July. However, now farmers are experiencing days with hot temperatures between May and July, similar to those found during the wet, hot season. When asked which month winter has been starting since 2000, responses from farmers were divergent. However, what was clear was that farmers thought winter was ending early because of increasing warm temperatures. At the same time, some respondents insisted that the length of the winter season is still the same, but they indicated that *ikozvino kuri kunyanyisa kutonhora* (it is now extremely cold) compared to some years back. As one respondent narrated, she started living in Nyakanyanga village in 1989. She had gotten married and moved from Mkumbura, Mashonaland Central. She remembered that when she settled in the village *kwaitonhora hakowo* (it was somewhat cold) but now there are days *ane kutonhora kwakawedzera* (which are very cold).

The majority (71.3%) of respondents in the study answered that that they were encountering extremes in temperatures and 28.7% said they were not. For some respondents, the problem was not just that they were experiencing extremes in temperature but days in which they experienced these were becoming more frequent. There were sentiments that *mwando wekupisa* (hot spells) and *mwando wechando* (cold spells) were becoming intense. From the survey results, 88.3% of respondents said they were experiencing intense heat and 11.7% said they were not. On the other hand, compared to the 1990s, 68.3% of the respondents thought the frequency of cold spells had increased since 2000, 19.7% said the frequency of cold spells had decreased and 12% said there was no change. These hot and cold spells were considered as random hence farmers were not able to predict their timing. In essence, just like they can no longer predict the start of the rainfall season, farmers pointed out that it was challenging to do the same with these cold and hot spells.

Furthermore, reference was made to cold and hot spells from different years. Common reference was made to the cold spell that lasted for almost a week in early April 2014. During continuous interactions and discussions with respondents, it became evident that some respondents attributed this cold spell to 'too much rain' they had received in January and February 2014. Some respondents also noted that that in February 2013 *kwakaita mapipi ezuva chibage chikapera nemakonye* (there was unbearable heat such that maize was destroyed by worms). These black worms were said to have been caused by high temperatures.

Finally, although most farmers alluded to the above, a few were of the view that hot and cold months were no longer clearly and strictly distinct. Respondents constantly made references to times when their parents were alive, their childhood times or times before they got married to explain this observation. Comparably, farmers were of the perception that during the aforementioned times they used to clearly distinguish cold and hot seasons. The period between November and April was regarded as *nguva yekupisa nekunaya* (hot, wet summer), May to July was *nguva yekutonhora isina mvura* (cold, dry winter) and August to October was *nguva yekupisawo kusina mvura* (a bit hot, dry summer). However, respondents reported that since the year 2000, they have found it increasingly difficult to apply these characteristics in clear terms.

Interpretation of changes in climate variability

Besides articulating the multifaceted concerns above, it is crucial to understand farmers' interpretations of the changes they are experiencing. The findings in the study reveal that farmers have diverse interpretations of changes in climate variability. From the survey results, 47% of farmers pointed to religious and cultural reasons as the main driver, 48% natural shifts in climate, 2% wars being fought in other countries and 3% said they did not know. These figures show that there is no significant difference in numbers between those who noted religious and cultural reasons and natural shifts in climate as main drivers of change. However, in the presentation below, the chapter deliberately focuses on religious and cultural reasons because a lot of intriguing findings around these aspects emerged during qualitative interviews.

Notwithstanding the decision to focus on cultural and religious facets, the fact that 48% of the farmers pointed to natural shits in climate remains an important discovery. To these farmers, these changes represent *kungochinjawo kunofanira kuitika* (it is just change that is supposed to occur). Only one male respondent commented that he did not understand why it was not raining properly when the water cycle occurs every day; therefore, he was convinced that these must be natural changes occurring in climate. Quite a number of respondents were of the view that *masandinisi* (scientists) and those with knowledge were saying weather is supposed to change. Therefore, if experts said that particularly through mass media, then the weather was changing and it is something that should happen naturally. One can therefore infer that these farmers regarded climate variability as a natural phenomenon.

On a different note, along the widespread perception that changes in climate variability were caused by natural shifts in climate, there was almost equal indication that they were induced by *Vadzimu* (ancestral spirits) and God. The two entities were responsible for the 'good' and 'bad' seasons and other climatic extremes that farmers were experiencing. Contrary to the current discourse on global warming that predominantly supposes anthropogenic causes, changes in climatic variability in Charewa are perceived and understood by farmers as reactions to provocation by these two extra-human entities. As such, farmers postulated a direct relationship between climate and the spiritual realm.

Vadzimu (ancestral spirits) were perceived to be angry over increasing cultural defilement and moral decadence. Dominant among the signs of the decadence and defilement were failure to follow traditional religious practices such as *kuwombera Vadzimu* (honouring the ancestral spirits) and traditional environmental practices. The subversion of local traditions and religious practices was regarded as evidence of increasing disorder in the religious, social and moral lives of people of Charewa. In general, people in the area were regarded as no longer interested in conducting traditional religious ceremonies, which angered Nehoreka (spirit of the land). One key reason it was perceived why people were no longer interested in rain ceremonies was the fragmentation of traditional religious beliefs owing to intruding modern values and apostolic religious discourses. Basically, these promoted *kurasa tsika dzechivanhu* (abandoning peoples' traditional values).

Generational rupture in terms of who bears the responsibility for the perceived increasing cultural defilement and moral decadence was also evident. However, this should not be read in terms of elders versus the young as there were also respondents (among both the young and old) whose perceptions were different. On the one hand, the perceptions of disruption of and deviation from valorised traditional religious practices, social mores and cultural values by young people were common amongst elders. It was generally perceived that there is a disconnection between the young generation and various traditional practices. The young generation was particularly blamed for *kurasa tsika* (abandoning tradition), *kuita zvisina hunhu* (engaging in immoral acts) and *kuita zvechirungu* (following modern ways). For example, one elder noted that: "*Vapwere vari muno vari kundoita zvechirungu. Zvino ino inzvimbo yaNehoreka, ndiye anonaisa mvura* [Young people is this area are following modern ways, but then this land belongs to Nehoreka, he is the one who makes it rain]." The ostentatiousness of modern habits was also pointed out in relation to traditional marriage practices. In conversations, elders lamented that appropriate marriage rites were being ignored as *vana vari kungotizisana* (children are eloping). In the end, marriage as it is construed and valued in the traditional sense is being downgraded. Consequently, *Vadzimu* (ancestral spirits) were angered and they retaliated in various ways including inducing drought as punishment.

On the other hand, young people in the study thought that those responsible for leading the traditional rain seeking ceremonies and other practices were no longer consistent. They cited that elders no longer visited Mutimuchena in

Mt Darwin and Dzivaguru where they are instructed on what to do regarding various facets of their lives. It was noted that over the years the elders had stopped visiting these areas and increasingly disregarded the centrality of the spirits in their lives. Some respondents however noted that the elders resumed visiting these areas in 2012, and that is why they had received a lot of rainfall in the 2012/2013 and 2013/2014 seasons. Nonetheless, it was also highlighted that when the rains become too much within the season, the elders have to hold ceremonies to appeal to the ancestral spirits to reduce the rains; but this was not done and that is why rainfall ended up causing *kundondovera* (leaching).

At the same time, others blamed the current chief and her messengers for not being firm regarding people who were engaging in what angered the ancestral spirits or Nehoreka. Furthermore, it was pointed out that there were people who were practicing *makunakuna* (breaking taboos) by engaging in incest. Other unacceptable practices that angered *Vadzimu* (ancestral spirits) included using black tins and pots to draw water from *zvisipiti zvinoera* (sacred springs).

In this case, the spiritual and the natural worlds were often presented as not dichotomous. The spirits were regarded as the guardians of the sacred springs and trees, among other natural resources and areas found locally. In return, these springs and trees provided abundant water and fruits respectively. Therefore, the use of tins or pots to ferry water from sacred springs and the destruction of scared trees attracts wrath from the spirits and they cease to protect people. They let the environment respond to the provocation by bringing droughts and cyclones.

There were also interpretations that pointed to climate variability as the ultimate response of God to inappropriate human behaviour. Besides angering the ancestors, it was cited that what was happening was God's doing. God was angry because of increased evil doing. Some people thought *zvivi zvawandisa* (sins have increased) and others suggested that there was a lot of Satanism and therefore God is angry. However, it did not necessarily mean that people who were engaging in evil doings were from Charewa all the time, but from other areas as well.

What was clear from respondents' descriptions was that *kusanaya kwemvura mutongo waMwari* (that it was not raining properly was God's punishment) regardless of who had sinned. It was common among those who attributed droughts and hunger to God's anger to quote Bible verses. In particular, they referred to the story found in Genesis 41:15 "… seven great years of abundance are coming throughout the land of Egypt, but seven years of famine will follow them". Related to this, respondents believed that changes in climate variability were signs of a coming apocalypse. They therefore perceived increase in droughts and hunger as signs foretold in the Bible that the world was coming to an end.

Finally, although a lot of studies do not pay attention to how farmers define and interpret climate variability in Zimbabwe, some scholars have noted views consistent with the foregoing. For example, others discovered that perceived climate changes were linked more to natural and human forces (in Makoni), and unknown forces as well as a breakdown in cultural norms and beliefs and rise of Christianity (in Wedza) (Mtambanengwe *et al.* 2012). In other African contexts, scholars have found that scanty rains can be taken as the sign that God and the spirits of the ancestors are displeased with local people because of their conduct; in contrast, abundant rains can indicate divine or cosmological favour (Orlove *et al.* 2010).

Conclusion and policy insights

Fully understanding climate variability in Zimbabwe requires broad conceptualisations that incorporate voices of farmers living on the frontiers of various changes. Farmers in Mutoko are concerned about patterns of rainfall and temperature trends. These are articulated in view of past and present observations and experiences. In this regard, taking increasing unpredictability and unreliability of rainfall as the ultimate concerns, what is problematic for farmers are: high intensity rainfall, inadequate rainfall, poor rainfall quality, late onset of rainfall season, early rainfall season cessation and poor rainfall distribution. At the same time, rising temperatures, extremes in temperatures, and increasing and intense cold and hot spells, dissatisfy farmers. In the same context, farmers are knowledgeable about climate issues and therefore they are able to contest the dominant framings of climate change and its impacts. They have different interpretations from 'scientific' explanations of causes of climate change. What all this tells, especially to climate change policy makers, is that climate variability has local meanings and changes are experienced in very specific ways. Farmers themselves can only capture these meanings through analysing narratives, stories and observations. This approach should be the basis for novel approaches to adaptation policy and practice in contemporary environments based on the recognition of the centrality of farmers' perceptions, experiences and practices. This enables policy makers to make better decisions to build farmers' resilience and promote sustainable adaptation. Therefore, my chapter encourages a shift from policy response frameworks based on assessments that are blind to local people's concerns to more encompassing or locally inclusive adaptation response frameworks.

References

Archer, M.S. 2003. *Structure, Agency and the Internal Conversation.* Cambridge, UK: Cambridge University Press.

Bhatasara, S. 2015a. *Understanding Climate Variability and Livelihoods Adaptation in Rural Zimbabwe: A Case of Charewa, Mutoko,* Unpublished Thesis, Rhodes University.

Bhatasara, S. 2015b. Rethinking Climate Change Research in Zimbabwe, *Journal of Environmental Studies and Sciences* 7 (1): 39–52.

Brown, D., Chanakira, R., Chatiza, K., Dhliwayo, M., Dodman, D., Masiiwa, M., Muchadenyika, D., Mugabe, P. and Zvigadza, S. 2012. *Climate Change Impacts, Vulnerability and Adaptation in Zimbabwe.* International Institute for Environment and Development (IIED) Climate Change Working Paper 3.

Chagutah, T. 2010. *Climate Change Vulnerability and Preparedness in Southern Africa: Zimbabwe Country Report.* Heinrich Boell Stiftung, Cape Town.

Chikodzi, D., Simba, F.M. and Murwendo, T. 2012. Perceptions, Vulnerability and Adaptation to Climatic Change and Variability in Masvingo Province. *Greener Journal of Political Science* 2 (5): 156–116.

Cooper, P.J.M., Dimes, J., Rao, K.P.C., Shapiro, B., Shiferaw, B. and Twomlow, S. 2008. Coping Better with Current Climatic Variability in the Rain-fed Farming Systems of Sub-Saharan Africa: An Essential First Step in Adapting to Future Climate Change? *Agriculture, Ecosystems and Environment* 126 (1/2): 24–35.

Demeritt, D. 2001. The Construction of Global Warming and the Politics of Science. *Annals of the Association of American Geographers* 91 (2): 307–337.

Foucault, M. 1980. *Power-knowledge: Selected Interviews and Other Writings, 1972–1977.* Hassocks: Harvester Press.

Freeman, T. 1994. *Investigation into the 1994 Malaria Situation of Mutoko District.* GTZ.

Gwimbi, P. 2009. Cotton Farmers' Vulnerability to Climate Change in Gokwe District (Zimbabwe): Impact and Influencing Factors. *JÀMBÁ Journal of Disaster Risk Studies* 2 (2): 81–92.

Hulme, M., Dessai, S., Lorenzoni, I., Nelson, D.R. 2009. Unstable Climates: Exploring the Statistical and Social Constructions of Normal Sciences. *Geoforum* 40 (2): 197–206.

Intergovernmental Panel on Climate Change (IPCC). 2001. *Climate Change 2001: Synthesis Report. Contribution of Working Groups I, II, and III to the Third Assessment Report of the Intergovernmental Panel on Climate Change.* Cambridge, UK: Cambridge University Press.

Makonyere, L. 2011. *Mutoko District Agricultural Information.* Paper commissioned by Miombo Eco-Region Programme. Harare: WWF Zimbabwe.

Mano, R. and Nhemachena C. 2006. *Assessment of the Economic Impacts of Climate Change on Agriculture in Zimbabwe: A Ricardian Approach.* Centre for Environmental Economics and Policy in Africa (CEEPA), University of Pretoria Discussion Paper No. 11.

Masanganise, J.N. 2010. *Climate Variability and Change and its Potential Impact on Maize Yield in North-eastern Zimbabwe,* Unpublished Thesis, University of Zimbabwe.

Meze-Hausken, E. 2004. Contrasting Climate Variability and Meteorological Drought with Perceived Drought and Climate Change in Northern Ethiopia. *Climate Research* 27 (1): 19–31.

Ministry of Environment and Natural Resources Management (Climate Change Office). 2008. *National Self-assessment for Climate Change, Biodiversity and Land Degradation in Zimbabwe.* Government of the Republic of Zimbabwe.

Mtambanengwe F., Mapfumo P., Chikowo R., Chamboko T. 2012. Climate Change and Variability: Smallholder-Farming Communities in Zimbabwe Portray a Varied Understanding. *African Crop Science Journal* 20 (S2): 227–241.

Mudowaya, P.F. 2014. An Exploratory Analysis of the Effects of Climate Change on Vegetation: The Case of Mutoko District in Mashonaland East Province, Zimbabwe. Unpublished Thesis. Midlands State University.

Mutasa, C. 2008. *Evidence of Climate Change in Zimbabwe*: paper presented at the climate change awareness and dialogue workshop for Mashonaland Central and Mashonaland West Provinces held at Caribbea Bay Hotel, Kariba, Zimbabwe, 29–30 September 2008.

Mutekwa, V. 2009. Climate Change Impacts and Adaptation in the Agricultural Sector: the Case of Smallholder Farmers in Zimbabwe. *Journal of Sustainable Development Africa* 11 (2): 237–256.

Orlove, B., Roncoli C., Kabugo M. and Majugu, A. 2010. Indigenous Climate Knowledge in southern Uganda: The Multiple Components of a Dynamic Regional System. *Climatic Change* 100 (2): 243–265.

Simelton, E., Quinn, C.H, Antwi-Agyei, P., Batisani, N., Dougill, A.J., Dyer, J., Fraser, E.D.G., Mkwambisi, D., Rosell, S., Sallu, S. and Stringer, L.C. 2011. *African Farmers' Perceptions of Erratic Rainfall.* Centre for Climate Change Economics and Policy Working Paper No. 73.

Unganai L.S. 1996. Historic and Future Climatic Change in Zimbabwe. *Climate Research* 6: 137–145.

Unganai, L.S. 2009. Adaptation to Climate Change Among Agro-pastoral Systems: Case for Zimbabwe IOP Conf. Series. *Earth Environmental Science*, 6, Article ID: 412045 http://dx.doi.org/10.1088/1755-1307/6/1/412045.

10 Livelihoods vulnerability among riverbed farmers in Negande, NyamiNyami District

Felix Tombindo

Introduction

This chapter analyses the interface between the vulnerability context and rural livelihoods in the semi-arid Negande community in Omay communal land, NyamiNyami district. Adverse agro-ecological conditions (such as poor soils, high temperatures and recurrent droughts) militate against agriculture, which is the immediate safety net for the Negande community. The central reference for the analysis is a case study of a 'rural survival innovation' in the form of riverbed farming (hereafter *mabbonzyi* as the locals call it). In the environmentally sensitive age that characterises today's world, one is bound to question the sustainability of cultivating on the riverbed, both in terms of the long-term sustenance of people's livelihoods and in terms of conserving the physical environment. In discussing the *mabbonzyi* farming practice as a *sine qua non* for Negande people's survival, the study also assesses the resilience of the survival strategy, its contribution to the well-being of Negande households, as well as the prospects and capacity of the strategy in continuing to serve the immediate consumption needs of households. In taking cognisance of the influence of external institutions as well as the 'mixed-bag' nature of rural livelihoods (as rural livelihoods scholarship notes the diversified character of rural livelihoods), the study also briefly probes alternative survival strategies other than agriculture.

Background to the study area

Omay communal land is one of three communal lands that make up Nyami-Nyami district (Mubaya 2008, Sibanda 2001). The other two are Makande and Gatshe-Gatshe. NyamiNyami district is in the north-west part of Zimbabwe and falls within the Zambezi Valley. There are nine wards in Omay communal land. Of the nine wards, eight of them are under the traditional jurisdiction of four chiefs, namely Mola, Negande, Msampakaruma and Nebiri. Chiefs Mola and Negande are Tonga chiefs and the other two are of Shangwe origin. Highlighting ethnic identity is important for two reasons. First, *mabbonzyi* is an agricultural practice linked to the Tonga people and their historical connections with life in the hot and semi-arid Zambezi Valley. Second, the Tonga constitute the "traditional population of NyamiNyami district" (Mashinya 2007:14). As such, I refer mainly to the Tonga people in this background and the rest of the chapter.

At the time of this study (in 2014), an agricultural extension officer asserted that Negande has 756 households. Negande is located approximately 20 kilometres from Siakobvu growth point and has poor connections to the outside world. A dust road that is mostly inaccessible during the rainy season due to the flooding of Mawena River connects Negande to Siakobvu. *Mabbonzyi* farming is practiced on the Mawena riverbed during winter. Poor physical capital (road networks) is detrimental to the realisation of positive livelihood outcomes because roads are vital for linking an area to external markets. Roads also make livelihoods outsourcing viable through unhindered migration of people in search for work. Many a time people from Negande have to travel on foot the 20 kilometre distance to Siakobvu where they can access transport in the form of one bus that connects the area to either Karoi town (210 kilometres away) or to Chitekete growth point (40 kilometres away) in Gokwe district.

The settlement of Tonga people in NyamiNyami district dates back to their forced displacement to pave way for the Kariba dam construction in the 1950s. The Tonga's displacement involved only limited compensation for their disturbed livelihoods and this has turned them into one of the most impoverished, least developed and unconnected communities in Zimbabwe (Basilwizi 2010, Musona 2011). NyamiNyami district lies in Zimbabwe's natural region 5 (which is semi-arid) and this explains the susceptibility of the area to persistent droughts. The United Nations Development Programme in 2003 ranked NyamiNyami as the poorest of Zimbabwe's 55 districts (Save the Children 2004).

Although livelihoods experts point to the exposure of everyone (rich or poor, rural or urban) to livelihoods vulnerability, the case of the Tonga in Negande is even worse because of limited diversification options and, where there are attempts to pursue diversification, chances of realising positive livelihood outcomes are severely meagre. Reminiscent of the classical development of capitalism, a protracted history of neo-enclosure of productive assets from the rural population exists in the case of NyamiNyami. Colonial and post-colonial governments have systematically impacted natural resource management for the worse around NyamiNyami, preventing inhabitants from accessing natural resource endowments, including wildlife, in their area.

Authoritative natural resource management institutions[1] refer to the Tonga people as poachers (Dzingirai 1999:41); while their limited agricultural produce is annually destroyed by wild animals like elephants, hippos and buffaloes, which are strictly protected by the state (Musona 2011, Dzingirai 2003a, 2003b, Mashingaidze 2013). The area is characterised by chronic poverty because of limited social and educational development opportunities, isolation from markets, poor soils and erratic rainfall. As such, NyamiNyami is a site of countless relief projects (Metcalfe 1994, Mashinya 2007). In the end, these relief projects do not enable people to be self-sufficient, as they tend to tackle the 'symptoms of the problem' of starvation and hunger. Rather, programmes must be initiated which capacitate the people to stand on their own by addressing the root of the problem (that is, by supporting people to at least eke out their own livelihoods through, say, availing them of required resources/inputs).

Research methods

The study was qualitative, including focus groups, transect walks, key informant interviews and unstructured interviews as data soliciting instruments. I used purposive sampling to select participants for research. More than 50% of the respondents were *mabbonzyi* farmers (those who were not directly involved in *mabbonzyi* farming were included for comparative reasons, and to get a holistic overview of livelihoods strategies in Negande). Data was collected through face to face interviews, tracing respective life histories of households in Negande to get a description of 'how', 'why' and to what extent *mabbonzyi* farming contributed to people's survival. A qualitative approach enabled open-ended questions and provided room for further probing. I also conducted two focus groups, with males and females. The focus was on old people with assumed rich 'cultural capital' (knowledge) about the origins of *mabbonzyi* farming due to their long stay in the area.

Data collection coincided with the time for *mabbonzyi* farming and the majority of respondents were working in the fields, and this made the combination of transect walks and interviews inevitable. I also undertook unstructured interviews with fifteen households. Five of these fifteen households were not *mabbonzyi* farmers. This was to enable a more nuanced, 'representative' and holistic understanding of livelihoods in Negande, which might not have been possible if the focus had solely been on *mabbonzyi* farmers. One key informant interview took place with an employee at NyamiNyami Rural District's environment department to obtain its views on *mabbonzyi*, as well as to confirm whether what respondents in Negande said tallied with the position and perceptions of natural environment conservation authorities.

The Why and how of *mabbonzyi* farming in Negande

Agricultural communities engage regularly in either agricultural extensification or intensification for livelihoods construction (Nkamleu 2011, Chirau *et al.* 2014) but for Negande inhabitants neither of the two options is viable. Extensification is not possible due to lack of abundant arable land while intensification is difficult because of unavailability of modern inputs and technology. As such, people resort to *mabbonzyi*, comprising of very small plots per household and with meagre inputs. *Mabbonzyi* is augmented (in some cases) by cotton contract farming and cultivation of drought resistant sorghum. Cultivation of sorghum and contract farming occur during the conventional rainy season.

Mabbonzyi farming is an innovative way of using scarce natural capital (land and water). It is a centuries-old farming practice linked to floodplain cultivation practiced in the Zambezi Valley before displacement of the Tonga people. *Mabbonzyi* emanated from people's lived experiences as a mechanism to cope with livelihoods stress in the severely hot Zambezi valley, and Negande residents 'inherited' it from their ancestors who used to farm three times a year as an adaptation strategy given the adverse climate conditions in the area. As one farmer said:

> We adopted this from our forefathers; they used to farm three times a year along the Zambezi River ... The Zambezi Valley has always been hot and characterised by low rainfall and constant flooding ... But before the forced displacement, it was easy to be food secure due to the availability of the perennial Zambezi River, which enabled our fore fathers to farm throughout the year.

Before the displacement of the Tonga from the Zambezi valley, *mabbonzyi* was a form of livelihood coping strategy from natural disaster shocks (persistent droughts due to flooding and sometimes limited rainfall) and it was not subject to prohibitive external policies or institutions.

Mabbonzyi is now subject to a constraining environmental policy framework that does not fully appreciate people's unremitting struggle for survival under the severe natural environment conditions. These are the challenges of the rhetoric of 'sustainable development'. Environmental management regimes condemn livelihoods practices that go against the objectives of conservation, but these may in fact facilitate livelihoods. Scott's (1985) 'everyday forms of resistance' describe the subtle ways through which 'less powerful' people silently but significantly resist powerful structures. *Mabbonzyi* practice is an animation of passive resistance in the face of environmentally induced strain on livelihoods and restrictive environmental rules. It provides some agency vital for coping with livelihoods stress although the extent of this agency is limited in terms of its contribution to household self-sufficiency. One resident (named Chatembwa) explained the origins of *mabbonzyi* in Negande thus:

> When we relocated to Negande, there was no room for us to continue the practice of *mabbonzyi*; [this was] due to government laws that prohibit us from farming near the rivers. Local authorities – the chief and headmen – do not prohibit *mabbonzyi* because they know the predicament that we are in. *Mabbonzyi* is a realisation that adherence to prohibitive environmental conservation laws does not make us food secure ... Chronic hunger and poverty made us see the need to ignore the law.

Livelihoods scholarship is concerned among other issues with the ability of a livelihood to continue to serve its purpose while at the same time maintaining the natural source on which it is based (Chambers and Conway 1992, Scoones 1998). Pioneers of *mabbonzyi* farming in Negande claim that their conventional fields, near the Mawena River, became subject to erosion by floods, thus prompting them to eventually farm directly on the riverbed. It started as flood plain cultivation became more viable, compared to the small harvests that people got from conventional farming. However, this resulted in erosion and siltation of the river until the demarcation between the river channel and its banks became unnoticeable.

Relatives of the pioneers of *mabbonzyi* gradually became interested in this 'unorthodox' farming practice, which yielded better returns. This led to a subsequent apportionment of the river in total. People with usufruct rights and thus access to portions on the river generally base their claims on the notion that their ancestral fields were eroded away into the river; hence their undisputed entitlement to cultivate on the river. Social capital, involving connections to those with access to riverbed portions, is important as it gives people without direct access to portions on the riverbed access to riverbed farming. In this sense, *mabbonzyi* farming claims are 'socially-embedded' (Sakdapolrak 2014) and thus any understanding of *mabbonzyi* means going beyond the household as the sole unit of analysis. However, social capital also exposed some households to vulnerability because the more they cut off their portion in giving to relatives, the less their own crop yields. As such, social capital can be a source of livelihoods vulnerability, just as it can be a means to obtaining a sustainable livelihood. Siachakanzwa had this to say:

> I have allocated my *mabbonzyi* to three of my married sons. I cannot leave them starving but this means the harvest I get is too small. I now have only 46 lines [approximately 100 square metres] on which to farm. The harvests can last for only a month or even less.

During the interviews and transect walks, marked boundaries were evident in the form of pole fencing and dugout soil ridges. The respondents cited no form of conflict over boundaries. No formal allocation from the local authorities (chiefs and headmen) was required. Siabwanda elaborated on the allocation rules as follows:

> These are ancestral fields, the *sibbuku* or *simwaami* [village head or chief] does not have the right to reallocate or distribute *mabbonzyi* land. If the headman or chief wants a *mabbonzyi* portion, he has to have ancestral inheritance to the land or relations who may voluntarily cut their pieces and give him.

The majority position was that *mabbonzyi* was a result of claimants making up for their eroded fields due to flooding. But a divergent view emerged that asserted that the actual erosion in the first place came as a result of intensive flood plain cultivation as people realised that they could reap comparatively higher harvests from *mabbonzyi* than from the conventional farming season.

This divergent perception reveals the endowment of scientific capital (knowledge) by Negande residents concerning the causes of environmental degradation and hence the need to protect it. In an environment where enabling incentives from the government or private actors for alternative livelihood options are absent, *mabbonzyi* is a last gasp alternative in pursuing survival by the community. *Mabbonzyi* farming reveals that rural people engage in 'environmentally unsustainable' practices because of lack of alternative sources of livelihoods. In worst-case scenarios, the natural environment has to suffer as people look for means to survive. One of the respondents asserted:

> As we realised better harvests from flood plain cultivation, we became eager to expand our fields. Erosion and siltation of the river were a result of us farming on the banks of the river ... This [erosion] was helpful as it enlarged our farming territory.

The cultivation method employed by the farmers further substantiates the fact that they are not ignorant of the need to conserve their fields. *Mabbonzyi* has some tenets of 'cost-benefit analyses' on the part of the farmers as they attempt to maintain the resilience of their respective fields. An overarching concern to obtain a livelihood is there, but they also try to avoid undercutting their source of livelihood. While there are no local/traditional regimes governing the conservation of the riverbed (only the Environmental Management Agency which was cited as opposing the practice altogether), the farmers were aware of the need to conserve the natural resource base (the riverbed) in order for them to continue to make a living from it. They did so by applying significant conservation methods (such as minimum tillage and planting of flowers to avoid erosion of their portions) which contributed somehow to the 'sustainability' of the practice over the long period of time for which it has been in existence. The 'calculative' nature of *mabbonzyi* farmers is evident through their use of hoes only to dig holes in which they sow the seeds, which is reminiscent of modern day conservation farming and minimum tillage. These big holes are the ones in which the maize crops grow until they are ripe for harvest. This significantly reduces erosion unlike in the case of draught-power driven cultivation practices. Apart from the minimum tillage technique, a few households also made sure their fields do not erode away through planting an indigenous flower that bound the soil.

With undeniable evidence of erosion and siltation of the river explicitly leading to the undermining of the natural resource base from which this livelihood strategy emanates (hence evidently unsustainable in the long run), respondents were quick to point to a simultaneous comparative 'economic advantage' vis-à-vis 'natural disadvantage' conundrum that came with *mabbonzyi*. In the end, most of them acknowledged the severity of erosion but saw the economic advantage as more important to them:

> My friend, you have to come here and experience the hardships that we face year in, year out for you to appreciate how important *mabbonzyi* is to us. If you could spend just a day on an empty stomach, then you will probably have a different view altogether ... Soil erosion yes, but it is better to erode

the soil than die with hunger when God has given us this redemptive river … He is the one who knows what to do if eventually this river dries up because he is the one who gave it to us in the first place.

Reinforcing the above respondent's sentiments were perceptions by most respondents of *mabbonzyi* as a 'self-sustaining livelihood strategy'. They argued that when the rainy season comes, reeds and grass grow all over the river, and this kept the soil bound and safe from erosion. Also cited were rich alluvial soil deposits (deposited on the riverbed during the rainy season, which is usually characterised by floods). These alluvial deposits became a substitute for inorganic fertilisers that many households lamented they could not afford due to unavailability of financial capital. The substitution of fertilisers by the alluvial soils meant an avoidance of salinisation of the soil and pollution of Mawena River which during the rainy season served as a source of another, though short-lived, livelihood strategy through fishing. Komichi asserted that:

> This crop is very rich as you can see but I did not apply even a spoonful of chemical fertilisers. *Mabbonzyi* helps me because I do not have to incur expenses for purposes of making the soil fertile. The soil is already fertile on its own, as it is fed naturally … There is a difference between conventional farming and *mabbonzyi* because we have reeds and grass that keep the soil together during the rainy season, and we also do not use ploughs. It has been a long time since we started cultivating on this river but even today we are still cultivating on it without any problems [of erosion].

Despite the decades-long farming on the riverbed without fertilisers, some relatively affluent households were contemplating further innovation through application of fertilisers to maximise outputs. This is a fact which further validates my contention that, when people are faced with the most pressing of constraints on their livelihoods, they end up engaging in coping strategies that – no matter how harmful to the natural environment – may serve the purpose of their survival.

Comparatively, *mabbonzyi* farming was less demanding than conventional farming in relation to the intensity of labour required within households as well as machinery used for cultivation. For *mabbonzyi*, children participate in the clearing of fields. Women participate in guarding against wild animals such as monkeys during the day. Men however participate during the night guarding against dangerous wild animals such as elephants and hippos. Households only weeded the field once because it was during winter and no more weeds grew, unlike during the rainy season when two or more sessions of weeding are required. Also, because they engage in minimum tillage, *mabbonzyi* was appreciated because it used simple machinery in the form of hoes only (unlike conventional farming which required draught power and machinery such as ploughs which most households professed not being able to afford).

Mabbonzyi had the advantage that households could grow maize as well as some other crops such as vegetables like covo and rape, sweet potatoes and pumpkin plant, primarily for household consumption and to a limited extent for bartering or trading in cash with fellow villagers. The advantage of this was that unlike gardening during summer that required watering and hence the need for extra labour, vegetables could grow with the available moisture on the riverbed.

Vulnerability context

In this section, I consider some of the vulnerability factors, which impinge in various ways on the *mabbonzyi* practice, starting with environmental management institutions. *Mabbonzyi* farming in Negande serves the purpose of livelihoods coping in the light of the adverse effects of droughts, but it exists in an external policy context that subjects it to institutional constraints. These challenges involve social exclusionary factors as well as conflicts in the form of the district's environmental regulation department that is the major hindrance against positive livelihood outcomes. When I met the chief's representative seeking his permission to conduct this study, he advised me to start by asking about other livelihood strategies. He advised that asking questions around *mabbonzyi* at the beginning of the interviews would frighten away people from participation for fear that I might be an employee of the environmental regulation authorities. In this regard, the Environmental Management Agency (EMA) is seen as a constraining rather than an enabling structure for the attainment of positive livelihoods.

Respondents cited the disruption of preparations and planning for much needed early planting before moisture on the riverbed portions dried up with the approaching of the winter season. People feared environmental authorities would destroy their crops. Lydia noted that:

> EMA is as bad as elephants that occasionally destroy our crops. They disrupted our planning for the farming season ... You see, these crops are still in their early stages ... because we were afraid of EMA. Conventionally, we would have planted our crops in February and by now [June] most of the crops should have been ripening for consumption and harvesting.

At the time of conducting this research, there was still uncertainty about whether EMA employees would come to destroy the crops. Farmers were afraid that there would be destruction of their crops, most of which were still a month or two away from maturing. Gifta explained thus:

> This is our only source of livelihood. If EMA sends someone to come and destroy our crops that will mean death for us. They have already inflicted immense damage by disturbing us from preparing well; ... we are living in constant fear, guarding the crops against wild animals and EMA officials during the day and night.

Additionally, there were conflicts and disgruntlement that came from those without access to riverbed farming portions. Those with access to portions on the riverbed cited the conniving of those without access with EMA in spreading the rumours about the illegitimacy of the farming practice and the liability of continued farming on the riverbed to possible legal consequences. One farmer (called Orders) claimed that:

> Year in, year out, those not practising *mabbonzyi* farming are the ones who spread rumours about its possible banning, thus disrupting our planting time schedule. In the end, though we plant on our respective portions, much loss incurs, as portions far away from the centre of the river are quick to dry…. Part of the reason for our susceptibility to hunger come from our fellow community members who do not want to see us continue, as they do not have that access. Some of them have other means of survival and they do not want to see the continued practice of riverbed farming for they do not directly benefit from it.

An interview with one of NyamiNyami district's environmental department employee, Chitemere, revealed contrasting perceptions regarding how environmental authorities treat *mabbonzyi* farming. He claimed that EMA recognises the precarious nature of livelihoods in Negande, and has approved of *mabbonzyi* farmers continuing to farm on the riverbed. He said:

> We know that *mabbonzyi* is detrimental to the river in the long run but *mabbonzyi* farmers have been given the green light to continue cultivating on the riverbed because of the adverse climatic conditions in Negande. In other areas, it is not allowed; … Cultivated land must be 30 metres or more away from the riverbanks but in Negande, where there is little production during the rainy season, relevant authorities have agreed to let the people continue with that farming system. Sometimes we have to value human life over the environment and we have allowed for this for Negande villagers.

Such contrasting views between the respondents in Negande and the environmental official could be because of two reasons. First, it could be a fabrication of fellow villagers without access to *mabbonzyi* portions conflicting with those with access, hence spreading the rumours. Second, it could be that indeed EMA has really been threatening to destroy the crops. In either case, this has exposed *mabbonzyi* to vulnerability through disturbance and delaying of the planting process, thereby constraining the optimal yield that could be realised. If one takes EMA's position that it has given the villagers the green light to continue with riverbed farming, then one could argue that external structures within which *mabbonzyi* exist are enabling it as opposed to the constraining picture that villagers painted.

Access to credit for inputs such as seed and fertilisers is another constraining and vulnerability factor. No government or private sector support provides inputs for *mabbonzyi* farming. The government only provides seed and fertilisers for the conventional farming season and not for the purposes of farming on the riverbed. The seed and fertiliser donations from the government are selective and not everyone receives them. Diverse criteria including old age and widowhood are the basis for selection.[2] Because *mabbonzyi* farmers face uncertainty about whether they will be able to practise *mabbonzyi* every forthcoming winter season, they are compelled to also farm during the conventional farming season. As such, they end up using all the seed during the conventional farming season. Respondents emphasised that access to inputs such as seeds from the government was uneven with very few directly benefitting. Lenias explained thus:

> When we harvest, we have to make sure that we keep stock for next year's planting season despite the fact that the harvest is not enough for household consumption ... Our major challenge is seed from the previous harvest, which is prone to destruction by pests like green weevils, thus reducing their germination chances.

Social relations are important in accessing crucial inputs such as seed and fertilisers. Establishing firm relations with those benefitting from the limited government supply of seed and fertilisers gives some farmers access to inputs. Sometimes farmers can use such social resources to foster balanced reciprocity and gift exchange. Those with large *mabbonzyi* portions also gave part of their portions to those without portions but who had access to inputs. Spiwe noted that:

> My auntie is old and always has access to donations of seed from the government; ... as a result, we share the seed ... I also cut part of my portion on the river and gave her family 46 lines for her to cultivate ... We are a family; we help each other in times of need.

Contribution of *Mabbonzyi* farming to livelihoods in Negande

This section looks at the contribution of *mabbonzyi* farming in Negande. The magnitude of the contribution of *mabbonzyi* differs according to size of farming portion, household size, access to credit/cash for inputs, and means to pursue other augmenting livelihoods options. As such, the contribution of *mabbonzyi* varied from one household to another depending on their respective capital (financial, human and natural) endowments. The larger one's piece of land on the river, the bigger the harvest. Also linked to high productivity is the strategic position of the *mabbonzyi* portion. Portions in the middle of the river yield relatively huge harvests because they hold moisture for a long period. Farmers with alternative employment have comparatively higher yields than those who solely depend on *mabbonzyi* farming. Chatembwa, a teacher by profession noted:

> *Mabbonzyi* is invaluable in complementing my other survival strategies; ... last year, my off-river fields did not yield anything due to floods. I had to make up for the loss through *mabbonzyi*. This year again, I did not get anything from conventional farming due to floods ... I am heavily counting on

these mabbonzyi maize crops. Last year, I had two scotch cartloads of maize from *mabbonzyi*. The bulk of the produce is for household consumption. When I get good harvests as I did last year I also reserve some few buckets of maize, which I use for *maricho* [informal work assistance] from fellow villagers to clear the fields for the next season. Every year I have seed set aside for *mabbonzyi* in advance as part of my portion is quite some metres away from the middle of the river and it loses moisture.

In some instances, some who have access to larger portions of *mabbonzyi* land also directly turn natural capital (land) into a source of financial capital. These 'landlords' apportioned their *mabbonzyi* fields into smaller segments from which they received reasonable amounts of cash through renting them for a season. Tigere, one of the landlords, explained:

> I rent out part of my *mabbonzyi* as I have a large portion that I cannot farm on my own with limited access to seed … People would expect me to cut out portions to give to my kin and affine relations but if I do that, we will all starve because they are also poorly resourced. Hence, it is better for me to help them through remitting some of the accruing revenue from the rented portion; the least amount that I charge is US$25.00, but it varies with the size of the portion.

Those opting to rent are socially differentiated from the rest of 'common villagers' because they have access to other means of making money through for instance part time employment from occasional donors that came with food relief and related programmes in Negande. Tapera, who has been on contract with an NGO, CordAid since 2012 asserted:

> [Conventional] farming during the rainy season has been yielding very little returns for years. *Mabbonzyi* have been comparatively helpful. I do not have a portion of my own but I make sure that I keep some money aside for renting from Tigere every season. Fertilisers, draught power and intensive labour is required for conventional farming, unlike for *mabbonzyi*, so I will continue renting portions of *mabbonzyi* for my family's survival.

Rural communities worldwide are characterised by heterogeneity that results in differentiated livelihoods strategies and outcomes. The same was evident in Negande. While a few respondents took *mabbonzyi* as a temporary livelihood strategy, the majority of those who engaged in the activity were largely dependent on it for their very survival. Paradoxically, *mabbonzyi* is a seasonal activity and can only take a household through an average of three to four months from the time that they harvest the crop between late June and August. This renders most people prone to chronic food shortages. The majority who depended heavily on *mabbonzyi* were those from lower societal groupings especially widowed women without sufficient human capital to diversify their livelihoods. Melody, one of the female focus group participants highlighted:

Mabbonzyi is where our lives entirely rest on but it does not last us the whole year. It lasts only for a few months. We do not survive from even *sadza* … Look at our skin; does it reflect the skin of people who survive from *sadza*? Usually I get three to six 50kg bags and this, given the size of my household, barely lasts us three months. By December, the stock will have dried up and I have to wait for food donations that usually come in February.

Mabbonzyi and livelihoods studies

Data in this study substantiate the generalisation in rural livelihoods scholarship (Chirau *et al.* 2014, Jowah 2009, Bernstein 1992) that 'agriculture is the mainstay of rural economies'. The influence of agro-ecological regions though is significant (Phiri and Dube 2013) because it directly affects the contribution of agriculture for rural households in different regions across space and time, including within Zimbabwe. A relativist and comparative approach that takes cognisance of regional peculiarities reflective of different rural economies avoids generalisations in terms of our understanding of rurality. As such, this study concludes that rurality is context specific and has differentiated susceptibility to vulnerability as well as in terms of the strategies that people devise to cope with crop failure.

The study also resonates well with the livelihoods framework and literature that rural households try to diversify their livelihoods to cope (and even to adapt) in the face of vulnerability to livelihoods constraints. *Mabbonzyi* is a conscious attempt to traverse the persistent failure of conventional farming. The capacity of *mabbonzyi* farmers to cope in terms of activities that are beyond the farm depend on an array of capital endowments inclusive of human capital (knowledge), access to natural capital (for those that rented their portions in exchange for cash) and social resources (access to *mabbonzyi* portions, seed and food donations though relations).

Environmental institutions, notably the EMA in this regard, are social structures that constrain riverbed farmers' attempts to construct livelihoods because of the illegal status they impose on *mabbonzyi*. *Mabbonzyi* therefore is a land use practice that falls outside the norm of environmental conservation discourse. Here, one sees the broader challenges faced given the mantra of sustainable development. *Mabbonzyi* farming reveals clearly that livelihoods are context-dependent in terms of their construction and viability. Social institutions can play a fundamental role in enhancing households' capabilities to be resilient, and to overcome ill-being and starvation. EMA, instead of enhancing the capacity of households to move out of the risk posed by the persistent flooding and droughts, added to the risk by making *mabbonzyi* illegal.

Paradoxically, institutions in Negande also play an enabling role; they help households to adapt to livelihoods risk, for instance by augmenting the meagre agricultural produce of the farmers through food donations. Such inputs especially by NGOs are invaluable. However, we should not exaggerate the importance of this support as it tends to be seasonal and focuses only on reducing the problem and not alleviating or overcoming the problem. A question not peculiar to this study is then: what role should external support play in terms of aiding vulnerable households to overcome risk and be self-reliant?

Francis (2010) suggests that we must think of people's livelihoods as reactions to the external environment rather than as 'coping strategies'. The use of 'coping', 'survival' and 'strategies' conceals the depth of despair in which people find themselves (Mate 2010, Taru 2013). These arguments concur with the realities faced by *mabbonzyi* farmers. Looking at their livelihoods options and pursuits in terms of ad hoc and fluctuating reactions better suits the empirical reality. Viewing farmers as 'strategising' at all times easily leads to the depiction of all households being endowed with the capability to cope with livelihoods in a highly rational manner.

Mabbonzyi farming exudes a multi-dimensional social embeddedness of livelihoods. First, if EMA has indeed legalised *mabbonzyi* in Nengade, then livelihoods are entangled in social conflicts. The spreading of false rumours by those who do not own *mabbonzyi* portions exposes *mabbonzyi* farmers to livelihoods failure through a delay of their planting preparations. Second, the use of social relations to access inputs also points to the dependence of livelihoods on the social context in which they exist. There is, however, need to avoid romanticising the role of social relations because in some cases it leads to limited yields for farmers who helped their relations by cutting off their *mabbonzyi* portions. Hence, livelihoods studies need to be sceptical about the contribution of social capital to livelihoods construction.

Mabbonzyi is unsustainable in the end. In even using minimum tillage techniques, farmers are eroding the riverbed despite concerns not to do so. This is attributable to ecological marginality and the context in which the people's livelihoods exist. Conventional natural resources conservation and popular environmental degradation narratives attribute environmental degradation to the lack of capacity by locals to be custodians of their natural environments. On the contrary, it is alienation from resources that results in risky livelihoods by locals and this, in the process, depletes the natural resource base. Further, due to poor physical capital development (road networks especially), *mabbonzyi* farmers are incapacitated in terms of seeking outward safety nets (migration to other areas to seek alternative employment). Migration of household members in search of paid income can be of significance, but we must take cognisance of the fact that contexts exist in which to migrate is a mammoth task on its own.

Inter- and intra-household stratification along the lines of capital endowments and capabilities (Francis 2010) is important because such dynamics shape the success or failure of individuals to cope or be resilient during times of livelihoods stress and shocks. Vulnerability of livelihoods to stress and shocks, just like poverty more broadly, also has a gendered dimension. This study reveals that female-headed households appeared less able to 'constructively react' and meaningfully 'cope' with persistent flooding, droughts and hunger. This concurs with livelihoods scholarship that emphasises the gendered nature of access to vital livelihoods resources (particularly land) and the marginalisation of women (Bhatasara 2011, Prowse 2010, Chirau *et al.* 2014). Rather than looking at rural livelihoods with a general focus on the household as a unit of analysis, livelihoods research must also narrow its analysis to individuals and how they fare.

Conclusion and policy insights

Overall, rural livelihoods in Zimbabwe cannot be generalised as they take place within different ecological conditions that determine people's respective reactions to the vulnerability conditions to which they and their households find themselves subjected. Many invaluable analytical tools for livelihoods studies (such as diversification and coping strategies) need to be considered carefully because what works for one household, village or district may not apply in another. In the case of Negande, while households engaged in a number of activities for survival (but most notably, *mabbonzyi*) in the face of severe vagaries of environmental marginality and hazards, these were mostly seasonal and not sufficient for adequate survival and well-being for most households. The study thus agrees with Cannon's (2008) claim that households, in responding to livelihoods shocks and stress, may not in fact improve their livelihoods and may experience deterioration. Therefore, making simplistic assessments of households as being resilient to shock might be a misguided conclusion.

Responsible authorities should put measures in place to curb siltation as well as conserve the little rain that obtains in Negande during the rainy season. This might involve rainwater harvesting and educating people in Negande on how they can harness the water resources in Mawena River without degrading the river. If a viable water-harvesting scheme were to arise, it could result in the establishment of an irrigation system that does not lead to siltation of the river as *mabbonzyi* does. The government can also consider revising the fast track land reform programme and move Negande people to areas that are suitable for agriculture. There is also need for adequate and equitable provision of credit and inputs for all the residents of Negande. Finally, the government should consider developing good roads in Negande to necessitate easy livelihoods outsourcing and access to markets.

Notes

1 This refers in particular to the Department of National Parks and Wildlife Authority and the Communal Areas Management Programme for Indigenous Resources (CAMP-FIRE) arrangement. The NyamiNyami Rural District Council controls the latter. All these institutions vest ownership of land and natural resources in the hands of the state and curtail rural livelihoods options by restricting natural resource use and access by rural communities in NyamiNyami.
2 Such criteria were also not straightforward and some respondents claimed that they did not receive any support despite meeting the requirements.

References

Baslwizi Trust. 2010. *Sustainable Development Support for a Poverty Free Zambezi Valley* Strategic Plan 2010–2015.

Bhatasara, S. 2011. Women, land and poverty in Zimbabwe: Deconstructing the impacts of the Fast Track Land Reform Program. *Journal of Sustainable Development in Africa*, 13 (1): 316–330.

Cannon, T. 2008. *Reducing people's vulnerability to natural hazards communities and resilience*, Research paper/UNU-WIDER, No. 2008.34, ISBN 978-92-9230-080-7.

Chambers, R. and Conway, G. 1992. *Sustainable Rural Livelihoods: Practical Concepts for the 21st Century*. IDS Paper No. 296. Sussex: Institute of Development Studies.

Chirau, T., Nkambule, S. and Mupambwa, G. 2014. Rural Livelihoods in Zimbabwe: Heterogeneity, Diversification and Vulnerability. *International Journal of Innovation and Applied Studies*, 5 (1): 5–15.

Dzingirai, V. 1999. *Human Migration and Natural Resources Management in Communal Lands: The Case of Binga in Zimbabwe:* Dphil. Centre for Applied Social Sciences: University of Zimbabwe.

Dzingirai, V. 2003a. CAMPFIRE is not for Ndebele Migrants: The Impact of Excluding Outsiders from CAMPFIRE in the Zambezi Valley, Zimbabwe. *Journal of Southern African Studies*, 29 (2): 445–459.

Dzingirai, V. 2003b. The New Scramble for the African Countryside. *Development and Change*, 34 (2): 243–263.

Francis, E. 2010. Rural Livelihoods, Institutions and Vulnerability in North West Province, South Africa. *Journal of Southern African Studies*, 28 (3): 531–550.

Mashingaidze, T.M. 2013. Beyond the Kariba Dam Induced Displacements: The Zimbabwean Tonga's Struggles for Restitution, 1990s-2000s. *International Journal on Minority and Group Rights*, 20 (3): 381–404.

Mashinya, J. 2007. *Participation and Devolution in Zimbabwe's Campfire Program: Findings from Local Projects in Mahenye and Nyami-Nyami*. Phd Dissertation. University of Maryland, College Park.

Mate, R. 2010. Feminist Responses to the Neo-Liberal Global Economic Order. *Buwa!* 1(1), www.osisa.org/buwa/womens-rights/regional/feminist-responses-neoliberal-global-economic-order [Accessed 30 October 2017].

Metcalfe, S. 1994. The Zimbabwe Communal Area Management Programme for Indigenous Resources. In D. Western and D. Wright (eds), *Natural Connections: Perspectives in Community-based Conservation* (pp. 161–192). Washington, DC: Island Press.

Mubaya, C.P. 2008. *Community-Based Natural Resources Management (CBNRN) in Distress: Experiences from Omay Communal Lands, Zimbabwe*. Indiana University: Digital Library Commons.

Musona, M. 2011. *An Exploration of the Causes of Social Unrest in Omay Communal Lands of Nyami Nyami district in Zimbabwe: A Human Needs Perspective*. Nelson Mandela Metropolitan University https://dlc.dlib.indiana.edu/dlc/handle/10535/1195

Nkamleu, G.B. 2011. *Extensification Versus Intensification: Revisiting the Role of Land in African Agricultural Growth*. African Development Bank: C\conference\AEC\AEC.

Prowse, M. 2010. Integrating Reflexivity into Livelihoods Research, *Progress in Development Studies*, 10 (3): 211–231.

Sakdapolrak, P. 2014. Livelihoods as Social Practices – Re-energising Livelihoods Research with Bourdieu's Theory of Practice, *Geographica Helvetica*, 69: 19–28.

Save the Children. 2004. *Household Economy Assessments, Binga and Nyaminyami (Kariba Rural) Districts, Matabeleland North and Mashonaland West Provinces, Zimbabwe*. April–May 2004. Save the Children (UK), Harare.

Scoones, I. 1998. *Sustainable Livelihoods: A Framework for Analysis*. IDS, Working Paper 72, IDS, Brighton, UK, June 1998.

Scott, J.C. 1985. *Weapons of the Weak: Everyday Forms of Peasant Resistance*. New Haven. Yale University Press.

Sibanda, B.M.C. 2001. *Wildlife and Communities at the Crossroads: Is Zimbabwe's Campfire the Way Forward?* Harare: SAPES Books.

Taru, J. 2013. NGO Projects and Urban Livelihood Activities: Lessons from Institutionalized Urban Gardens in Masvingo. *Basic Research Journal of Social and Political Sciences*, 2 (1): 4−11.

11 "Let them starve so that they 'hear' us"

Differing perspectives on unresolved land occupations and livelihoods at Mushandike smallholder irrigation scheme, Masvingo District

Jonathan Mafukidze

Introduction

Since 1999 black producers at Mushandike Smallholder Irrigation Scheme, in the Masvingo District in Zimbabwe have experienced unprecedented invasion of their land by hundreds of land-seekers. The land-seekers occupied grazing land across the entire irrigation scheme, built homes, opened up crop fields and grazed their animals at will. Many more continue trickling in, to this day. This unceremonious entry altered the social space, imposed new relations and pro-voked a delicately negotiated yet unavoidable coexistence between irrigators and land-seekers. This case study, based on findings from interviews, observation and focus group discussions, interrogates prevailing perceptions of this phenom-enon and its implication on local lives. It examines the challenges experienced and the understanding of issues by locals and by politicians.

Findings suggest that local views weave a complex mosaic of perspectives studded with emotion. Politics, power, greed, maladministration, corruption, land hunger and 'ignorance' emerged as explanations of causes of the invasions and their deferred resolution. Explaining his view of why the issue remains unsolved, a Zimbabwe African National Union – Patriotic Front (ZANU-PF) stalwart and Member of Parliament argued, "We are concerned with stability, not expediency, we can't reserve land for cattle when people need it: do cattle vote?" As talk rages on, livelihoods rapidly deteriorate due to acute land short-age. The study recommends that land should be allocated to the land-seekers on two neighbouring farms purportedly occupied by local Chief Charumbira and the late Minister Stan Mudenge.

This chapter thus provides an understanding of diverse perspectives on black-on-black land invasions, deferred state intervention to resolve them and their impact on livelihoods. It pays attention to how socio-economic and political real-ities shape these matters and how they subsequently affect relations within and between the Mushandike Smallholder Irrigation Scheme's farming population, land-seekers and other stakeholders. The main goal of this chapter is to identify and analyse how contestation for access and ownership of resources (notably land and water) becomes framed, negotiated and resolved at the local level (the Mushandike Irrigation Scheme). Secondary goals include the following: to identify and examine the socio-spatial environment that triggers contestations and how certain interests gain dominance; to analyse how local communities as agents participate in processes of inclusion and exclusion; and to discuss the role of the state and political parties in exacerbating or resolving contestations at the local level.

Irrigation scheme literature on Zimbabwe

The establishment of Mushandike, like that of other state-instituted smallholder irrigation projects across Zimbabwe, is aimed at modernising smallholder agriculture to improve food security, to help break the cycle of rural poverty and to increase incomes (Musara *et al.* 2010, Samakande *et al.* 2004). However, at Mushandike, the occupations beginning in 1999 (and continuing unabated) derailed this. There is a rich body of literature on smallholder irrigation in Zimbabwe. This literature focuses on themes such as: the evolution and location of smallholder irrigation schemes (Harvey *et al.* 1987, Manzungu 1995); water availability and management, inputs, infrastructure availability, technology provision and productivity (Mupawose 1984, Pazvakawambwa and Van Der Zaag 2001); and food security, employment creation and non-agricultural uses of water and electricity (Svubure and Zawe 2010). But the multi-faceted and ambivalent social relations that develop within a 'community' of irrigators and between them and land-invaders and surrounding communities are not significantly addressed, and it is this lacuna in particular that this study seeks to fill.

Some studies do in part address this. For instance, Magadlela and Hebinck (1995) point to strained relations between resettled irrigation farmers and surrounding (indigenous) communities over land 'ownership' and the distortion of inheritance customs (*nhaka*) by external decision-makers. Such a distortion tends to affect social relations, identity and productivity. Because of such concerns, Samakande *et al.* (2004) argue for a reduction of external interference at the irrigation scheme level. Turning to internal contestations, Madebwe and Madebwe (2005) reveal, with reference to the Ndongoma irrigation scheme, that some women farmers' productivity is constrained by spousal interferences. Pazvaka-wambwa and van der Zaag (2001) and Samakande *et al.* (2004) also touch on contestation and consensus over distribution and use of irrigation water within some irrigation schemes. Therefore, improvement in the performance of smallholder irrigation schemes lies in addressing both socio-political and technological issues (Manzungu 1995). This chapter points to another dimension hitherto inadequately addressed, and that is the complications drawing from scheme invasions not only in relation to production but also around how this phenomenon is framed by external actors and the impact that has on multi-stakeholder involvement.

Black-on-black land invasions that occurred at Mushandike Smallholder Irrigation Scheme from 1999 do not have much of a precedence in the recent history of Zimbabwe; and they mean many things to many different people. One old man conceptualised them as ZANU-PF's "political bad breath", throwing an undeniable yet embarrassing stench on the world arena. They are also seemingly discordant with the supposed logic of struggles for land in Zimbabwe, which are invariably seen as racially based. To others, the invasions are a blow to developmental efforts; to many more, they led to devastation on livelihoods, identity, sense of community and belonging.

It seems clear that questions around identity and interest are at the centre of these land invasions and subsequent contestations for domination and struggles for survival. Sociologically, identities tend to be a vital resource deployed to open or close entry into socio-spatial and economic realms during contestations (Harris 2002). In the case of Mushandike, this entails groupings of people who share (and differ at times on) national, racial, regional and ethnic identities. Importantly, identity-based groupings co-existed in the Mushandike area for many decades. After the invasions, both scheme and non-scheme members use varied constructions of insider-outsider binaries to include and exclude others. The practices of the (national and local) state and political parties often contributed to this.

The study area

The Mushandike Smallholder Irrigation Scheme lies approximately 20 kilometres southwest of Masvingo City. It is located in the southern tip of Masvingo District, which borders six other districts namely Bikita, Chiredzi, Chivi, Gutu, Mwenezi and Zaka. Much of Masvingo Province (56,566 square kilometres in size) is found in agro-ecological regions IV and V (arid and too harsh for crop farming) except for small parts of Gutu, Zaka, Bikita and Masvingo districts that are in agro-ecological region III. In essence, the province is largely unsuitable for crop production, and more so for rain-fed cultivation. The rural poor in Masvingo Province clearly live in a harsh environment. That is why Mushandike is an attractive destination for those seeking to engage in crop production.

Mushandike was established in the 1980s. Scheme members treasure and cherish it. Their adoration is encapsulated by one female scheme member, namely Mazvi's, words: "Mushandike is Canaan, overflowing with milk and honey". This somewhat hyperbolic view however speaks more of Mushandike's past and potential as opposed to the chaos currently obtaining on the ground. The scheme comprises of sections known as villages. Villages 1–9 and 17–20 are not part of the irrigation scheme as they practice rain-fed cultivation. The irrigation scheme initially comprised of villages 11–16 and 21–23. According to findings, Village 23B was later added on at the behest of the then Chief Charumbira for people from his area. Village 10 remained uninhabited many years after all other villages were fully operational. It was only occupied after Chief Charumbira requested to resettle his people who were being evicted from privately owned land at Morgenster College. Although Village 10 (unlike the rest of the villages under the irrigation scheme) has no overnight dams − nor any concrete secondary or tertiary canals, or properly designed irrigation fields – beneficiaries were allowed to irrigate.

The first group of beneficiaries arrived at Mushandike in 1986 and was allocated land in Village 13. Gradually many others followed. Upon arrival, beneficiaries were given government support that included training, inputs and assistance with land preparation. They were also trained in environmental conservation, flood irrigation, and crop and animal husbandry among other things. Every Zimbabwean was free to try to join; however, the most preferred, according to Agricultural Technical and Extension Services (Agritex) officials were "poor, landless farmers who were prepared to be fulltime farmers". Government officials, under the leadership of a Resettlement Officer, were to hold interviews to choose the most suitable candidates.. Successful candidates were allocated plot numbers by lot for transparency purposes.

Most scheme beneficiaries came from the land-starved communal areas of Chivi, Nyajena and Mapanzure, all of which lie a walkable distance from Mushandike. A few others came from neighbouring Charumbira communal area and other parts of the country. Each farmer was allocated 1.5 hectares of irrigated land, a residential stand and had access to communally controlled grazing land. Many people, even those within the vicinity such as Charumbira communal area, refrained from joining because they were averse to being 'exploited' by the government; rumours circulating at the time suggested that the government was going to demand a share of the produce from every farmer. Similar concerns were also recorded at Murara irrigation scheme in Mutoko (FAO 2000). This suggests that communication might have been ineffective during the inception phase of such smallholder irrigation schemes.

The scheme was designed to carry 417 smallholder farmers. This number was linked to the capacity of the dam to supply sufficient irrigation water, according to Agritex officials. The initial idea, again according to Agritex officials, was that the capacity of the dam would allow it to supply sufficient irrigation water for a period of three years even without receiving a single raindrop (with each of the 417 farmers irrigating a maximum of 1.5 hectares per season). However, there was no adherence to this idea during implementation. For undisclosed reasons the scheme started off with over 600 farmers excluding those of Village 23B and Village 10 who joined at later stages.

After it started operating, Mushandike gave beneficiaries better access to natural resources (including land) compared to those who remained in communal areas. In light of their ongoing restricted access to land and water, residents of Charumbira and other communal areas in the province soon began to seek access to the scheme. The findings suggest that Chief Charumbira took it upon himself to ensure that his people also benefited. His efforts resulted in the establishment of Village 23B, which borders his communal area, just for his people. Later on, as discussed below, he was also able to resettle many others in Village 10. Further efforts by him to control Mushandike form part of the complexities of the land invasions. The government bequeathed the land to beneficiaries, and issued them with occupancy cards but no title deeds. This fertile land was acquired from large-scale white commercial farmers under the willing-buyer willing-seller arrangement governing commercial land transfer in the 1980s (Palmer 1990). The main canal and dam were already in place. However, the government made several improvements such as turning the canal from gravel into concrete. The scheme now has hundreds of land-seekers settled on the grazing land. There is no clarity on how they ended up there, and what the future holds for them. These are some of the issues discussed in this study.

Research methods

The study was explorative in nature hence it employed a qualitative approach to data collection and analysis. It was carried out within weekly intermittent periods between 2014 and 2017. The case study method was used with Mushandike being the socio-spatial environment selected for the study. The case study method helps with the investigation of contemporary phenomena within a real-life context (Yin 2003). More importantly, it allows for investigating the extent to which relations vary across time-periods and seasons (Harvey *et al.* 1987). Additionally, it facilitates contextual encounters with perceptions, views, emotions, ideas, narratives, stories and voices of a people within a life-world. Permission to enter the field area was sought from Village Heads upon arrival at every village. Their positivity was highly commendable. Generally, the field experience was characterised by a high level of cooperation. The District Administrator (DA) was deliberately visited much later due to the fear of encountering bureaucratic delays. He was not amused that I visited his office after spending close to three weeks in the field. I offered an apology and all went well.

Respondents (both irrigators and invaders) based at the scheme were selected through purposive sampling also known as judgemental sampling. This technique accords researchers the leeway to use their discretion or judgement to select respondents influenced by such factors as gender, age, marital status, socio-economic status, political affiliation and so on (Palys 2008). This was purposively done to enrich findings. Thirty respondents were purposively selected and interviewed. I also conducted four focus groups, engaged in transect walks and held sixteen key informant interviews. Key informants were drawn from local people in authority. Information was thus gathered through in-depth interviews (structured and unstructured), observation and focus group discussions.

The in-depth interviews were held with various respondents including government officials, politicians, farmers, traditional leaders, land-invaders, and extension and veterinary officers. Furthermore, numerous days and long hours spent in the field allowed for both participation and observation. Observation is very valuable as it allows for accessing data through encounters and interactions rather than through the use of questions (DeWalt *et al.* 1998). As regards participation, I attended several meetings and gatherings. I also participated in various farming activities with different households. This gave respondents ample time to freely tell their story. It also affirmed the agency and selfhood of each respondent. Narratives, as observed by Brubaker and Cooper (2000), help in understanding how individuals and groups have relationally progressed over time. As pointed out by Denzin (1997), this produces sufficient data to allow for the production of a life-story of a people as interpreted by me, the investigator. Data was thematically analysed both in-field and post-field. Prominent themes were identified and used to shape the analytical framework. Themes helped with describing, understanding and discussing the prominent issues that emerged.

Analysing the social dynamics at Mushandike

Three important findings are discussed here. First, the apparent black-on-black Mushandike land invasions (which entrenched the marginalisation and exclusion of the poor) were 'deliberate' and power-led illegal political land allocations, subtly framed and articulated by the state. The political goals were long-term (to effect significant favourable demographic changes that would influence electoral outcomes), hence the land-seekers at Mushandike were 'overlooked' by the government-led, nationwide Fast Track Land Reform Programme (FTLRP) that began in June 2000 and resettled most of the people who had invaded white owned farms. Second, findings also suggest that the poor tend to stay close to the state, regardless of its form, because they view it as their last feasible hope of accessing resources. This explains why, as long as there is a flicker of hope of some possible gain, the poor tend to acquiesce to exploitation or other forms of ill-treatment. Third, immiseration remains an effective political tool, though diabolic. Evidence shows that the land invasions (which were largely illegal allocations) had a negative impact on the livelihoods, security and sense of community of both the host and incoming populations.

These findings give impetus to Miriro's (a female irrigator) view that the government, manipulated by politicians, is saying: "Let them starve that they 'hear' us". This view suggests that there is a perception amongst some at Mushandike that people in power deploy the tactic of controlling through impoverishment. Engaging with these findings, this section begins with a discussion of perspectives on causes of 'land invasions', then proceeds to perspectives on how the land allocation played itself out, and ends with perspectives on the implications on livelihoods.

Black-on-black land invasions: ignorance and in the name of politics

Perspectives discussed here are those of the state represented by the District Administrator. He succinctly gave 'ignorance' as the factor that caused land seekers to occupy peripheral land at Mushandike, at a time when the land-hungry across the country were occupying white-owned land. He suggested that, "People were genuinely looking for land and thought all open land … was free, they did not realise … it was earmarked for other activities, they were ignorant".

Importantly, the many study visits I had to Mushandike over three years, did not yield a confirmation of his perspective from numerous other stakeholders. Asked to explain how hundreds would be so naïve that they all blindly invaded the wrong place whilst there were two white-owned farms bordering Mushandike and none strayed into them, he was brief: "I can't explain it". In addition, asked what he thought about the claim that land-seekers were channelled into Mushandike because Chief Charumbira and late Minister Mudenge were going to occupy the two neighbouring farms, he simply said, "I can't speak for politicians". He then shifted focus to what he thinks matters now: "All we want now is stability, let no one compromise stability, those people will be moved, I don't know to where and when but for now we want peace". Interestingly, many of the initial arrivals amongst the land-invaders (land-seekers) were from Charumbira communal area; therefore, they somehow already knew Mushandike as the two communities are simply separated by the old Beitbridge-Masvingo road. More importantly, to reach villages 11, 12, 13, 14 and 15 like some did, from Charumbira area, one has to walk past the two above noted formerly white-owned farms.

By framing the arrival and stay of hundreds of land-seeking households on an occupied, black-owned smallholder irrigation scheme as an act of ignorance, the official deliberately tried to frame the land occupations in accordance with official discourse. The official view, according to our findings, was that this had to be understood as a genuine mistake that occurred during a process of land seeking. This was because the invasions went contrary to the dominant racialised historical discourse and practice of recovering land from whites whose ancestors colonised it (Palmer 1990). Such framing helps to project issues to the advantage of the speaker/writer in this case through deliberate lack of analysis (Chari 2013:292). Furthermore, framing accords one the liberty to promote a particular view and allows one to bend the truth so as to influence others to think in a certain way. The ignorance argument is therefore a political rather than an administrative explanation of a phenomenon. Land invasions were deliberately framed as based on ignorance rather than actual intent to occupy black-owned land, in order to create a positive view of the situation.

The dominant perspective amongst scheme members, encapsulated in the voices of John and Samuel, is that people were allocated land at Mushandike for political reasons. It is common knowledge around Mushandike that from the scheme's inception and until the late 1990s a Resettlement Officer (RO) administered it. Chiefs had no direct leadership role to play in the scheme. This view finds support in Jacobs (1991:522) who notes that all land resettlement schemes were established in spaces declared independent of the jurisdiction of traditional authorities. Elected officials at the village level assisted the RO. Each village was led by a Production Chairman (in charge of production) and a Village Chairman (in charge of domestic issues in the village), who were assisted by other elected members.

The withdrawal of the RO by government due to a change of administrative thrust in the late 1990s is alleged to have created a power vacuum, which many players, the Chief included, pounced upon. Backed by politicians for purposes discussed below, the Chief gained entry and took charge. To consolidate power, he quickly removed the elected Village Chairmen and replaced them with his self-appointed Village Heads. In supporting the Chief to gain control of Mushandike, ruling party politicians sought to win it back politically from the Movement for Democratic Change (MDC) (the largest opposition party at that time) which had just established dominance amongst irrigators. The Village Heads were the Chief's foot soldiers, tasked with populating the scheme with supporters of the ruling party (ZANU-PF) so as to outvote the opposition during voting at every level of social organisation at the local level, it was reported in interviews.

When land-seekers began to arrive and settle on grazing land in late 1999, scheme members reported the issue to government, only to be advised that it was a political issue and could only be addressed by politicians. The FTLRP that began in June 2000 targeted land issues everywhere else except at Mushandike. The reason a government official gave for this was "Mushandike was overlooked". Findings suggest that ironically in 2000, politicians continued to bring in more land-seekers instead of removing those already there. A prominent politician from ZANU-PF is said to have brought in a large group of land-seekers and spoke at a rally saying, according to Samuel, "Where we come from, every metre of land has a person on it, don't complain that we brought too many people here". At another rally, similar sentiments were echoed by another politician, who as noted by John argued, "Where we live, if a person gets stubborn, we resettle people in his own house. You want to keep land for cattle: do cattle vote? Let us neutralise the enemy first, then we will deal with the rest". From then on, it was clear that land allocations were for neutralising the MDC through resettling ZANU-PF supporters.

Practice here projects a state entrenching marginalisation through manipulating land-seekers for political reasons in the guise of land allocation. It contradicts the views of Hendricks (2003:1) that, in a post-colonial democracy, redistribution should necessarily promote participation in social, economic and political spaces. Land allocation should assuage rather than entrench marginalisation. The Mushandike experience legitimates the view that at times the post-colonial state compounds the predicament of the poor instead of redressing historical injustices related to access to resources (Peters *et al.* 2002). Legitimate expectations are that the post-colonial state has to avail productive land to the poor to solve economic, productivity, poverty and identity issues (Walker 2005:807). When individuals or groups access land, their sense of identity, community and national belonging is expected to change for the better (Woodward 2000). Access to land therefore, addresses identity concerns and improves the diversity and quality of livelihoods and in so doing enables the formerly excluded to enjoy social citizenship (Hendricks 2003).

We are not invaders

The purpose of this subsection is to pay attention to perspectives of land-seeking immigrants themselves, with regards to how land was accessed. Our findings suggest that the Village Head allocated land. Evidence portrays the poor not as victims but proactive people striving to better their existence, though in unorthodox ways. Their vulnerability is clear but they do not construct themselves or their relationship with the world as characterised by victimhood but by aspirations and hope for a positive change.

Mhandami, a land-seeker, argued that on their own, land-seekers would not have succeeded in invading black-owned land because they would have met ZANU-PF orchestrated violence that was directed towards all those purported to be derailing the land struggle. He argued that land-invaders would have positioned themselves as enemies of the ruling party, opposing the idea of taking land from whites and that could have proved futile. He said that, "If we had done that I could be showing you a couple of graves. Instead getting land here was the easiest thing ever". He revealed that he heard, whilst in Masvingo town, that land was available at Mushandike and immediately went there. Upon arrival, he spoke to the Village Head who allocated him a residential stand about an acre in size and two more acres for crop cultivation. Land was allocated to Mhandami at no charge although he had to pay a US$25 "administrative fee". To Mhandami, the Village Head is a man who understood the plight of the landless evidenced by the fact that "he addressed the landlessness of so many".

To substantiate that such allocations were above board, Mhandami indicated that every year their Village Head takes them to the chief's farm where they cultivate the fields "according to *Zunde raMambo* tradition". This is a tradition predominantly practiced by the Shona people where members of a community either cultivate grain crops in the chief's fields or make contributions of a certain quantity of a specific grain or grains which will be stored at the chief's place for feeding orphans, the sick and the needy in the event of a drought. He argued that he knows that what they are doing is not exactly how the tradition works. However, the main importance of the visits, for him, is that each time the chief allows them to work on his land he indirectly acknowledges their stay at Mushandike. More importantly, he views tilling the chief's land as a gesture of gratitude to the "Chief of Chiefs" who gave them land. Many affectionately call Charumbira Chief of Chiefs because he is the President of Zimbabwe's Council of Chiefs.

Even Ndondo, who arrived more than a decade after others, reveals that land is accessed for free. However, he argues that there is nothing wrong with showing from the beginning that you will express your gratitude monetarily if allocated land. He said, "Some say I corrupted the Village Head to get land. But I only thanked him for rescuing me, I had been condemned to Masangura in Chiredzi, imagine, of all places". Allegedly, Masangura is one of the barren places where people who were removed to make way for the Tokwe/Mukosi dam were resettled. Views of land-seekers in this study confirm the observation elsewhere that, "many remain drawn to the state because ... it remains a major source of spoils and one of the only available channels for getting what little there is to get" (Cruise O'Brien 1996:56). It is evident from these findings that the state, regardless of its character and even failings, remains the axis of socio-economic and political life for the rural poor (Neocosmos 2003). The state evidently functions as the central organ for the distribution of resources (Post 1996). The Village Heads distribute land belonging to fellow irrigators with impunity, reflecting that the state represents a concentration of power for those in control.

Furthermore, it is evident that, in the struggle for access to resources, those who are well represented within the state benefit from it more than others do. For instance, ruling party supporters ended up assuming part-ownership of land already owned by others. It is also evident that the state in Africa responds favourably to the desire of those in power for 'predatory' accumulation, as Neocosmos (2003) observes. To confirm this, a chief and a government minister openly occupy a nearby farm each, while hundreds of households at Mushandike remain excluded. However, the poor, as shown above reveal agency as they strive to improve themselves. As social actors, they position themselves, strategise and negotiate, seeking to maximise benefits while minimising damages (Gould 1997, Woodward 2000). However, the gamble of settling at Mushandike is a huge one. Whether or not this gamble will prove profitable to land-seekers is yet to be seen.

The state's impoverishment of the local population

In this context, this subsection interrogates the role of the state at the local level in relation to how it impacts people's lives. It confines itself to "low politics" as opposed to "high politics", that is, simply to the "politics of everyday life" as above (Webner 1996:7). Customary authority (chiefs and headmen) here represents the state. In this regard, the state orchestrates immiseration at Mushandike so as to enact control of local populations. As it was summed up in Miriro's words: "Let them starve that they 'hear' us". The research findings show that the politics of land allocations made immiseration possible. It led to poor productivity as the dam dried up, draught power was reduced, and labour demands heightened and crime increased.

Many factors led to the drying up of Mushandike dam. The dam, according to Agritex officials, had the capacity (as indicated previously) to supply sufficient irrigation water to 417 farmers, irrigating 1.5 hectares of land throughout the year, for up to three years, without rainfall. However, increased human and animal presence and land usage exacerbated degradation, which caused increased dam siltation. Animals also damaged the main canal leading to increased seepage. These factors, coupled with increased water usage, evaporation due to high temperatures and poor rainfall patterns led to the drying up of the dam.

Loss of irrigation led to serious suffering, inadequate food supplies and emotional stress. According to Moto, a scheme member,

> We lost much of what we had worked for, we had no income; our land is too small for rain-fed farming ... these granaries will for long be reminders of the suffering we endured, we never had them, we always sold our maize green, but then we had to harvest the little we got for food from 2010 when we could not irrigate because the damn had dried up.

During the drought years, animals strayed into the irrigation fields seeking pasture and caused huge damage to secondary and tertiary canals. When irrigation resumed, the canals needed repairs and this made life much more difficult for the poor farmers.

Loss of grazing land affected the farmers in a number of ways. For the first time, they started herding cattle. Some who did not want to herd had to sell. Others allowed their cattle to graze on their own but some stray onto the Masvingo-Beitbridge highway where a few were killed by speeding haulage trucks. The area stretching a few kilometres either direction from Bhuka Township along the highway is now a notoriously famous black spot due to accidents caused by stray cattle. It is alleged that cattle stray because barbed wire that kept them away from the highway disappeared following the arrival of land-seekers. Now the only available land for cattle grazing is a forest up north used by the army for training. However, it exposes both cattle and herdsmen to explosives. Some explosives do not explode during training thus posing a great danger to intruders. Although there are warning signs around the army site stressing that civilians should not enter, many do not heed that. In 2014, a 21-year-old boy from village 14 detonated an explosive, which killed him instantly.

Population increase was accompanied by a rise in crime. Large numbers of cattle were said to have been stolen at night. The police advised owners to construct kraals closer to homes, which only led to a reduced frequency of stealing but not a stoppage. The police fail to investigate properly the thefts. Locals suspect that resident thieves are working closely with butcheries from Masvingo because animals were in large part slaughtered on site. The community therefore suspects the involvement of someone who sells carcasses. Suspects seek refuge in the ambits of their political parties such that the politicisation of the social space impedes security provision. A Village Head for instance found a senior politician with his 13 missing beasts. The politician only released two oxen and refused to give the rest back, using political muscle in doing so. The overpowered Village Head could not do anything about this.

In response to increasing poverty, locals have diversified their livelihood strategies to survive. Some have migrated to towns across the country while others left for neighbouring countries mainly Botswana and South Africa. Others who remained behind took to gold panning, moulding and selling bricks and/or collecting and selling firewood, activities considered illegal unless one is licensed. Enactment of power appears to have succeeded in turning irrigation farmers and land-seekers into deeply marginalised groups. The thought of 'becoming somebody' has become but an illusion. The lamentations of a young woman summarise this reality:

> I came here as a newlywed, now I am a mother of a teenager, all I have done is wait. Waiting for the unknown, I have endured insults and name-calling. But does it matter; I am just a poor woman.

Conclusion and policy insights

The chapter has shown that although the poor, in striving to make the best of a resource-stressed rural context, tend to innovate, negotiate and improvise for the best possible outcome. However, they come out worse off when they collide with a state that in particular is not impressed with their political allegiances. What is obtaining at Mushandike shows that correcting historical injustices is studded with difficulties, especially due to a lack of resources. Furthermore, it reveals that when an excluded citizenry challenges a state, the latter can be deeply insensitive. Its behaviour oscillates between "domination and the grotesque" (Webner 1996:1).

Cousins' (1997) discussion of the poor elsewhere helps understand why the poor saw it worthwhile to invade other people's land, whether duped or otherwise, and remain there for 16 years. He stresses that the marginalised lack options to the extent that unruly social practices help them challenge legal rules of resource entitlement (Cousins 1997). In so doing they rethink, if not contest, property rights. This usually occurs when many are deprived while a few seem privileged (Cousins 1997). Mushandike appeared as an island of hope and opportunity in a province characterised by immense deprivation. It therefore stood as a symbol of privilege easily attracting admiration and envy. In that regard, formal rules governing ownership and utilisation of resources were challenged causing problems between 'owners' and 'intruders'. However, the meddling of the state makes it difficult to identify where local agency ends and interference by power begins.

It is evident that Zimbabwe's poor who live in marginal, infertile and water stressed regions are prone to political manipulation and abuse due to poverty and marginalisation. This study recommends the following corrective measures to address anomalies and to assuage the suffering of poor going forward. First of all, inclusive land and water reforms should be biased towards resettling people in productive habitable regions so as to begin phasing out farming in peripheral regions. There should be plans to ensure that in the long-run all farmers in regions IV and V have access to irrigation. Second, customary and chiefly authority should be transformed through training in administration, leadership, democracy and human rights. Third, the poor should be equipped to deal with the state through training on citizenship rights and how to seek recourse in the face of the abuse of rights by a state bent on excesses.

The chapter concludes that people's struggles are best understood through critically paying attention to the context in which they occur. This requires seeking to understand the present in relation to place and people, history and culture. This helps understand locally produced realities and perspectives coming out of contestations and struggles. For instance, it would be difficult at first for one to understand why the poor at Mushandike appear to disrespect the name of a chief revered in other parts of the country. However, looking at what obtains on the ground helps one understand, but not necessarily approve of the situation. The chapter also concludes that livelihood strategies, which are intricately related to place, shape local relations and influence responses to inclusion and exclusion. Therefore, the way the weak and vulnerable live reflects their understanding of their socio-political and economic circumstances.

References

Brubaker, R. and Cooper, F. 2000. Beyond "Identity". *Theory and Society*, 29 (1): 1–47.

Chari, T. 2013. Media Framing of Land Reform in Zimbabwe. In S. Moyo and W. Chambati, *Land and Agrarian Reform in Zimbabwe. Beyond White-Settler Capitalism* (pp. 291–329). Dakar: CODESRIA and AIAS.

Cousins, B. 1997. How Do Rights Become Real?: Formal and Informal Institutions South Africa's Land Reform. *IDS Bulletin*, 28 (4): 59–68.

Cruise O'Brien, D.B. 1996. A Lost Generation? Youth Identity and State Decay in West Africa. In R. Werbner and T. Ranger, *Postcolonial Identities in Africa* (pp. 55–74). London: Zed Books.

Denzin, N.K. 1997. *Interpretive Ethnography: Ethnographic Practices for the 21st Century.* Thousand Oaks, London and New Delhi: SAGE Publications.

DeWalt, K.M., DeWalt, B.R. and Wayland, C.B. 1998. Participant Observation. In H.R. Bernard (ed.), *Handbook of Methods in Cultural Anthropology* (pp. 259–299). Walnut Creek: AltaMira Press.

FAO. 2000. *Economic Impact of Smallholder Irrigation Development in Zimbabwe: Case Studies of Ten Irrigation Schemes.* Harare: Sub-Regional Office for East and Southern Africa (SAFR).

Gould, J. 1997. *Localizing Modernity: Action, Interests and Association in Rural Zambia.* Helsinki: Finnish Anthropological Society.

Harris, B. 2002. Xenophobia: A New Pathology for a New South Africa. In D. Hook and G. Eagle, *Psychopathology and Social Prejudice* (pp. 169–184). Cape Tow: University of Cape Town Press.

Harvey, J., Potten, D.H. and Schoppmann, B. 1987. Rapid Rural Appraisal of Small Irrigation Schemes in Zimbabwe. *Agricultural Administration and Extension*, 27 (3): 141–155.

Hendricks, F. 2003. Class and Citizenship in Contemporary South Africa: President's Address South African Sociological Association Annual Congress, 2002 Citizenship, Living Rights and the Public Intellectual 30 June–3 July, East London. *Society in Transition*, 34 (1): 1–12.

Jacobs, S. 1991. Land Resettlement and Gender in Zimbabwe: Some Findings. *The Journal of Modern African Studies*, 29 (3): 521–528.

Madebwe, C. and Madebwe, V. 2005. Women and Access to Land in Smallholder Irrigation Schemes: The Case of Ngondoma Irrigation Scheme in Zhombe (Zimbabwe). *Pakistan Journal of Social Science*, 3 (7): 922–927.

Magadlela, D. and Hebinck, P. 1995. Dry Fields and Spirits in Trees: A Social Analysis of Irrigation Intervention in Nyamaropa Communal Area, Zimbabwe. *Zambezia*, 22 (1): 43–62.

Manzungu, E. 1995. Engineering or Domineering? The Politics of Water Control in Mutambara Irrigation Scheme, Zimbabwe. *Zambezia*, 22 (2): 115–135.

Mupawose, R.M. 1984. Irrigation in Zimbabwe, a Broad Overview. In M. Blackie, *African Regional Symposium on Small Holder Irrigation* (pp. A1–A12). London: Hydraulics Research Limited.

Musara, J.P., Chikuvire, T.J. and Moyo, M. 2010. Determinants of Micro-irrigation Adoption for Maize Production in Smallholder Irrigation Schemes: Case of Hama Mavhaire Irrigation Scheme, Zimbabwe. *African Journal of Food, Agriculture, Nutrition and Development*, 10 (1): 2050–2069.

Neocosmos, M. 2003. The Contradictory Position of Tradition in African Nationalist Discourse: Some Analytical and Political Reflections. *Africa Development*, 28 (1–2): 17–52.

Palmer, R. 1990. Land Reform in Zimbabwe. *African Affairs*, 89 (355): 163–181.

Palys, T. 2008. Purposive Sampling. In L.M. Given, *The Sage Encyclopaedia of Qualitative Research Methods*, (pp. 697–698). Sage: Los Angeles.

Pazvakawambwa, G.T. and van Der Zaag, P. 2001. *The Value of Irrigation Water in Nyanyadzi Smallholder Irrigation Scheme, Zimbabwe: Principles and Method.* Delft: IHE Delft.

Peters, P.E., Ferguson, A.E., Darroch, M., Derman, B., Fuller, B., Gonese, F. and Rugube, L. 2002. *2002 Gender and Broadening Access to Land and Water in Southern Africa. Basis Brief Number 12, August 2002.* Davis: BASIS.

Post, K. 1996. *The State, Civil Society and Democracy in Africa: Some Theoretical Issues.* Dar es Salam: Dar es Salam University Press.

Samakande, I., Senzanje, A. and Manzungu, E. 2004. Sustainable Water Management in Smallholder Irrigation Schemes: Understanding the Impact of Field Water Management on Maize Productivity on Two Irrigation Schemes in Zimbabwe. *Physics and Chemistry of the Earth, Parts A/B/C*, 29 (15): 1075–1081.

Svubure, O. and Zawe, C. 2010. The Elusive Multiple Uses of Irrigation Water: Some of the Forgotten Issues in Smallholder Irrigation Schemes Designing in Zimbabwe. *Journal of Sustainable Development in Africa*, 12 (3): 70–86.

Walker, C. 2005. The Limits to Land Reform: Rethinking "the Land Question". *Journal of Southern African Studies*, 31 (4): 805–824.

Webner, R.P. 1996. Introduction: Multiple Identities, Plural Arenas. In R.P. Webner and T.O. Ranger, *Postcolonial Identities in Africa* (pp. 1–26). London: Zed Books.

Woodward, K. 2000. *Questioning Identity: Gender, Class, Ethnicity.* London and New York: Routledge.

12 "Other people inherit property, but I inherit people and their problems"

The role of kinship and social capital in providing care and support for the HIV infected and AIDS affected, Chivanhu informal settlement, Masvingo Province

Loveness Makonese

Introduction

This chapter is a case study of a cluster of households in an informal settlement in Masvingo Province in relation to resilience to HIV and AIDS. The Machekeche cluster provides an opportunity to find out the role of social capital (notably kinship relations) in sustaining resilience and reducing vulnerability to the impacts of HIV and AIDS. Three sets of orphans are linked to Machekeche and their case studies are presented here. The history of each set of orphans shows how accessing care and support through social capital is embedded in negotiated relationships and networks which may even extend beyond a specific locality (beyond the informal settlement of Chivanhu in this case). The case studies identify how decisions on orphan care are made within the households and how resilience is possibly strengthened over time. The three cases outlined focus on the households of the following women: Precious, Respina and Rumbidzai. The cluster consists of four households, with the household headed by Machekeche absorbing most of the impacts across all the households. Overall, the case studies reveal the ways in which different households forming a cluster share critical resource flows and how kinship networks (as an example of social capital) cope with the impacts of HIV and AIDS over time and potentially facilitate resilience. In doing so, the chapter attempts to address some of the existing gaps in available literature on HIV and AIDS and livelihoods (Drinkwater *et al.* 2006, Samuels *et al.* 2006, Seeley *et al.* 2008, Samuels and Drinkwater 2011, Gandure and Drimie 2005).

Background and case study site

HIV and AIDS affect all facets of people's livelihoods, including through chronic illness, death and the subsequent care of orphans. Not all households and individuals are affected by the loss of livelihood security and not all HIV- and AIDS-affected households dissolve or discontinue. Some households survive and continue, and are able for instance to maintain key livelihood assets. But the challenge in most HIV and AIDS studies has been to show which households dissolve and which households continue, and to offer a full account of the processes leading to dissolution or continuity. In this respect, a range of factors condition people's ability to respond to the impacts of AIDS. This chapter explores the concept of resilience in the context of HIV and AIDS related adversity and suffering. Resilience is seen as the response which enables households to persist or at least to adapt to the difficulties caused by HIV and AIDS. Resilience is the opposite of vulnerability. Whereas the condition of vulnerability encompasses an inability to cope, the disruption of livelihoods and loss of livelihood security, resilience denotes an ability to cope with the impacts of HIV and AIDS.

One of the main objectives of this study is to show and emphasise that households are rarely self-contained units and that a complex array of interrelationships often (but not always) exist between groups of households (or clusters). The household case studies that are presented and discussed in this chapter demonstrate that a fuller picture of HIV and AIDS vulnerability and resilience over time requires an examination beyond the level of the individually affected household. In this chapter I move beyond a household analysis in order to offer a nuanced analysis of the complex interrelationships within and between households. In particular, the chapter shows how the illness and death of a household member usually affects more than just the immediate household, and how households in the cluster become active and mobilised in handling the loss and minimising its effects. The case study of the Machekeche cluster therefore brings to the fore coping strategies and resilience, and over an extended period of time.

The Chivanhu settlement where the case study members reside is situated in Nemanwa, which is found in Masvingo Province in the southern part of Zimbabwe. Masvingo Province falls in regions 4 and 5 of the country's ecological zones, which are characterised by intermittent rains of less than 500 mm per year. The population is of mixed ethnic origin. Some of the households originated from deep rural areas and some originated from the Masvingo urban centre. Households that settled earlier occupy more land compared to households that settled later. Even among the latter occupiers, those who have the means can buy or seek favours through gifts to the village heads in order to gain more land. The Chivanhu settlement is a dynamic zone, operating outside of the mainstream of rural Zimbabwe. The majority of the population has reduced and restricted participation in public decision-making and are often discriminated against, stigmatised by the broader population in the area. The spatial and socio-economic location of Chivanhu settlement provides a unique opportunity for exploring and understanding HIV and AIDS affected coping strategies of those households surviving at the periphery of mainstream economic, political and social processes.

Methodology

The study adopted a mixed methodology approach. Both quantitative and qualitative methods of data collection were used. Interviews and focus group discussions were used during the initial phases from 2008 to 2010. Data and insights gathered during this phase helped in framing and formulating the research assumptions and questions, and laid the foundation for the survey-based household livelihood questionnaire. The household survey captured basic demographic and socio-economic information on households, along with orphanhood, chronic illness, AIDS related deaths, land sizes, consumption patterns and social services in Chivanhu. The information collected through this survey was critical for guiding the research in the identification of specific households for in-depth case histories .The cluster approach was adopted in this study and was used for identifying interconnected households. This approach facilitated the mapping out of the impacts of HIV and AIDS across households; and it helped to identify the existence and relevance of livelihood decisions across clustered households in responding to the impacts of HIV and AIDS.

Social capital and resilience of the HIV infected and AIDS affected

HIV and AIDS affected coping and social capital research evidence on long-term adaptation mechanisms – what they are and how they work – is still limited (Rugalema *et al.* 2010:29). While the term 'vulnerability' attempts to describe the likelihood of experiencing adverse consequences as a result of HIV and AIDS, the term 'resilience' encompasses the ability of HIV and AIDS affected households to bounce back from a shock. Resilience means that a livelihood system is able to absorb the impacts of disturbances due to AIDS, without resulting in significant changes to its structural features or declines in livelihood outputs. It thus refers to the ability of HIV and AIDS affected households to adopt responsive livelihood strategies to avoid negative consequences in order to rebuild their livelihoods faster and on a surer footing (Loevinsohn and Gillespie 2003). Resilience is normally analysed through proxy indicators like the ability to preserve some assets, the condition of the homestead, the quality of life before and after, and the ability to re-bounce out of a crisis. This chapter considers the matter of resilience and, in doing so, also profiles the contribution of Anti-Retroviral Therapy (ART) in strengthening resilience. In the context of my study of a marginalised community, particularly considering that most households are poor and generally asset deficient, social capital and political capital become critical for long-term coping and resilience.

HIV and AIDS and the stigma and discrimination which accompanies it causes a deterioration in an individual's social capital by disrupting social networks, institutions, organisations and social support mechanisms. Infected individuals regularly face social exclusion, loneliness, and lack of support and comfort from families and broader networks. Taylor *et al.* (1996:55) argue – in relation to both the infected and affected – that care-giving by household members and AIDS-based illnesses prevent individuals and households from creating and sustaining networks (Seeley *et al.* 1993). UNAIDS (2002) also notes that social cohesion within households is heavily compromised.

Households in some instances will eventually dissolve, as parents die and children are sent to relatives for care and upbringing.

The growing impact of the AIDS pandemic is weakening community safety nets (Forster and Williamson 2000). Reliance on social networks (involving reciprocal arrangements for sharing resources through gifts, loans of cash, food and labour between relatives) becomes more difficult as the demand for resources and assets has been intensifying with the progression of the condition. The loss of labour (both productive and unproductive) often strains the capacity of a household to mobilise social capital. Topouzis (1998:9) argues that HIV and AIDS may "create a crisis of an unprecedented proportion particularly among the extended family and kinship systems, with implications not only for the spread of HIV but also for the viability of rural institutions and of traditional social safety mechanisms". Studies are confirming that families are failing to cope as demands for support are increasing and the social safety system is overburdened with the demands for care-giving, cash and labour needs (Forster and Williamson 2000). The number of affected persons increasingly undermines community labour and credit groups, which have existed historically. Findings from a study conducted by TANGO (2003), revealed that HIV and AIDS affected households had challenges getting assistance from kinship networks and there were challenges in mobilising the HIV and AIDS affected to participate in community activities. HIV and AIDS have led to the straining of local community based institutions to the point of collapse (TANGO 2002).

Findings and discussion

The Machekeche cluster consists of four HIV and AIDS affected households. Machekeche is the central household that absorbs most of the HIV and AIDS affected from the other three households (for Precious, Respina and Rumbidzai). The total number of households in this cluster is 15 as shown in Figure 12.1. Precious' kinship networks and movement of the chronically ill and the orphans with represented by the blue colour. Respina's kinship networks and movements of chronically ill and orphans are represented by the red colour and Rumbidzai's networks are represented by the green colour. The Machekeche cluster reveals the long-term dynamics that influence coping with the impacts of HIV and AIDS. The case studies of the households are going to be discussed and analysed in the following sections to reveal how the impacts of HIV and AIDS are absorbed beyond the household as well as the ways in which resilience in the face of HIV and AIDS is embedded within the kinship social system in this context.

Insights from the Precious case study

The insights derived from the study of Precious are discussed in terms of chronic illness, looking after orphans and livelihood resilience over time. The first household in the Machekeche kinship network involved Bonnie, his wife Precious and

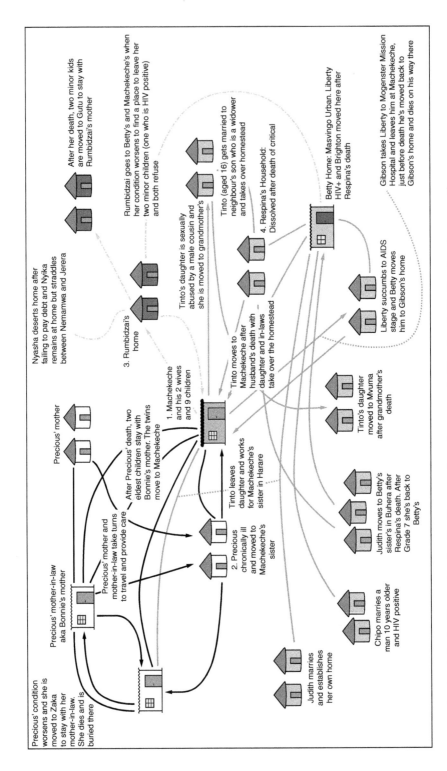

Figure 12.1 Machekeche Cluster showing kinship networks and movement of the chronically ill and orphans over time.

Precious' condition worsens and she is moved to Zaka to stay with her mother-in-law. She dies and is buried there

Precious' mother-in-law aka Bonnie's mother

Precious' mother and mother-in-law take turns to travel and provide care

Precious' mother

After Precious' death, two eldest children stay with Bonnie's mother. The twins move to Machekeche

Tinto leaves daughter and works for Machekeche's sister in Harare

1. Machekeche and his 2 wives and 9 children

2. Precious chronically ill and moved to Machekeche's sister

Judith marries and establishes her own home

Chipo marries a man 10 years older and HIV positive

Judith moves to Betty's sister's in Buhera after Respina's death. After Grade 7 she's back to Betty's

Tinto's daughter moved to Mvuma after grandmother's death

Nyasha deserts home after failing to pay debt and Nyika remains at home but straddles between Nemamwa and Jerera

3. Rumbidzai's home

Tinto's daughter is sexually abused by a male cousin and she is moved to grandmother's

Tinto moves to Machekeche after husband's death and in-laws take over the homestead

Tinto (aged 16) gets married to neighbour's son who is a widower and takes over homestead

4. Respina's Household: Dissolved after death of critical

Liberty succumbs to AIDS stage and Betty moves him to Gibson's home

Betty Home: Masvingo Urban. Liberty HIV+ and Brighton moved here after Respina's death

After her death, two minor kids are moved to Gutu to stay with Rumbidzai's mother

Rumbidzai goes to Betty's and Machekeche's when her condition worsens to find a place to leave her two minor children (one who is HIV positive) and both refuse

Gibson takes Liberty to Mogenster Mission Hospital and leaves him at Machekeche, just before death he's moved back to Gibson's home and dies on his way there three children. The family had migrated from Zaka, which is about 121 kilometres from Chivanhu. The family was asset poor and survived on remittances from Bonnie's mother and his sister. But the sister married and this affected Bonnie's household; the sister could no longer send money for Bonnie's sustenance because of her own household's demands. Bonnie moved to Norton and ended up at Porta Farm engaged in fish poaching. He immediately got involved with a woman from the area and did not send any remittances to his wife in the Chivanhu settlement. As the wife grappled with the absence of Bonnie, the settlement was burned down by police officers and she was uprooted with the children. They went back to Zaka. As the farm occupations in the year 2000 resulted in local governance breakdown, the settlement dwellers took another chance and came back to settle again. Bonnie tried poaching in Lake Mutirikwi, but he did not get enough proceeds to sustain his family. He got involved in stealing cattle, and was caught and sent to prison. While Bonnie was in jail, the wife became engaged in affairs.

After he returned, he found it hard to live with the stigma of having been in jail, so he moved to South Africa and immediately got involved with another woman there. By this time, Precious had become HIV-positive and was progressing to the AIDS stage, suffering from AIDS-related chronic illnesses. The extended kinship system experienced a shock. Precious had to be looked after and there was also the demand of maintaining the homestead. Coping mechanisms during the illness are challenged because, at the end of the day, there is only Machekeche (Bonnie's brother) and his wife (and no other relatives and close extended family members in the settlement to assist with the care-giving). The other challenge is that the household had not stayed in the area long enough to maintain reciprocal support in the community. There was no sense of community; hence, it was difficult to cope with Precious' HIV chronic illness. Although staying close by, Machekeche's wife could not adequately offer any kind of support, as she was young and had three young children. The other reason was that she was maintaining dual homes in Harare and Chivanhu; at the same time, her husband was in the process of formalising his relationship with his soon-to-be second wife. Precious' mother and Bonnie's mother stayed in Zaka and they had to take care of their own individual homesteads. Precious' two children were too young to take care of her. As the family searched for ways to cope, they made a decision that Machekeche should bring his extramarital partner, who has since had a son, to come to stay in Precious' homestead and take care of Precious. She agreed because for her it was an opportunity for her relationship with Machekeche to be formally recognised. Precious was later moved to her aunt, Bonnie's sister in Harare, where she was nursed before being moved to Zaka, a week before she died in early 2006.

The impact of HIV and AIDS and the demands of care do not affect the household alone. The impacts and coping demands extend beyond the household to the extended family. In the absence of material and financial resources to provide care to the chronically ill, households engage in a suite of responses in order to make sure that the caring service is provided. However, some of the strategies have a negative impact on certain individuals on whom demands are placed. In this case Machekeche's first wife, due to her powerless position within the extended family network, ended up bearing the greatest burden of the impact of HIV and AIDS.

The Precious case study shows how HIV and AIDS affect a household over time. During the start of the research, this was a typical example of a household that was going to dissolve and have its assets disposed of. Social capital has proven to be a critical element in the livelihood security of the HIV and AIDS affected in this household cluster. The nature of the livelihood portfolio has increased the risk of getting HIV infection. The social capital proved in this case study to be a critical household asset that influenced coping during chronic illness and coping after the death of a critical adult due to AIDS. Social capital may compensate for the lack of other types of capital, as in this case. The household is asset poor to begin with, and it has weak financial, human, and physical capital to draw on in times of crises; however, the kinship network draws on its resources to provide the support on behalf of the household. Very few individuals and households in Chivanhu settlement had adequate social capital to draw on, as is the example of the Precious case study (Seeley *et al.* 1993, Taylor *et al.* 1996, Portes 1998, Wiegers 2008).

The Precious case study reveals that household resilience is achieved, but at a cost for the wider extended family system. The demands and pressures on households do not end with the death of the chronically ill person, as the presence of orphans presents further challenges. Machekeche, as a way of forcing his first wife to contribute to the caring of the inherited orphans, destroys his wife's kitchen and ends up making certain decisions. Current AIDS and livelihoods studies might fail to account for the challenges faced by other households, especially Machekeche's household and his first wife as the kinship system tries to absorb the impacts of HIV. Literature has recorded sub-optimal coping strategies in HIV and AIDS affected households. However, the behaviour by the whole Machekeche kinship network proves that there are times when other non-household members also make suboptimal decisions in order to deal with the consequences of HIV. The kinship system assures the care of the survivors but at a cost to some members within the system.

Machekeche's mother in Zaka wields considerable power in this regard. She insists that since Bonnie was the first to settle in Chivanhu (before Machekeche) and he was the eldest of the two brothers, his home should be maintained for family traditional rituals like *kurova guva.*[1] As a result, when Machekeche was supposed to conduct the ritual of *kurova guva*, he had to renovate and renew the thatching on Precious' homestead because that is where the family ceremony was going to be conducted. He was in fact cultivating the fields and paying the yearly US$3 tax to the village head in order to retain the land and the homestead. Other affected households in Chivanhu that failed to do that were dispossessed of their land. From this life history of Precious' coping with HIV and the resilience shown, it seems in this instance that resilience was deeply embedded in the cultural, traditional and spiritual frameworks of the cluster. More specifically, ceremonies like *kurova guva* presented the larger extended family with an opportunity to make demands on repairing and preserving assets like houses.

This study has managed to penetrate deeply into the households and intra-household relations to capture and analyse the issues that influence resilience and preservation of assets within households. I expected to find low levels of resilience due to the nature of the economic and social configurations. However, despite initial observations of a poor asset-base overall for most of the households, it soon became clear that there was another story to tell. For clusters like the Machekeche cluster, the household's social networks and resources were mobilised beyond Chivanhu settlement, including in Zaka and Harare. The study revealed intra- and inter-household decisions about coping with chronic illness and orphans and how to redistribute and maintain the human and physical capital base in HIV and AIDS affected households.

Insights from Rumbidzai's case study

The second household belonged to Rumbidzai and her four children, Nyasha, Nyika, Joyce and Grace. Rumbidzai was Machekeche's half-sister and had four children from three different relationships. She did not have a stable place to call her home, and the multiple displacements and a sense of hopelessness led her to depend on commercial sex work as a coping mechanism. Her mother had remarried and the husband did not want to assume the responsibility of looking after her. She is left to reside with her maternal grandmother who is powerless to defend her against being chased away. She has unstable marital unions and in each case they end in divorce. Insecure livelihoods produce suitable conditions for getting HIV infection.

Rumbidzai's last partner was HIV positive. It is not known whether she got HIV from the man she recently married, or whether she had already been HIV positive, considering the past sexual relationships she had been engaged in. The marital union produced two children, Joyce and Grace, but she did not have a male heir. In the event of the death of this husband, the husband's child from his first marriage would inherit the homestead and she would be dispossessed of the homestead. After her dispossession, because her husband did indeed die, she returned to her maternal grandmother to re-join her other two children from her first two marital unions. The extended family was wary of taking her in, and they forced her to make arrangements about where her children would stay in the event that she died. The situation was complicated further by the fact that her first child had already had a child of her own out of wedlock. In order to cope, she embarked on selling firewood and getting extra support from Machekeche to buy a homestead. Nevertheless, she was setting up a homestead when she was already in the advanced HIV stages of infection.

Most child-headed households in Chivanhu settlement facing adverse conditions came from households that were set up in this way. The HIV-infected household head, on realising that he or she might die at any time, would look for a home in which to die and leave the children there. In cases such as these, the household head would not have adequate time to build and strengthen social networks that would be critical for the orphans' survival in the event that the chronically ill household head dies from AIDS-related complications. As a way of ensuring food security, Rumbidzai encouraged her eldest child to leave her 10-month-old baby so that she can work as a house cleaner in South Africa. However, the daughter soon returned after becoming pregnant from someone in South Africa and on return entered into another relationship. In the process, this created a vicious cycle for her increased susceptibility for getting HIV infection. In order to get food during her illness, Rumbidzai gets support from Machekeche; the other relatives were exhausted and did not want anything to do with her and her household.

Despite the fact that she was on ART, Rumbidzai's condition did not improve. At the same time, like all AIDS sufferers with dependents, she had the challenge of ensuring that her children are taken care of. When I met with Rumbidzai in February 2011 she was wasted physically; she was carrying her HIV-positive daughter (who was also chronically ill) on her back because she had difficulties moving. The situation presented the pathetic condition and situation of AIDS sufferers. It also leads to the prevalence of child-headed households, as the now dead parent or parents are sometimes unsuccessful in securing a place for the orphaned children amongst relatives or other guardians. The extended family and the whole cluster in the case of Machekeche were already overstretched. Machekeche had three different sets of orphans to look after and he could not look after all of them anymore.

In this instance it shows that, although eventually the AIDS-infected person failed to secure a suitable stable place for the survivors, the associated households in the cluster actively sought a place that they deemed to be the best place for the upkeep of the orphaned children. None of the older surviving orphans in fact had the capacity or resources to sustain themselves. In a patriarchal system, where lineage is traced from the father's side, the children are not valued in their mother's family. In the case of Precious, the extended family system made important sacrifices so that her children were taken care of, but the same family system was reluctant to take responsibility for the children of Rumbidzai who are deemed to be born out of unsuccessful marital unions.

Attending the funeral of Rumbidzai was Betty, who represented her late brother (Rumbidzai's father). Machekeche, in order to avoid having any responsibility for the orphans, does not go to the funeral. Rumbidzai's mother takes over the minors (Joyce and Grace) and moves them to Gutu. The two eldest children, Nyasha and Nyika, despite the fact that they are not engaged in any meaningful livelihood activity, are effectively left to fend for themselves. Nyasha borrows as a coping mechanism to provide food, but she fails to pay back and runs away from the homestead. Only Nyika is left at the homestead but he has challenges accessing food. He moves to Machekeche's household and then is forced to go back. Orphans, especially older ones, are not passive victims only but are active agents looking for a place where they can be looked after. Because the extended family considers Nyasha an adult, she ends up in full time commercial sex work in Masvingo, creating further HIV susceptibility and AIDS vulnerability for her children. For the first three months, when all the survivors seem to have moved away from the homestead, the homestead can be deemed dissolved. However, a year later, Nyika is still there due to pressures and after having failed to secure an alternative place to stay. He looks to the church networks for survival and, in the meantime, it helps. He is not cultivating the land left by his mother, but he is able to scrounge for food and basic upkeep.

This also shows the way claims are made on social networks (or social capital broadly), including kinship networks. The first claim is made on the social capital of kinship and, when this fails in the context of Nyika, he opts for getting support from the church system. The case history of Rumbidzai also demon- strates that it is not a given that survivors automatically receive support through social networks; any support is contingent on the character of pre-existing rela- tionships and the stresses currently embodied in those relationships. While Nyika is able to capitalise on the church system for survival, Nyasha fails to capitalise on networks because of her lifestyle decisions. This case study thus highlights the limitations of the kinship system in providing care for survivors.

Insights from the Respina case study

The third household in this kinship system belonged to Respina, Machekeche's aunt, and her five children; Chipo, Tinto, Judy, Brighton and Liberty. The youngest Liberty was HIV positive and already chronically ill. The eldest daugh- ter, Chipo, got married to an elderly man who was HIV positive. Interviews with survivors show that the main push factor for the union that Chipo got into with her current husband was finding a place to stay and someone to look after her. After Respina's death, a male neighbour (who was already sick) took advantage of the second eldest daughter (Tinto), and married her despite the fact that she was a minor. This man died after two years living with Tinto, who is now a widow at 19 with a two-year child to support. Judy was moved to Buhera to stay with her aunt. Brighton was moved to Masvingo to stay with another aunt. Liberty, the youngest and already chronically ill by the time of his mother's death, was forcibly left at Machekeche's homestead – because, according to Machekeche, he was sick and nobody in the kinship system wanted to take care of him. In the case of Respina, her children had no original homestead to call their own and they were forced to move from one place to another as a way of coping. The relatives of the mother did not have the resources to look after them such that five years after her death, the children broadly speaking have had troublesome times and are not doing well. HIV and AIDS create a trap where it becomes difficult for the survivors to escape or survive the situation in which they find themselves. Wiegers (2008) argues that the nature of coping across time is not documented in existing literature. When a parent like Respina dies, who does not have a fixed place to call home and always struggled financially (without any physical or financial capital) then surviving becomes an even greater challenge for surviving orphans.

The vulnerabilities not only affect the children, but also the grandchildren of Respina. While first generation adults who succumbed to AIDS left the children with their grandparents, people in the situation of Tinto do not have parents to look after their children in the event that they die or fall sick. After moving to Harare to work as a domestic worker, Tinto has a dilemma. Other affected children were relying on their mothers to look after their children, but Respina is not there for her, and she has no option other than to leave her child at Machekeche's home. Machekeche, due to the pressure, started having problems with his first wife. The first wife moved back to her homestead of origin with her biological children and left Tinto's daughter at Machekeche's home in the custody of a distant male relative who later sexually abused her. Again, despite the fact that the child is abused, Tinto has no option other than to move her daughter to her mother-in-law. The mother-in-law, who was now staying with Tinto's daughter, died after six months in mysterious circumstances according to the family members. Tinto moves the child to her late mother-in-law's sister's homestead in Mvuma, which is about 120 kilometres away. In addition, when her boyfriend deserts Tinto, after she has been impregnated with a second child, she cannot go and stay at her late first husband's homestead. In this instance, her late husband's father is saying that culturally it is not possible to bring another man's child into the homestead. She wants to go back to Machekeche's homestead, but by this time Machekeche is feeling overwhelmed because he has other orphaned children to look after. By the time of finishing the research, Tinto was staying in Masvingo urban where she was working as a house cleaner, but the employer could only accommodate her and her younger child (the eldest child was still staying in Mvuma). Where the social capital, in this case kinship relations, is overwhelmed with responsibilities, those who are HIV and AIDS affected experience adverse conditions.

Despite the high level of resilience shown in Tinto, coping with the impact of HIV and AIDS for households that are not stable provides a challenge. A closer analysis of what happens in households over time is very critical for understanding the household and intra-household dynamics brought about by people affected by HIV and AIDS. In the case of Tinto's child in this cluster, apart from having the burden of being an orphan, she is also facing the challenge of abuse in the process. She needs extra support in order to heal from the abuse, but she is finding herself being moved from one homestead to another. At the time of finishing my fieldwork, one of the siblings (Chipo) and her husband were chronically ill from AIDS. This means that the cluster, which is currently struggling to sustain itself, may soon be confronted with a new set of orphans; and this means a further burden for individuals who are barely managing to achieve a livelihood. The Respina case study shows that the challenges brought about by HIV and AIDS in the household do not only affect the generation of surviving orphans of the deceased person or persons. Rather, the consequences are widespread and affect households of relatives whose resources are already stretched; in addition, future generations of surviving children (in this case Tinto's child) and even more orphans (possibly Chipo's children) are also affected by the HIV and AIDS pandemic.

The cases of Judy and Brighton show that, in situations where orphans are split, it is possible to find some orphans fairing much better than their siblings who remain behind. Of the five siblings, only Brighton had managed to attend secondary education, although he failed. However, by the end of the research he was aged 17 and being pushed to look for a homestead of his own so that he could provide a home for his sisters and their children. Succumbing to these pressures and also by the fact that he was unemployed, he was now being accused of petty theft in the settlement. Machekeche's first wife chased him away and his whereabouts were not known. In Shona culture, sending some children to wealthier relatives has been one of the coping mechanisms. However, social capital is showing its limitations in providing care and support for orphans such that, in this sense, social capital or social networks are effectively safety nets with holes. Unlike in the Precious case study, where the whole kinship system got together to ensure that orphaned children are taken care of, in this instance relatives seemingly select which children to support and which children not to support.

The case of Liberty (Respina's youngest child who is also HIV positive) shows the plight of children who are orphaned and at the same time HIV positive. The kinship system, although it would wish to assist, in this instance shows that when the costs of looking after a chronically ill orphan are increasing, households would prefer to preserve their financial capital and in the process look for the next person within the kinship system to give the burden of caring for an HIV infected child. The relatives would offload the sick Liberty but, at the same time, remain with his brother Brighton because Brighton was providing agricultural labour during his school holidays. The situation was made worse towards the end of Liberty's life, as his caregivers were more concerned about the implications of him dying in their custody. Moving him from one homestead to another as a way of avoiding paying the burial penalties from the traditional authorities added to this problematic scenario. In most cases, people were complaining about him in his presence and I had felt compelled to talk to them about the impact of what they were doing to the chronically ill child. The complaints from Machekeche's wife, that no one was benefitting from the very existence of Liberty, reveals that when extended families make decisions to look after orphans, they also look at benefits from them: in this instance the provision of labour.

The plight of children who were in similar circumstances as Liberty is disturbing. I identified three children who were HIV positive and orphans at the same time. It appeared during the interviews as if the guardians were regretting that they opted for taking custody of the children in the first place. According to them, they are dealing with a double burden: looking after orphans and dealing with their own HIV-positive status as well. In the Chivanhu context, the plight of the children is worsened because of insensitive and opportunistic village heads. Whilst penalties like *Ndongamabwe*[2] according to the people are meant to deter people from burying *vatorwa* (aliens), traditional leaders needed to assess each situation before applying a blanket penalty. The researcher lobbied with the village heads to review this practice, but it was a challenge because it was a source of livelihood for the village heads in the area. Compared to Rumbidzai's children who did not have many options to access and negotiate care and support within the kinship system, Betty was willing to make occasional sacrifices. According to Betty, Respina's children belonged to her sister; whereas in the case of Rumbidzai's children, according to the extended family, "she grew up with her mother's relatives and they should take responsibility for the children". At the same time her mother's relatives were reluctant to take over the children. They had looked after Rumbidzai when she was growing up: but they could not look after her children again. A lot of children in similar circumstances end up with little opportunities for achieving positive life outcomes.

Conclusions and policy insights

The chapter has discussed the long-term coping mechanisms of individuals and households affected by HIV and AIDS, particularly in relation to surviving orphans. In doing so, it shows in sequence the steps which are taken by HIV- and AIDS-affected individuals and households to ensure survival – the steps of both the chronically-ill person who is in the throes of death and the associated cluster households (in this case, focused on Machekeche) which face the pro- spects of caring for the orphans. There is no necessary and universal response by households (even kin-related) to the death of a member in an associated house- hold. In the end, the response is a negotiated one, and one which is the subject of considerable controversy and conflict at times. The type of response is therefore a contingent one dependent on a range of variables such as the age of the orphans, the specific status of the deceased person, the stresses currently borne by associated households and the influence of patriarchal practices. These vari- ables also impact on the persons or households that eventually bear the respons- ibility of orphan care, if indeed anyone takes that responsibility. In the end though it is important to note that, even in marginalised informal settlements like Chivanhu, the possibility of some kind and level of resilience (as arranged at the cluster scale) exists. The chapter results and implications show that there is a need for multisectoral responses for HIV and AIDS to revise programmatic approaches. These approaches should respond and adapt to the needs and chal- lenges on the ground. Apart from that, the issues for the marginalised cannot continue to be ignored; there is a need for strong advocacy strategies for responding to the challenges on the ground.

Notes

1 *Kurova guva* is a ceremony or process where the dead man or woman's spirit is accom- modated or brought home to the village. It is normally conducted a year after the deceased has died.
2 *Ndongamabwe* is a penalty paid in the form of money or a cow for burying someone considered to be an alien in the community. It varies depending on the community in Zimbabwe.

References

Drinkwater, M. and McEwan, Samuels, F. 2006. *The Effects of HIV/AIDS on Agricultural Production Systems in Zambia. A Re-Study 1993–2005.* Lusaka: IFPRI/RENEWAL.

Forster, G. and Williamson, J. 2000. A Review of Current Literature on the Impact of HIV/AIDS on Children in SubSaharan Africa. *AIDS Care* 14 (3): 275–284.

Gandure, S. and Drimie, S. 2005. *The Impacts of HIV/AIDS on Rural Livelihoods in Southern Africa: An Inventory of Literature Review.* Harare: FAO.

Loevinsohn, M. and Gillespie, S.R. 2003. *HIV/AIDS, Rural Livelihoods and Food Security: Understanding and Responding.* RENEWAL Working Paper No.2.

Portes, A. 1998. Social Capital: Its Origins and Applications in Modern Sociology. *Annual Review of Sociology* 24: 1–24.

Rugalema, G., Mathieson, K. and Sentongo, J. 2010. Resilience and (Dis)continuity in Households Afflicted by AIDS: Some Preliminary Insights from a Longitudinal Case Study Analysis. In A. Niehof and G.S. Rugalema (eds), *AIDS and Rural Livelihoods: Dynamics and Diversity in Sub Saharan Africa*, (pp. 29–42). London: Earthscan.

Samuels, F., Drinkwater, M. and McEwan, M. 2006. *Understanding HIV/AIDS and LIVELIHOODS: The Contribution of Longitudinal Data and Cluster Analysis*, London: ODI.

Samuels, F. and Drinkwater, M. 2011. Twelve Years on: The Impacts of HIV and AIDS on Livelihoods in Zambia. *Ännals of Anthropological Practice*, 35 (1): 148–166.

Seeley, J., Biraro. S., Shafer, L.A., Nasirumbi, P., Foster, S., Whitworth, J. and Grosskurth, H. 2008. Using Indepth Qualitative Data to Enhance our Understanding of Quamitative Results Regarding the Impact of HIV and AIDS on Households in Rural Uganda. *Social Science and Medicine*, 67 (9): 1434–1446.

Seely, J., Kajura, E., Bachengana, C., Okongo, M., Wagner, U. and Mulder, D. 1993. The Extended Family and Support for People with AIDS in a Rural Population in South West Uganda. *AIDS Care*, 5 (1): 117–122.

TANGO. 2002. *Impacts of HIV/AIDS in East and Southern Africa: A Livelihood and Systems Analysis approach*, Tucson: TANGO.

TANGO. 2003. *HIV/AIDS Vulnerability: An Overview of Micro, Meso and Macro level Implications.* Johannesburg, TANGO.

Taylor, L., Seeley, J. and Kajura, E. 1996. Informal Care for Illness in Rural South West Uganda: The Central Role that Women Play. *Health Transition Review*, 6: 49–56.

Topouzis, D. 1998. *The Implications of HIV/AIDS for Rural Development Policy and Programming: Focus on Sub-Saharan Africa*, Study Paper No.6. UNDP.

UNAIDS 2002. *Global AIDS Epidemic*, Geneva: UNAIDS.

Wiegers, E. 2008. Resilience and AIDS: Exploring Resilience in the Case of AIDS Among Female Headed Households in Northern Zambia. *Medische Antropologie*, 20 (2): 25–277.

Wiegers, E., Curry, J., Garbero, A. and Hourihan, J. 2006. Patterns of Vulnerability to AIDS Impacts in Zambian Households. *Development and Change*, 37 (5): 1073–1092.

13 Insecure land tenure and natural resource use in a post-fast track area of Zimbabwe

Takunda Chabata

Introduction

Zimbabwe has experienced a number of reconfigurations in its land tenure systems over a number of years. As noted by Moyo (1995), the post-colonial state inherited an economy whose land holdings were largely skewed in favour of the white minority. The government immediately embarked on a steady land redistribution process meant to address the colonial historical imbalances. In the first phase of the land reform, which stretched from 1980 to the late 1990s, insignificant levels of land redistribution took place and this gave rise to a more violent, disorganised and accelerated fast track land reform programme from 2000 (Scoones *et al.* 2010). The fast track land reform programme, in a swift and unplanned way, altered the land tenure systems and availed more land to smallholder farmers through its A1 Model. This chapter examines the underlying relationship between land tenure and natural resource utilisation on one A1 farm. The focus is on establishing how small-scale farmers in an A1 Farm (in the Sovelele Resettlement Area) interact with the natural environment in the context of insecure land tenure, and to explore how this affects household and agricultural investment. It became clear that insecure land tenure does not incentivise A1 farmers to conserve the environment and to invest in the resettlement area. Small-scale farmers hesitate to invest resources on land in which they feel they do not have complete control over in terms of rights of possession and usage. It was also discovered that an open access system was created by the existence of villagisation resettlement (homesteads concentrated in villages) and this exposed biodiversity to a depletion risk. Securer land tenure is very important, among other things, in fostering investment confidence and promoting the sustainable use of natural resources among the resettled small-scale farmers.

Case study site and methodological note

This study focused on a post fast track community organised under the A1 fast track resettlement model. This particular settlement is known as Sovelele and it falls within Masvingo Province in the southern part of Zimbabwe. It is home to hundreds of families and households who were resettled on the land through the

Fast Track Land Reform Programme (FTLRP) that started in the year 2000. The area in which it is located has heavy soils, is very dry and was – prior to fast track – a ranching/wildlife area (Scoones *et al.* 2010:38). According to Zimbabwe's agro-ecological regions, Sovelele falls under region V, where rainfall patterns are highly unreliable and therefore not suitable for dry-land agriculture. Rain-fed agriculture has failed to provide sustainable livelihoods for these smallholder farmers due to erratic rainfall patterns. The situation obtaining in this area makes natural-resources-based livelihoods a better alternative to agro-based livelihoods.

This research for this chapter relied on a qualitative research design. The data presented here are part of my doctoral fieldwork that began in January 2014. The following are specific research instruments that I employed in data gathering:

a   *Close-ended questionnaire*: One hundred households were randomly selected for a survey, and were proportionally dispersed across four areas each under a particular sub-chief. A close-ended questionnaire was administered to establish the levels of economic investment and utilisation of natural resources in a context of insecure land tenure.

b   *Key Informant Interviews*: This involved respondents who had been in the resettlement area since 2000 and had adequate knowledge of the different patterns and changes of natural resource utilisation. Such people included sub-chiefs, kraal heads, war veterans, councillors and agricultural extension officers.

c   *Focus Group Discussions (FGDs)*: Different households were randomly selected to participate in eight FGDs, with two FGDs carried out in each of the four areas. These FGDs allowed for an in-depth and collaborative discussion of experiences and understandings around the linkages between land tenure, natural resource utilisation and agricultural investment.

d   *Observations*: To corroborate information elicited from respondents through the above research instruments, observations on natural resource utilisation and investment commitments were undertaken in the four different sub-chiefs' areas.

Zimbabwe's land reform and land tenure systems

The post-colonial government inherited a system of land tenure that recognises both public and private ownership of land which include: freehold, leasehold, common hold (communal), easement (servitude), resettlement permit hold tenure, state lands tenure and unalienated land tenure (Blume 1996). However, by 1980, much of the land was under private freehold ownership. About 42% of Zimbabwean land was thus in the hands of some 6,000 large-scale farmers predominantly whites (Stoneman 2000). The government immediately embarked on a land reform programme that saw the acquisition by the state of a number of formerly white-owned farms. The idea was to decongest communal areas by resettling people from communal areas onto former white large-scale commercial farms, with common-hold land tenure as opposed to private ownership existing on these acquired farms. By 1990, only 52,000 families had been resettled on three million hectares or 16% of formerly white land. This was a worrisome development which raised doubts as to whether earnest resettlement of landless black people was going to be achieved in the near future on any significant scale. The pace of resettlement was inhibited by logistical and constitutional bottle-necks prescribed by the 1979 Lancaster House Constitution assented to by the nationalists in a bid to maintain a cordial relationship with the outside world (Dzingirai *et al.* 2012). These bottlenecks focused on the existence of a willing-seller willing-buyer market-led land redistribution process.

In the 1990s, further challenges, exogenous and endogenous, continued to frustrate the government's efforts to realise equitable land redistribution. Of note were the Structural Adjustment Programme of 1991 and the 1992 drought which, combined, led to an economic slowdown. Structural adjustment reinforced the commitment to the market-led redistribution, but also increased poverty levels amongst households in both urban and rural areas. By 1999, the government found itself in a serious political quandary as the popular demand for land increased throughout the 1990s (Kanyenze *et al.* 2011). The government was also faced with an agitated group of war veterans who claimed that the ruling party had not lived up to the liberation promise of land to the masses. It was at this time that a major opposition party (Movement for Democratic Change) was born from the labour movement and urban civil society groups, and it started to exert meaningful pressure on the government to address people's socio-economic needs (Moyo 2000). Faced with this tense political atmosphere, the government opted to allow for an accelerated compulsory acquisition of land as a way of appeasing in particular its rural electoral supporters in communal areas. Thus, the FTLRP was born out of social, economic and political chaos that threatened the regime's legitimacy and power base.

The FTLRP was a spontaneous, unplanned, haphazard and violent way of 'grabbing' land from the commercial white farmers (Dekker and Kinsey 2011:3). This grabbing happened through a swift movement code-named 'Third *Chimurenga*' or '*Jambanja*' denoting the violence that characterised it (Marongwe 2011, Scoones *et al.* 2010:45, Dzingirai *et al.* 2012:287). Though the war veterans were definitely at the helm of these farm invasions, there is still an acrimonious debate on whether the FTLRP was a genuine peasant-led move-ment or pushed by political elites to achieve land distribution to enhance their own political legitimacy (Scoones *et al.* 2010:22, Moyo 2000). As well, while some scholars like Bernstein (2003) and Moyo and Yeros (2005) have argued that the FTLRP brought about some benefits if only by correcting the historical imbalances in land ownership and utilisation, other more critical scholars (Masiiwa and Chigejo 2003, Sachikonye 2003, Raftopoulos 2002, Wily and Mbaya 2001, Rutherford 2001) writing in the early years of FTLRP, were of the opinion that its negative impacts outweigh its benefits.

In the end, landless and land-short people, together with the ruling elite (Marongwe 2011), managed to appropriate land from the large commercial farms for different purposes. Chaumba *et al.* (2003) argue correctly that plans for land use after the FTLRP were only drawn up after the invasions or occupations, but only limited institutional support for fast track farmers arose in the immediate years after 2000. What mattered then was simply giving people land (Dekker and Kinsey 2011). The political frenzy characterising the occupation was a reflection of the country's atmosphere charged with massive tension and animosity. Of particular significance for this chapter is that specific plans on how to provide secure land tenure on the fast track farms were not formulated and implemented in the haste to redistribute, with tenure on A1 farms in large part reproducing communal land tenure.

The FTLRP followed two distinct resettlement models that are the A1 and A2 models. A1 was designed to decongest communal areas and ensure livelihoods for newly resettled farmers through small-scale farming (Makhado 2006, Chingarande 2008). These small-scale A1 farmers now pursue different and diversified livelihood strategies, the main being dry-land small-scale agriculture (Wolmer 2007, Moyo *et al.* 2009). They also engage in livestock keeping, firewood harvesting for own use as well as for sale, wildlife harvesting, mopane worms harvesting, gold panning, hunting and gathering, fisheries and petty entrepreneurial activities (Moyo *et al.* 2009, Scoones *et al.* 2010). Many of these livelihood activities as pursued by A1 farm occupants entail an intimate and intricate interaction with available natural resources. The A2 model is commercially oriented and therefore targeted people with capital, assets, agricultural skills and entrepreneurial abilities. These farms were either taken over as an entire unit or subdivided into commercially viable land areas.

Land reform and the natural environment utilisation

It is imperative to address existing literature on the link between the FTLRP and environmental or natural resource utilisation. Sutton (2004) notes that environmental sustainability is a key area of focus within academic and development circles essentially because of the role that the environment plays in sustaining livelihoods. The natural resource base that regularly sustains human livelihoods has for many years been the focus of debates and research (Scoones *et al.* 1996:22), including in relation to Zimbabwe. Attempts have been made to try to link sustainable resource management and meaningful rural development in Zimbabwe (Mutimukuru-Maravanyika 2010). Different types of resources have been considered in this context, including minerals and forests (Katerere *et al.* 1993), land itself (Chaumba *et al.* 2003, Moyo *et al.* 2004, Gadzirayi and Mutandwa 2006), water (Manzungu 2004, Kujinga and Manzungu 2004, Forner *et al.* 2006), and wildlife (Murombedzi 1995). Efforts to conserve natural resources especially wildlife in Zimbabwe have been witnessed through the implementation of CAMPFIRE (Communal Areas Management Programme for Indigenous Resources) Programme from 1989 (Murphree 1991). This programme was at times useful in conserving wildlife while, at the same time, giving producer communities the chance to enjoy the profits of managing natural resources in a sustainable way. However, despite some efficacy within the CAMPFIRE programmes, they have since disappeared. As it stands, Zimbabwe probably has one of the most 'suffocating' and restrictive operational environments where issues pertaining to sustainable environmental resource management are concerned (Manzungu 2012).

Early on, the Government of Zimbabwe (2001) reported that there was accelerated destruction of the natural resource base following the FTLRP, with serious tree cutting, poaching and gold-panning. With limited institutional support and ill-planned land use arrangements in place, compounded by insecure land tenure, this destruction almost seemed inevitable. This is in part chronicled by Dzingirai (2009) who argues that the FTLRP had adverse effects on ecological life, especially forestry and wildlife. Wildlife decimation in fact worsened during the peak of Zimbabwe's political crisis after the year 2000. Dzingirai *et al.* (2012) thus highlight the severe impact on wildlife by raising the following points: a) Poaching threatened to desolate certain wildlife species; b) Deforestation destroyed wildlife habitats and, browsing and grazing areas; and c) Resettlement made it very difficult for wildlife to live in areas with larger human populations. Lindsey *et al.* (2012) also claim that about 80% of large game in private game farms was eradicated within ten years. Dzingirai *et al.* (2012) however acknowledge that the degree of environmental damage is difficult to accurately assess due to limited systematic data.

Stunning evidence shows that in Masvingo province, by 2009, an estimated 6.8, 13.3 and 23.7 hectares of land per household had been cleared – in the main for cultivation purposes – in model A1 villagised farms (with homesteads concentrated in villages), A1 self-contained farms (in which homesteads are dispersed) and A2 farms respectively (Scoones *et al.* 2010:78). This massive clearance of land could be attributed to many reasons such as farmland expansion, establishing possession over a given piece of land, the formation of new human settlements, and collecting subsistence-based fuel wood supplies (Dzingirai *et al.* 2012:290). Mubvami (2004) opines that the FTLRP had destructive impacts on biodiversity with major impacts on vegetation cover, soil erosion and water quality. His further argument is that because Zimbabwe lacks a well-formulated and integrated environmental policy, the FTLRP failed to ensure land use planning in which conservation measures are properly incorporated, and that the negative environmental impacts of the FTLRP were a clear result of human-induced processes. Additionally, environmental management in resettled fast track areas was compromised due to the lack of proper institutional structures to manage the environment. In the same vein, Masiiwa and Chipungu (2004) argue that the FTLRP lacked coordinated institutional roles to monitor natural resources utilisation.

Though a large corpus of literature exists on FTLRP focusing on livelihoods in the post fast track period (Moyo 2009, Mandizadza 2010, Chamunorwa 2010), "none of these has offered a comprehensive insight into livelihood patterns and changes over time" (Scoones *et al.* 2010:60). Any such changes in livelihood patterns however need to be studied in relation to access to and use of natural resources since the two are intricately intertwined. A more detailed story of the relationship between land tenure, rural livelihoods and natural resource utilisation is therefore cardinal in our understanding of the ongoing impacts of the FTLRP. A few researchers such as Chigumira (2010) have looked at the interplay between livelihoods and natural resource utilisation but – in Chigumira's study – the focus was on a different agro-ecological region, i.e. Region III, where the soils and rainfall patterns are relatively suitable for dry-land agriculture. Livelihood options available for A1 small-scale farmers in Region III are different from the ones available for resettled families in agro-ecological region V in which Sovelele is located and where there are poor soils and erratic and unreliable rainfall patterns.

Land tenure and access in Sovelele resettlement area

Resettlement in Sovelele follows a villagised model, such that the new emergent communities are organised in villages where they share common resources. The A1 land at Sovelele is divided for three land uses, that is, for residence (homesteads), for cultivation and for pastures for grazing. Individual households have absolute control of the land meant for residential settlement and over their arable land. However, they only control the land for cultivation during the farming season and, after that (or between growing seasons), this land tends to be used as pastures over which the household often has no direct control – other households bring their livestock onto any arable land during the off-season. This off-season land, as well as the land reserved all year for grazing specifically, thus becomes subject to communal use or an open-access system regarding the utilisation of natural resources on this land.

There are five villages that are run by village heads who were selected from the war veterans who led the invasions. These village heads are responsible for settling disputes over land boundaries between and among different households. Each village has its own grazing land. The village heads sometimes try to control grazing patterns especially when they realise that the land within their areas of jurisdiction is being overgrazed. Each village has between 15 to 20 households. A household is ordinarily run by a male figure who is the father of the house. In a few cases, especially where the father has died, his widow becomes the de facto head. Some households also have a 'missing' husband due to frequent migrations to nearby South Africa. Most men cross the border into South Africa in search of employment especially menial jobs on South African farms near the Zimbabwean border. In the absence of these men, women are often left to make decisions in the home. But these women do not see themselves as acquiring control over land, as they are simply tending to it on behalf of the absent male figure. When interviewed on the role they might play in ensuring that their homestead's arable land is not 'invaded' during the off-season, the women confessed that they had neither the wherewithal nor capacity to stop anyone from herding their cattle on this land.

The challenge of land tenure in the newly resettled areas was captured by the solemn confession of one key informant who was at the helm of the land invasions in the year 2000, when he said that "the land invasions happened in a rushed way without any preparedness on the part of both the occupants and the government itself". Most people interviewed also displayed anxiety at the way the land occupations occurred as well as the timing of the land occupations. In particular, they argued that the occupations started at an awkward time of the year (in mid-October 2000) when they, as farmers in the communal areas, were supposed to start working in their fields for the coming agricultural season. There was no prior warning of the impending invasions such that the people literally rushed onto the nearby commercial farms. However, they do not regret becoming involved in the invasions as they conceptualised the invasions as 'correcting' land ownership by way of transferring land into the hands of the 'rightful owners'. They argued that occupying these farms was very necessary because they had waited far too long to gain access to more, and hopefully better, land.

In this regard, having occupied the farms, one informant (a village elder) recalls that:

> No one was quite sure about the security of tenure; neither did anyone care at the time of occupation. We were all overjoyed for having eventually gotten the chance to take back our land. The war veterans only encouraged us to start working on the farms arguing that the government was very serious about land invasions. They however did not specify on what type of tenure system that we were going to use. They later informed us that the government was processing offer letters for us and at the same time discouraged us from destroying our homes in the communal areas where we had just vacated.

Within a year after occupation, the government sent district land officers to peg land for the occupants. Each household was allocated about six hectares of arable land. In doing so, the government replicated the communal areas set-up by dividing land into arable, grazing and homestead land (for residential purposes). This involved households being settled on one side of the village in a straight line shielding arable land from the grazing area that lay on the other side of their homesteads. The grazing areas for each village are characteristically much larger than the arable areas and normally cover *vleis* (marshy land where water pools) and mountainous land. These grazing lands stretch to the next village but it is not always clear where the grazing land for a particular village begins and ends. It is difficult to control livestock from other villages coming to graze on a particular village's grazing land. Further, some pasturelands do not have dams of their own, and this forces Sovelele farmers to drive their livestock onto an adjoining village's grazing lands for water.

The farmers who pioneered this resettlement area through invasions note that grass for cattle was abundant initially in the communal grazing areas at Sovelele. In 2002, however, Zimbabwe experienced a severe drought that complicated the lives of small-scale farmers in communal areas but also newly settled A1 farms such as Sovelele. In particular, since there was no mechanism in place to protect the common grazing resources in the new resettlement areas, people from neighboring communal areas had a free reign on Sovelele's natural resource base including grazing land. This was captured in the statement made by one interviewee who narrated his experience:

> The year 2002 was a very bad year in the country. Communal areas surrounding us received little rains creating drought for both people and their livestock. The pastures in our farm were quite abundant and more than what our livestock could take. People started importing their relatives' livestock from communal areas to the farm in a system of *kuronzera* [a system of loaning cattle to someone to keep them on your behalf]. More and more cattle were driven into the farm with some cattle owners from the communal areas practically coming to camp in the farms feeding their cattle on our pasturelands.

It was clear that the situation in the already-degraded nearby communal areas was dire such that pastures had not only dried up but had diminished.

Through existing social ties that people in communal areas had with those in Sovelele, they managed to 'smuggle' their cattle into the A1 farm. The Sovelele farmers explained that it would be immoral to try and block communal people from doing this since their livestock were in poor health. One of the respondents remarked:

> How can you chase away the people that you have known for a long time from your communal areas? They are as good as your neighbours. Some of them are even your in-laws. In our culture, it is morally wrong to deprive someone of the only chance to survive. Refusing their cattle to graze on our pastures is as good as denying them a livelihood.

All the Sovelele villagers concurred that controlling access to grazing lands, even if desired, was almost impossible as no one had the power to exclude anyone from using grazing land. This was despite the villagers bemoaning the fact that there was a grazing crisis in the area that affected their own livelihoods. In this sense, grazing land existed as an open access resource.

Natural resource depletion and livelihood activities

Natural resources are central to the livelihoods of the new A1 farmers, as they lived off different forms of these resources. Of particular significance were timber products, fish, wild fruits, *mopane* worms, wildlife and minerals (especially gold). Tree felling was rampant especially in the early years after the land occupation as people sought timber to construct their homestead structures. But Sovelele farmers continue to harvest timber for homestead roofing and also for fencing their homes and fields. Additionally, they harvest firewood for heating and cooking. In this context, the Sovelele farmers recognised that most of these natural resources had been plundered over a very short space of time. Most areas had been cleared of vegetation cover almost indiscriminately as people cut down trees. An elderly sub-chief also lamented the killing of wildlife that happened during the invasions and the early years of settlement:

> The occupants behaved like cattle that had been moved from a place without enough pastures as they cut the paddock wires, which they would use to trap wildlife indiscriminately. Any type of game could be trapped including elephants and rhinos. It is now very difficult to bump into small animals like bush rabbits since they had been killed.

Farmers turned to fishing as a source of protein, found in small dams and nearby rivers. This entailed the use of fishing nets that also trapped baby fish, thereby hindering the maintenance of fish stock levels. The fish was not only used to supplement food requirements, but was sold as a way to raise cash for household needs such as fees and clothes for school-going children. A reduction of fish stock in rivers and dams was only due in part to over-fishing, as river siltation also arose because people undertook gold panning in streams and stream bank cultivation. Over a number of years now, Sovelele farmers have experienced ailing and even failed crop harvests and stream bank cultivation is seen as a way of augmenting or replacing mainstream crop cultivation in fields. Most people face challenges of poor harvests and decide to augment their ailing harvests with stream bank cultivation. The failed harvests also contribute to gold panning as an alternative livelihood.

Unpredictable grassland fires are reportedly common during the dry season and are very difficult to control once started. In the dry season, especially immediately after any crop harvesting, the grass is usually tall making it very difficult to put out once caught alight. Farmers spoke about reckless causes of fires. People harvesting bee honey or simply smoking could start a fire for example. The village elders noted with concern that these grassland fires were very dangerous to the mopane worms' life cycle. The fires also meant that grass for livestock was burnt.

It seemed that Sovelele farmers were not totally alarmed about the overall destruction of the natural resources on the farm. This is because they were not even sure themselves if they were to stay on the farm permanently. Farmers only received offer letters from the government in 2007 (about seven years after occupation) and all this time people lived in perpetual fear of being evicted. Nor have the offer letters necessarily enhanced farmer security. People therefore stampede for the available resources, as was noted:

> If one is not sure of whether he/she owns a place, he/she has no incentive to conserve what is there. People will be competing to exploit the resources without any restraint. Each person will be thinking that, "I must get it first before the next person or the visitor".

This is not to suggest that livelihood failures at Sovelele are reducible to insecure tenure. When asked about what plans they had when they occupied the farm, most people pointed out that they wanted to improve their livelihoods and even be able to acquire some assets. Most people who occupied Sovelele were coming from 'poor' communal area backgrounds and saw this as an opportunity to break out of the poverty cycle. But it was clear from the responses proffered by the interviewees that they had not been able to build a strong asset base through various livelihood strategies at Sovelele. Different reasons were put forward to explain the low asset achievements, as depicted in the selected following quotes:

- There is no way we can improve our livelihoods without meaningful support from the government. We lack adequate farm inputs like fertilisers, seeds and chemicals (Focus group discussant, 27 January 2015).
- Our farm produce are mainly drought resistant crops like millet, rapoko and sorghum. Market for these crops is a problem. This problem is compounded by poor road networks to close towns and cities (Village elder, interview, 27 November 2014).
- No one knows, given the political instability of our country, what will happen to us here. A change of government may mean losing our land. And imagine what will happen to all our investment here (Village elder, interview, 13 June 2014).
- People here are not skilled. They do not know what to plant, how to plant what they plant and do not have what to plant (Agritex officer, interview, 20 November 2014).
- We have not received reliable rains since the occupations and the maize that most of us want to grow will not produce much.

> (Focus group discussant, 27 January 2015)

Lack of government post-settlement support, climate variability and change, infrastructural challenges and political uncertainly all combine with other factors to minimise sustainable livelihoods in Sovelele. Indeed, few farmers claimed to have made significant strides in improving their livelihoods and accumulating assets wealth. Some probing showed that the more successful Sovelele people were those who had draught power from the communal areas and/or were gainfully employed as either teachers or other civil servants in the area.

Insecure communal tenure and local governance arrangements

In 2000, when the invasions started, the government through its local political structures advised the new occupants not to pull down their homes in the communal areas until the finalisation of the land acquisitions. This announcement, the village elders argued, created uncertainties around the land occupation process and subsequent land tenure security. Most people believed that this meant that the land occupation and fast track settlement were not a guarantee of permanent tenure for the A1 farmers. This, no doubt, has contributed to the failure to invest meaningfully at Sovelele.

As noted by Maguranyanga and Moyo (2006:3), "to date, A1 settlers have not secured formal documentation and A2 farmers are still awaiting lease agreements, while some settlers have not received their offer letters, from the government". Sachikonye (2005) argues that this delay created uncertainty and insecurity of land tenure for particularly A1 farmers with the consequent result of reduced confidence and investment commitment on the farms. It is difficult for the resettled farmers to embark on serious investments on the A1 farms when their future lies not in their hands but in the hands of a ruling party that is subject to twists and turns in land policies and programmes. Certainly, in the early years of fast track, when the fear of eviction was particularly pronounced, natural resource depletion may have been at its height. Though the settlers at Sovelele are now armed with offer letters, they are still not confident about their security of tenure due to the ongoing political turbulence and conflicts between the ruling party and main opposition party. Also, once accustomed to using natural resources almost at will, it takes considerable effort to bring about a change of practices, which would need to be based on a local consensus around environmental conservation.

Security tenure systems are normally associated with a number of rights including use rights, transfer rights, exclusion and inclusion rights, and enforcement rights. Post-fast track resettlement communities on A1 farms have had in essence use rights of land only without any power to either transfer the rights to other people, or to exclude others. The permit system based on an offer letter therefore is quite limited in terms of rights and powers for Sovelele farmers. Commenting on the predicament of farmers in the resettlement areas of Zimbabwe prior to fast track, Blume (1996:20) argued that the permit system used by the government to guarantee some form of tenure for the resettled famers lacked "a specific term and may be withdrawn at any time without compensation having to be paid for any investments the farmer has made". It seems that the fast track permit system does not deepen A1 farmer security any more than what happened in Zimbabwe under the earlier resettlement programme.

There may be no immediate and direct links, at least not inevitably, between land tenure systems, tenure security, natural resource use and wealth/asset building. Even communal tenure in-itself does not necessarily entail insecure tenure, as many communal farmers in Zimbabwe have occupied land for generations. Regrettably, though, the offer letter has not facilitated a sense of permanence on A1 farms. Added to this is the failure to ensure a regulatory mechanism for natural resource usage under the communal tenure arrangement on A1 farms.

Though communal tenure in-and-of-itself does not translate into natural resource depletion, the failure by the local community to ensure clear systems of regulation over natural resource access and use has tended to result in an open access system. Natural resources under communal tenure do belong to the community (unlike under the private property regime), but at Sovelele the absence of local regulatory systems inhibits the sustainable usage of natural resources. In the case of Sovelele, with livelihood options minimal, households turn to natural resources to eke out a living. People make deliberate decisions to access certain natural resources to eke out a living. The exploitation of natural resources is rationalised on this basis and it entails deliberate competition for resources and even outcompeting each other.

Beyond land itself, natural resources in Sovelele are thus open to free access by both Sovelele farmers and visitors from nearby communal areas. As argued by Hardin (1968), communal land tenure systems lead (at least potentially) to free-for-all access to natural resources insofar as there are no localised control mechanisms in place that are respected by all. For Sovelele, this is particularly evident in the case of the harvest of *mopane* worms, fisheries, wildlife hunting and use of pasture land. Masiiwa and Chigejo (2003) highlight that the absence of institutional frameworks (or local governance arrangements) for governing natural resource access is a broader problem within the A1 resettlement areas.

It is clear that visitors from the nearby communal areas, using social capital involving kinship and social networks with Sovelele farmers, are able to come and access natural resources at Sovelele. In the case of the pasture land of Sove- lele, the incentive for communal people to invest in and to improve this shared resource is insignificant, while the incentive to 'free-ride' and exploit the resource in question to the maximum is very great. When pastures are depleted in communal areas, households with relatives in the new resettlement areas loan their livestock to them. This practice of *kuronzera* (of loaning out cattle to poor households in particular) also contributes to overgrazing and the overstocking of pastureland in Sovelele. This bridging social capital across the A1 farm/ communal area divide seems to outdo any bonding social capital between Sove- lele farmers in that the farmers are failing to protect their resources from what would ordinarily be seen as 'outsiders' intruding within their space.

Conclusion and policy insights

This study concludes that insecure land tenure and the absence of local regu- latory mechanisms combined play a key role in discouraging investment on farms and in encouraging the unsustainable use of natural resources. Secure tenure in particular is crucial in ensuring that the goals of both community- level development and natural resources conservation are met. Communities are both forced and attracted to resort to natural resource exploitation by a number of factors, which can be addressed in the first instance by ensuring a securer land tenure arrangement. Local governance systems, in the second instance, can likewise fulfil the same purpose. Meaningful development in fast track resettled areas though can be realised only if the government supports the occupants with basic infrastructure such as good roads and communication networks, education and health facilities, agricultural extension services and links to the market, among other things. The following are the policy implica- tions of this study:

- Land tenure rights in Zimbabwe must be very clear and final. The government should make sure that the occupiers of any piece of land have clear and absolute rights over that land to encourage responsibility.
- There is need for the government of Zimbabwe to recognise the importance of separating the land from the politics of patronage. Occupiers of land should not live in perpetual fear of being evicted if political regimes change.
- It is the responsibility of the government in conjunction with the local authority to ensure that their people are well educated on the need to conserve the natural environment since it is cardinal to both the present and future livelihoods.
- Communities must be encouraged to tightly control their resources from outsiders so that the natural environment is conserved.
- It is also imperative for the government to assist in the provision of basic social amenities in the resettled areas to make sure that the settlers do not entirely rely on natural resources for their sustenance.

References

Alexander, J. 2003. *The Unsettled Land: State-making and the Politics of Land in Zimbabwe 1893–2003*. James Currey: Oxford.

Blume, A. 1996. *Land Tenure in Rural Zimbabwe*. Orientierungrashmen: Bodenrecht und Bodenordnung Deutsche Gesellschaft Technische Zusammenarbeit.

Chamunorwa, A. 2010. *Comparative Analysis of Agricultural Productivity Between Newly Resettled Farmers and Communal Farmers in Mashonaland East Province*. Livelihoods after Land Reform in Zimbabwe, Working paper 8. Livelihoods after Land Reform Project, South Africa. PLAAS.

Chaumba, J., Scoones, I. and Wolmer, W. 2003. *From Jambanja to Planning: The Reassertion of Technocracy in Land Reform in Southeastern Zimbabwe*. Sustainable Livelihoods in Southern Africa. Research Paper 2.

Chigumira, E. 2010. *Zimbabwe's Fast Track Land reform*. LAP Lambert Publications.

Chingarande, S.D. 2008. Gender and the Struggle for Land Equity. In S. Moyo, K. Helliker and T. Murisa (eds), *Contested Terrain: Land Reform and Civil Society in Contemporary Zimbabwe*, Pietmaritzburg, South Africa: S and S Publisher.

Dekker, M. and Kinsey, B. 2011. Contextualizing Zimbabwe's Land Reform: Long-term Observations from the First Generation. *The Journal of Peasant Studies*, 38 (5): 995–1019.

Dzingirai, V., Egger, E.M., Landau, L., Litchfield, J., Mutopo, P. and Nyikahadzoyi, K. 2012. *Migrating out of Poverty in Zimbabwe*. University of Sussex: Brighton.

Dzingirai, V. 2009. The Impact of Political Crisis on Natural Resources: A Case Study of Zimbabwe. *Africa Insight*, 39 (3): 24–37.

Forner, C., Blaser, J., Jotzo, F. and Robledo, C. 2006. Keeping the forest for the climate's sake: avoiding deforestation in developing countries under the UNFCCC. *Climate Policy*, 6 (3): 1–20.

Gadzirayi, C.T. and Mutandwa, E. 2006. Land Degradation in a Changing Agrarian Context – Case of the Communal Areas in Zimbabwe. *International Journal of Agriculture and Biology*, 8: 708–709.

GoZ, 2001. *Land reform and resettlement: Revised phase II*. Harare: Ministry of Lands and Rural Resettlement.

Hardin, G. 1968. *The Tragedy of the Commons*. Toronto: York University.

Kanyenze, G., Kondo, T., Chitambara, P. and Martens, J. 2011. *Beyond the Enclave: Towards a Pro-poor and Inclusive Development Strategy for Zimbabwe*. Weaver Press: Harare.

Katerere, Y., Moyo, S. and Mujakachi, L. 1993. The national context, land and structural adjustment and the Forestry Commission. In P.N. Bradley and K. McNamara (eds), *Living with trees: Policies for forestry management in Zimbabwe*, (pp. 11–27). World Bank Technical Paper 210. Washington: World Bank.

Kujinga, K. and Manzungu, E. 2004. Enduring contestations: Stakeholder strategies in water resources management: The case of Odzi sub catchment council, Eastern Zimbabwe. *Eastern Africa Social Science Research Review*, XX (1): 67–91.

Lindsey, P.A., Balme, G.A., Booth, V.R. and Midlane, N. 2012. The Significance of African Lions for the Financial Viability of Trophy Hunting and the Maintenance of Wild Land. PLoS ONE 7 (1): e29332. doi:10.1371/journal.pone.0029332

Maguranyanga, B. and Moyo, S. 2006. *Land Tenure in the Post FTLRP Zimbabwe: Key Strategic Policy Development Issues*. Prepared on behalf of the African Institute for Agrarian Studies, Harare.

Makadho, J. 2006. Land Redistribution Experience in Zimbabwe: 1998–2004. In M. Rukuni, P. Tawonezvi, C. Eicher, M. Munyuki-Hungwe and P. Matondi (eds), *Zimbabwe's Agricultural Revolution Revisited* (pp. 165–188). University of Zimbabwe Publications: Harare.

Mandizadza, S. 2010. *The Fast Track Land Reform Programme and Livelihoods in Zimbabwe: A Case Study of Households at Athlone Farm in Murehwa District*. Livelihoods after Land Reform in Zimbabwe, Working Paper 2. Cape Town, South Africa: Institute for Poverty, Land and Agrarian Studies, University of Cape Town.

Manzungu, E. 2004. *Water for All. Improving Water Resource Governance in Southern Africa*. Gatekeeper Series No. 113. International Institute for Environment and Development Natural Resources Group and Sustainable Agriculture and Rural Livelihoods Programme. London.

Manzungu, E. 2012. Introduction: The Shifting Sands of Natural Resource Management in Zimbabwe. *Journal of Social Development in Africa*, 27 (1): 7–21.

Marongwe, N. 2011. Who was allocated Fast Track land, and What Did They Do With It? Selection of A2 farmers in Goromonzi District, Zimbabwe and its Impacts on Agricultural Production. *The Journal of Peasant Studies*, 38 (5): 1069–1092.

Masiiwa, M. 2004. *Post-Independence Land Reform in Zimbabwe: Controversies and Impact on the Economy*. Harare: Friedrich Erbert Stiftung Institute and Institute of Development Studies, University of Zimbabwe.

Masiiwa, M. and Chigejo, O. 2003. *The Agrarian Reform in Zimbabwe: Sustainability and Empowerment of Rural Communities*. Harare: IDS, University of Zimbabwe.

Masiiwa, M. and Chipungu, L. 2004. Land Reform Programme in Zimbabwe: Disparity Between Policy Design and Implementation. In M. Masiiwa (ed.), *Post-Independence Land Reform in Zimbabwe: Controversies and Impact on the Economy*, (pp. 1–24). Harare: Institute of Development Studies.

Moyo, S. 1995. *The Land Question in Zimbabwe*. Sapes Trust: Harare.

Moyo, S., Chambati, W., Murisa, T., Sisiba, D., Dangwa, C., Mujeyi, K. and Nyoni, N. 2009. *Fast Track Land Reform Baseline Survey in Zimbabwe: Trends and Tendencies, 2005/06*. African Institute for Agrarian Studies.

Moyo, S. 2000. *Land Reform under Structural Adjustment in Zimbabwe: Land Use Change in the Mashonaland Provinces*. Uppsala: Nordic Africa Institute.

Moyo, S., Mushayavanhu, D. and Gwata, C. 2004. *Review of the Zimbabwean Agricultural Sector Following the Implementation of the Land Reform Natural Resources and Land Reform.* African Institute for Agrarian Studies, Monograph Series, Issue No. 3/2004.

Moyo, S. and Yeros, P. 2005. The Resurgence of Rural Movements under Neoliberalism. In S. Moyo and P. Yeros (eds), *Reclaiming the Land: The Resurgence of Rural Movements in Africa, Asia and Latin America,* (pp. 165–208). London and Cape Town: Zed Books, David Phillip.

Mubvami, T. 2004. Impact of Land Redistribution on the Environment. In T. Masiiwa (ed.), *Post Independence Land Reform in Zimbabwe: Controversies and Impact on the Environment,* Friedrich Ebert Stiftung, IDS, University of Zimbabwe: Harare.

Murombedzi, J.C. 1995. *Zimbabwe's CAMPFIRE Programme: Using Natural Resources for Rural Development, Mimeo,* University of Zimbabwe: Centre for Applied Social Sciences, Harare, Zimbabwe.

Murphree, M.W. 1991. *Communities as Institutions for Resource Management.* CASS Occasional Paper Series – NRM; October 1991, University of Zimbabwe: Harare.

Mutimukuru-Maravanyika, T. 2010. Can we Learn our Way to Sustainable Management: Adaptive Collaborative Management in Mafungautsi State Forests, Zimbabwe. PhD thesis Wageningen University.

Raftopolous, B. 2002. *Key Note Address: The Crisis in Zimbabwe.* Paper presented at the Canadian Association of African Studies Annual Conference, University of Toronto, Toronto, Ontario, 29 May 2002.

Rutherford, B. 2001. Working on the Margins: Black Workers, White Land Beneficiaries in Post-Colonial Zimbabwe. Harare and London: Weaver Press: Zed Books.

Sachikonye, L. 2003. *The Situation of Commercial Farm Workers after Land Reform in Zimbabwe.* Harare: Unpublished Report prepared for FCTZ.

Sachikonye, L. 2005. The Land is the Economy: Revisiting the Land Question. *African Security Review,* 14 (3): 31−44.

Scoones, I., Chibudu, S., Chikura, P., Jeranyama, D., Machaka, W., Machanja, B., Mavedzenge, B., Mombeshora, B., Mudhara, M., Mudziwo, C., Murimbarimba, F. and Zirereza, B. 1996. *Hazards and Opportunities: Farming Livelihoods in Dryland Africa: Lessons from Zimbabwe.* London: Zed Books.

Scoones, I., Marongwe, N., Mavedzenge, B., Murimbarimba, F., Mahenehene, J. and Sukume, C. 2010. *Zimbabwe's Land Reform: Myths and Realities.* Harare and London: Weaver Press, Jacana Media and James Currey.

Stoneman, C. 2000. Zimbabwe Land Policy and the Land Reform Programme. In T. Bowyer-Bower and C. Stoneman (eds), *Land Reform in Zimbabwe: Constraints and Prospects.* Aldershot: Ashgate.

Sutton, P. 2004. *A Perspective on Environmental Sustainability? A Paper for the Victorian Commissioner for Environmental Sustainability.* www.green-innovation.asn.au/ [Accessed on 5 June 2011].

Wily, L.A. and Mbaya, S. 2001. *Land, People, and Forests in Eastern and Southern Africa at the Beginning of the 21st Century: The Impact of Land Relations on the Role of Communities in Forest Future.* Scan house East Africa: IUCN Eastern Africa Regional Nairobi.

Wolmer, W. 2007. From Wilderness Vision to Farm Invasions: Conservation and Development in Zimbabwe's South-East Lowveld. *Harare: Weaver Press.*

14 Fast track land reform programme and women in Goromonzi District

Loveness Chakona and Manase Kudzai Chiweshe

Introduction

In the year 2001, the government of Zimbabwe launched the large-scale Fast Track Land Reform Programme (FTLRP) as part of its ongoing Land Reform and Resettlement Programme (LRRP) that began in the late 1990s. The FTLRP emerged as a direct result of the land occupation movement that began in February 2000. The motive behind the FTLRP, as propagated by the ruling party, was to address the racially skewed land distribution pattern inherited at independence in 1980. Prior to 2000, land redistribution had occurred on an insignificant scale such that, by the late 1990s, Zimbabwe retained its colonial dualistic agrarian structure consisting of white commercial farm areas and black customary areas. The FTLRP has undoubtedly significantly addressed the racially based land injustices which emerged (and were consolidated) under colonialism and which were perpetuated during the first two decades of independence. However, crucial questions arise around other (unresolved) dimensions to the land question in Zimbabwe. One significant dimension is gender, in that women's relationship to land has been mediated historically through men.

Though less overt than the racial structuring of land relations in colonial Zimbabwe, patriarchy was intrinsic to colonial land dispossession and became embedded in the resultant agrarian structure. Historically, 'race' was invariably articulated as the key signifier for land in Zimbabwe and fast track over the past decade has sought to undermine the racial agrarian system. The pertinent question therefore becomes: has fast track addressed in any significant manner the patriarchal basis of land relations in contemporary Zimbabwe? A burgeoning number of broad overviews and specific case studies have been undertaken on the FTLRP, but few have had a distinctively gender focus in seeking to identify, examine and assess the effect of the programme on patriarchal relations and the socio-economic livelihoods of rural women in Zimbabwe. This chapter offers an empirically rich gendered study of land redistribution in one particular district in Zimbabwe, namely, Goromonzi District near the capital city of Harare. The focus is on women in new (heavily subdivided) A1 resettlement farms in the district (and specifically women who came from nearby customary areas) and on women who continue to live in the long established communal areas in the district. The chapter concludes that the FTLRP is seriously flawed in terms of addressing and tackling the patriarchal structures that underpin the Zimbabwean land question.

Women, gender and land in Zimbabwe

As attempted most explicitly by Sylvester (2000), many scholars of women and gender in Zimbabwe have investigated how women are located, defined, differentiated and shaped by dominant patriarchal discourses, practices and ideologies; as well as how they have used their agency to shape their identities and social spaces in colonial and post-colonial times. In this respect, as Goebel (2005:33) puts it, Zimbabwe is "undeniably divided into two groups, one called 'women' and another called 'men', with prescribed roles, rules of conduct and norms of relations between the two sexes". Boys and girls from an early age go through the socialisation process that produces and codes – as natural – gendered divisions of labour, access to economic and cultural resources, identities, roles, hierarchies of privilege, heterosexual marriage and childbearing (McFadden 1996, Zinanga 1996). This emphasises the widely accepted understanding of gender as entailing socially constructed roles between men and women that are deeply rooted in Zimbabwean cultures.

According to Goebel (2005), in her study of women and land in Zimbabwe, marital status and the way that the family mediates access to economic resources (land included), status and justice emerges over and over again in the work of feminist scholars of gender. This is because there are gendered categories with clear rigidities and consistencies that are especially salient to shaping women's experiences (Goebel 2002). This does not imply that women are a homogeneous group whose experiences can merely be assumed or asserted. Rather, as Rutherford (2001:150) highlights, the prevalence of gendered experiences suggests that there are modes of power that sustain "women" as a category – including varieties of marriage, and social practices that inform the administration and policies of the "state". For Sylvester (2000), this gendered regime involves discourses of knowledge and power, practices, laws, customs, social relations and ideologies that contribute to the differentiation of experience along gendered lines. And this runs through all regimes of truth in both colonial and post-colonial times in ways that disadvantage women:

> Viewed benignly, the gender regime "merely" enforces a commonplace designation of two major types of people – men and women. But this designation is rarely benign in its effects on people classified as women. Moreover the regime of gender, despite many historical permutations and challenges – not the least by women guerrillas during Zimbabwe's liberation struggle – continues to be openly advocated in the sense that many people defend "traditional" body-based gender distinctions as a true way of identifying people and designating their social places.
>
> (Sylvester 2000:86)

There is a strong justification for focusing on gender as a central site of struggle for rural women in Zimbabwe. In addition, though, other categories like class, ethnicity, race, lineage and totem are powerful forces in shaping women's experiences. Rather than simply being a Western feminist imposition on African social conditions, a focus on gender emerges as a legitimate field of inquiry in fieldwork studies in rural Zimbabwe. It is gender structuring that complicates women's position vis-à-vis land rights in Zimbabwe, leading to contestations over women's identities, positions and entitlements as read through complex cultural meanings and social practices (Goebel 2005). In Zimbabwe, the relations between land and culture are profoundly about the construction and reconstruction of masculinity (Kesby 1999). Men and masculinity require positioning women as outsiders in relation to land (notably in patrilocal settlements), just as it leads to distancing women from their children through constructing children as belonging to the patrilineage. Therefore, in claiming primary rights to land, women create distinctly "regime-defying identities" for themselves (Sylvester 2000:88). Historically, culturally, and within current 'regimes of truth', by claiming land in their own right in Zimbabwe, women step out of place due to patriarchy.

Goebel (2005:35) notes that it has become a truism that (in societies such as Zimbabwe that are historically hoe-cultivating) women are the main farmers but their subordinate cultural and social position often curtails their abilities to farm as productively as possible. In situations where rural-to-urban migration by men prevails, subsistence farming by women is difficult because husbands do not always support their wives; in fact, the urban migrants frequently become involved in expensive extra-marital affairs. African 'peasant' women farmers, therefore, may occupy a contradictory position – on the one hand, autonomy by way of de facto female headship in the household and, on the other, dependency and vulnerability with regard to male earnings and the prevailing gender ideologies that condone the supremacy of male authority even in the absence of men. In communal areas in Zimbabwe, there are many cases of women being beaten by their husbands after making key decisions about farming without the husband's authorisation.

Schmidt (1992) documents the gendered struggles over production in the African reserves (or communal areas) in Zimbabwe's colonial history. Although women had been the backbone of peasant agricultural production before colonial interference, male absence through the migrant labour system left women with an increasingly high farm burden, but not necessarily with decision-making authority over farm production. In the early 1900s, an increasingly harsh patriarchal ideology among African men (supported by chiefs) together with colonial measures (for example the introduction of passes for women in the 1920s), led to strict control over women's movement away from rural homesteads.

Another colonial practice in support of confining women in reserves was to hire men as domestic workers in urban centres; this subverted the "natural" association of women with domestic work and served the cause of creating a specifically male-waged workforce (Schmidt 1992, Jeater 1993, McCulloch

2000). In the 1930s, in order to stabilise the rural black workforce, the colonial powers encouraged men to bring their wives to live with them on commercial farms (Amanor-Wilks 1996). There was an increase in female labour on the commercial farms, as casual female labour became more popular and often preferable to permanent male workers.

While women have always been among the migrants to town (attempting to flee poverty or patriarchal control in the reserves), the dominant migration pattern under colonial conditions remained one of mobile men who maintained a home in the communal area, presided over by a wife or wives (Goebel 2005:36). In Zimbabwe, women's lack of primary land rights in customary (communal) areas was historically underpinned by the definition of their legal status as minors and the dual legal system (customary and civil law) that placed most African women under the dictates of customary law in the colonial period (Maboreke 1991).

After independence, in 1982 the new government instituted the Legal Age of Majority Act (LAMA) that gave women majority status at the age of 18. Despite the provisions of LAMA, customary law still dominated legal practice in communal areas throughout the 1980s (Maboreke 1991, Stewart 1992). This meant that women did not gain access to communal area land in their own right, and the practice of assigning land mainly to married men continued (Chimedza 1988). A clear example of the patriarchal character of the post-colonial state is in citizenship policy as expressed in the 1984 Citizenship Act. Zimbabwean men who marry foreign women can transfer their citizenship to their wives, but women who marry foreign men cannot transfer such rights to their husbands or children and also face the diminishment of their own citizenship rights (McFadden 2002).

This notion of citizenship reflects patrilineal patterns common in Shona culture, where a man stays within his patrilineal family upon marriage while a woman acquires obligations to her husband's family upon marriage. Rural women's lives in Zimbabwe have been distinctively tied to the land, but this relationship to the land has historically been mediated through male entitlement and control –involving the institution of marriage and the allocative powers of mostly traditional, chiefly authorities. As cited earlier, Rutherford (2001) notes that the gendered aspect of land allocation appears remarkably consistent and is marked by rigidities, becoming one of those "modes of power that sustain 'women' as a category"; and this cuts across colonial and post-colonial Zimbabwe. Securing land rights for women in Zimbabwe, and in Africa more broadly, is a common talking point in the literature on land (Razavi 2002), as this is seen as central to improving both women's livelihoods and food security more generally (Razavi 2002:16).

Women and fast track

Goebel (2005:145) highlights that land and fast track have been reduced, in competing discursive arguments, to volatile racial and class struggles. This emphasis on class and race is clear from the prevailing literature, which is largely critical of fast track. The government of Zimbabwe, in evicting white commercial farmers, has officially articulated the view that the redistribution of land serves the interests of the black peasantry. Certain critics of fast track, such as McFadden (2002), argue that the process was about the takeover of Zimbabwe's main economic asset (i.e. agricultural land) by the country's ZANU-PF political elite.

Another critic, Moore (2001), situates the 'land grab' within a more economistic framework; this involves an argument about stalled primitive accumulation brought on by the colonial and post-colonial structural impediments to economic development. At one level, fast track is a fundamental departure from previous philosophies, practices and procedures for acquiring land and resettling people in Zimbabwe. It certainly is a dramatic shift from the government's policy of constitution-based and market-led reforms (Chitsike 2003) that existed prior to the year 2000. But the critical question for this study is the relationship between fast track and the restructuring of patriarchy and land. Alone, racial and class restructuring of agrarian relations do not invariably entail gender restructuring. The discussion in this section seeks to highlight the position of women on both A1 farms and in communal areas in the light of fast track.

The Land Reform and Resettlement Programme (Phase 2), from 1998, specifies that any selection of land beneficiaries should seek to include special groups (for example women) and it refers to the need for poverty alleviation, particularly given that 75% of rural women live in poverty. Ensuing documents make reference to gender, targeting women as a special group, and seeking to mainstream gender throughout the land redistribution process. The fast track implementation plan does not specify any of this, and the policy documents and legislation setting out the basis of the fast track programme do not address gender issues in any sustained manner. In October 2000, though, the government stated that it would ensure a 20% quota for women to benefit from the programme. Interestingly, the Utete Report (2003) – a government-initiated audit of fast track – recommended a 40% quota allocation, especially for A1 peasant farmers.

Compared to land resettlement programmes that took place soon after independence, it seems that there has been a reduction in the number of female beneficiaries of land. It is estimated that, for schemes previous to fast track, 25% of the beneficiaries were women. Under fast track, actual female beneficiaries are close to but do not reach the target of 20% of the total (Chingarande 2008). In large part, the problem emanates from targeting families/households as units without addressing the prevailing property relations and rights within the family or household (i.e. the intra-household gender relations). In terms of fast track beneficiaries, the selection process was undertaken primarily by the Rural District Councils (RDCs) and District Land Committees (DLCs); although many informal processes also were important. The patriarchal character of these institutions (at least in terms of being male-dominated) disadvantaged women in the selection process. Issues of sexual harassment, sexual favours and gender violence against women were also visible. Some accounts indicate that women seeking allocation of a plot under the fast track scheme have been forced to exchange sexual favours to get on the redistribution lists and that war veterans and ZANU-PF militia members raped women in the course of the land occupations (Goebel 2007, Chingarande 2008).

Despite variations in belief systems and practices across rural Zimbabwe, women throughout the country did not benefit sufficiently from the fast track exercise. Overall, male-headed households benefitted most from FTLRP. Despite government commitment to addressing gender inequality in land distribution, women (whose rights to land in customary areas are weak) simply failed to benefit proportionately from the fast track process (Chingarande 2004). Thus, available evidence on statistics from all provinces indicates that, for both A1 and A2 fast track models, women did not benefit significantly from the FTLRP exercise compared to men. Model A2 is a commercial resettlement scheme, comprising small, medium and large-scale commercial resettlement. For model A2, the percentage is low for females in all provinces due to the fact that women in most cases do not have the necessary resources to be regarded as collateral in order to qualify for land allocation under this model. Model A1 was intended for landless people (officially with both villagised and self-contained variants) and women seemingly stood a better chance to qualify under this model. Female-headed households that benefited under model A1 constituted only 18% while women beneficiaries under Model A2 constituted only 12% (Hellum 2004:1796). Available statistics however, do not show the extent to which women received land as either de jure or de facto heads.

The Zimbabwean state has historically tended to reinforce patriarchy in relation to land, and this seemingly remains the case under fast track. Historically, as noted, men have been the central holders and heirs of land rights in both communal and (early) resettlement areas. Access to land in customary areas has not been easily conferred on single, married and divorced women, though customary law prevailing in these areas does not totally preclude this. Although women who (on a *de jure* basis) headed households in the early resettlement areas could access land and be given permits of occupancy, their married counterparts still in large part had to access land through their husbands (with no clear security of tenure should their husbands die). Occupancy of contemporary A1 resettlement plots is likewise based on a permit system (involving an offer letter) that is still marked by uncertainties. Female-headed households have possession of plots in their own right and, at least formally, plots occupied by married couples are held jointly in both their names. But this joint arrangement is optional rather than obligatory. Quite often, married men who obtained an A1 plot through the formal application channels have retained the plot in their name only. Action Aid (2009) reveals for instance that a significant number of female heads of households (on A1 farms) who have control over land are in fact widows who initially accessed land through their deceased spouses.

The sources of this gendered inequity in land allocation under fast track relate to a number of constraints faced by women in applying for land, including bureaucratic constraints, gender biases amongst selection structures (which compromise mainly men), lack of information on the process, and poor mobil-isation of women's activist organisations around the issue of applications (Moyo and Yeros 2007). The 2003 Utete Commission report in fact emphasises that the marginalisation of women during the implementation of FTLRP is related in par-ticular to the preponderance of men in relevant decision-making structures (PLRC 2003). It goes on to argue that the allocation of land on A1 farms (involv-ing the issuing of user permits) often directly involved the District Administra-tor, who followed the recommendation of the village head and headman (in customary areas) or the local councillor.

In most cases these people are men who are the custodians of culture and tra-dition, which they interpret as prohibiting women's 'ownership' of land allowing only secondary rights of access. Indeed, throughout Zimbabwe, a significant minority of A1 plot-holders has moved from customary areas, including A1 households headed by women. In these communal areas, during the colonial period and beyond (including the fast track period), the system of patriarchy has structured landholdings and land access (Blackwells 2003). Many unmarried women (single, divorced or widowed) from customary areas sought to escape the patriarchal confines of the communal areas (including the chieftainship system as the protector of patriarchal traditions) by seeking land during fast track on A1 farms. This is because, on A1 farms, women can more easily possess land either in their own right or jointly as 'owners' of plots. However, chieftainship arrangements are now emerging on A1 farms (including the appointment of headman by chiefs, though not on a hereditary basis) and this may have negative implications for women on these farms (Murisa 2011).

Research methodology

Goromonzi District, as the empirical site for the chapter, is one of nine dis-tricts in Mashonaland East Province. It is a district located 32 kilometres southeast of the country's capital Harare. The field work was carried out in late 2010 and early 2011 in three study areas: two contiguous A1 farms (Dunstan and Lot 3 of Buena Vista) and the nearby Gwaze Communal Area. The researchers randomly selected the two A1 farms from a list of A1 farms provided by the District Land Committee in Goromonzi. The study utilised a mixed method approach and four specific techniques were pursued: the admin-istration of a survey questionnaire, focus group discussions with farmers, in-depth interviews with key informants and simple observation. Sampling of respondents for a household questionnaire involved purposive and snowball sampling, with the focus primarily on women. In the case of the A1 farms (Dunstan and Lot 3 of Buena Vista) the target sample was primarily women who had moved from communal areas (either from within the district or from elsewhere in the province). In the case of Gwaze communal area, purposive sampling involved the targeting of mainly women. Selecting women from the A1 farms and the customary area were necessary for comparative purposes with regard to the lives of women.

In each of Dunstan, Lot 3 of Buena Vista and Gwaze, 25 households (selecting 20 women and 5 men) formed part of the survey. While women were the focus of the study, gathering evidence from men was crucial to identify the pervasiveness of patriarchal worldviews. Key informants included village heads for A1 farms, selected members of the governing Committee of Seven (for A1 farms), agricultural extension officers for all the study sites, members of the District Land Committee, the District Administrator, and the chief for Gwaze customary area. Direct observation was extensively used especially to identify the socio-economic quality of life in relation to the livelihood initiatives of A1 and customary farmers (such as numbers of livestock), and thereby verify empirical evidence collected using the other research methods.

Gendered distribution of land in Goromonzi

In the district, under FTLRP, 243 of the district's 257 farms were gazetted for resettlement, and 14 farms were left un-gazetted. According to the Utete commission report (PLRC 2003), 70 farms were de-listed for various reasons. Overall, 43% of the land went to the A1 schemes and 57% of the land in the district was redistributed under the A2 model. This went contrary to government's intentions, in which 60% of redistributed land was supposed to be for A1 farmers and 40% for the A2 farms. FTLRP in the district has resulted in a new agrarian structure in the light of both A1 and A2 farms. Pre-fast track, the district had four categories of commercial farms, namely, small-scale, medium-scale, large-scale and peri-urban commercial farms; in addition, there were communal areas. Post-fast track, the district consists of the following: only 1% of the land now belongs to large-scale commercial farming, 14% to medium-scale and small-scale commercial farming, 9% to peri-urban farming, 47% to small-scale farming in communal lands and 29% to the A1 model (Marongwe 2008). For the A1 model, a total of 33,933 hectares were allocated from 49 former commercial farms resulting in more than 1,800 new plots created. The average was 10 hectares for small plots and 47 hectares for bigger plots. New plots were generally larger than in the old resettlement period of 1980–1999, where a typical settler got 5 hectares of arable land in relation to the villagised model. Under the A1 model, the spatial distribution of the farms allocated seems to have been influenced by the proximity of the farm to the surrounding communal areas which are Seke, Chikwaka, Musana, Chinamhora, Gwaze and Rusike.

Of the 25 households interviewed through a household questionnaire in each of the three sites, results indicate that, for Dunstan, 20 of these households (or 80%) involve married women 'owning' land through a male; the respective figures are 70% for Lot 3 and 25% for Gwaze. The other households are composed of widows, single women and divorcees who often have land registered in their own names. Focus group discussions conducted in Gwaze highlight the significance of patriarchal practices: preference is invariably given to men in terms of land possession and – even in the case of the death of the husband – other men of adulthood age are regularly given priority over the wife in terms of inheriting land. Women in communal areas continue to be marginalised in this regard, such that fast track land reform has not addressed questions of land and patriarchy within the confines of customary areas. Women therefore in Gwaze communal area are heavily marginalised in terms of 'owning' land in their own right; this however may not be the case for divorcees, widows and single women. The specific reason for this is the existence of the chieftainship system, which governs access to land on a distinctively gendered basis. This system is considerably more pervasive and entrenched in communal areas compared to the fast track areas; as indicated, in the latter, at least on A1 farms, a modified or new traditionalism (based on nonhereditary headmen appointed by chiefs living in customary areas) has emerged but its impact remains uncertain. In terms of land access, communal area women suffer more from the effects of patriarchy than do women on A1 farms.

In Dunstan and Lot 3 of Buena Vista, the position of women is comparatively better. In A1 farms, the position of married women has improved in terms of land access. The explanation for this by married women in both Dunstan and Lot 3 is that land could be registered jointly with their husbands. The possibilities for joint ownership on A1 farms are evident (20% in the case of Lot 3) whereas joint ownership seems non-existent in Gwaze. Generally, for A1 farms, the names of the wife and husband tend to appear on the offer letter (although women on A1 farms still often speak about accessing land through their husband); whereas in Gwaze women access land through marriage in the light of chieftainships, with the latter effectively designating the man as the head of the household. In Gwaze, the traditional authority is responsible for land distribution and access, and therefore men 'own' and control the means of production. This is significant considering that a large number of households on the two A1 farms came from customary areas – hence, women from communal areas in particular may have been advantaged by this 'relaxation' of customary law on A1 farms.

Comparison between Gwaze and Dunstan/Lot 3

One of the key goals of this study is to compare the livelihoods in Gwaze communal area and the two A1 farms. There is the specific need to compare the experiences of women in the A1 farms who came from the communal area and those who continue to live in the communal areas, in terms of their livelihoods and livelihood strategies. Of importance in this regard is agricultural production. Overall, production on the two A1 farms has almost trebled compared to Gwaze and other nearby communal areas, with a marked increase in the standard of living of those households which moved from customary areas. The testimony from one woman who came with her family from Gwaze Communal Area to Dunstan Farm is revealing. She notes:

> The agricultural situation is good compared to Gwaze. Our yields have improved very much from where we were with a household producing an

average of 3–4 tonnes of maize and 8–10 bales of cotton. The soils we now till do not demand as much fertilizer compared to where we came from. The agricultural situation is good basing on what we have seen so far because there are rich soils and good yields.

In summer this household (like other households) also has a small garden for vegetables –they sell the produce to local farmers and to Seke communal lands which acts as a readily available market for them. At Dunstan and Lot 3, there is abundant pasture and vegetation for grazing (as well as wild game), which the A1 farmers said they never imagined prior to fast track land reform. There was concern though amongst the farmers that if current practices are not stemmed (deforestation and uncontrolled hunting), they will soon be back to the communal area situation.

One respondent exclaimed:

> I am excited about the new place and now being a proud owner of livestock and a piece of land. I know I will never go hungry as long as I am here. I started here as a pauper without anything but now I own 7 herd of cattle, goats, sheep and implements.

This married woman claimed that those farmers who are complaining are lazy because her life has been transformed since coming onto the farm. She went on to say:

> We are producing enough to consume and sell annually. In the reserves [customary areas] I never reached a tonne of maize despite working very hard. Now I can now afford to produce about 5 tonnes annually which is very different from where I came from. Now I have my own piece of land which no one has control over; it is only for me and my family.

This woman is amongst those households which were considered the poorest in their former home (communal) areas. Such households had come to the A1 farm with minimal property but had managed to obtain a plot of their own, and to acquire livestock and other moveable assets. In this regard, another female A1 farmer argued that her family's life has changed dramatically (alluding to the fact that they no longer survive on donations but have their own produce and income from farming).

There is however a challenge in terms of agricultural inputs at Dunstan and Lot 3 of Buena Vista. Farmers do not obtain inputs on time and the local shops do not sell the inputs they need (fertiliser and seeds). The shops they rely upon are located around 20 kilometres away in Goromonzi Business Centre. Besides the unavailability of inputs, they also do not have cash to access what they need for farming. However, in the 2010 agricultural year, they benefitted from and received inputs (seeds and fertilisers) through the Presidential Inputs Programme that was launched in most of the districts countrywide, despite the fact that the quantities received were low. There is a committee chosen by the local farmers which is responsible for distribution of inputs. But there are claims by A1 farmers of corruption by the committee leadership, as the leaders are accused of diverting some of the inputs for their own use.

Markets for agricultural products are also a big challenge with prices being low. As one A1 farmer exclaimed:

> Last year I grew sunflower but when I wanted to sell to those who buy sunflowers they told me that they would only buy from the farmers that they had given inputs. Adequate information should be availed to the farmers. The current prices are demoralising. We are buying fertilizer for $35 per bag but when selling our cotton we sell 200 kilograms (a bale) for $60. As a result of such poor pricing the farmer would end up as the final looser. In terms of outputs, yes we are farmers but if they cannot buy our produce at a good price this means our capacity to buy enough inputs for ourselves is limited.

Another woman reiterated this: "Last year I grew sunflowers. But I am still stuck with the sunflowers since those who bought that crop in the area said that they would only buy from specific farmers whom they had supported." Coupled with this is also a lack of information about markets for some of their products like peanuts and sunflower. This problem is particularly evident among women as they are the ones who were engaged in the growing of these crops. Despite the obstacles that they are facing in the fast track areas, one male A1 farmer at Dunstan exclaimed: "Of course we have new challenges but we are living comfortably here. Comparing with where we came from, we are living comfortably and cannot complain as long as we have the rains".

Overall, both male and female A1 farmers appear very pleased about their new place. There is increased productivity (with higher rainfall and good soils) and a degree of social harmony: "We now have a place where we are free, free from the troubles of rumours and gossips that were characteristic of the polygamous family, which is common in communal areas", one A1 woman in Dunstan in a focus group discussion put it. She went on to explain that "we lived in constant shortage of food in communal areas and even the ones we left are facing food problems now".

Overall, it would seem that A1 women farmers emanating from communal areas have improved their livelihoods. But this has not impacted significantly on the form that agricultural production takes, notably in terms of gendered relations of production and a gender based division of labour. The ongoing existence of men's and women's crops (and fields), with women seen as responsible for minor crops such as groundnuts, is of some significance in this respect. The gendered relations in Gwaze have in many ways simply been reproduced at Dunstan and Lot 3.

Fast track implications for women

The FTLRP in Zimbabwe has had a range of social outcomes, some progressive and some regressive. The programme caught global attention and caused intense local conflict. Its consequences led to a number of entrenched myths, including the idea that agricultural production on A1 farms is negligible or even non-existent. Fast track has been heavily criticised for resulting in rising levels of poverty, food insecurity and a declining economy, and benefitting political cronies mainly. Oddly, the gendered dimension of the programme has been subject to significantly less criticism, if only because land redistribution in Zimbabwe has always been predominantly articulated in racial terms. Generally speaking, land reform in Zimbabwe (in the form of fast track) has simply perpetuated patriarchy. This is a key finding to the study, thereby confirming the overall conclusion of the few earlier gender-sensitive studies of fast track. Women remain marginalised with regard to A1 farms, and there does not appear to be any reason to believe that there will be a significant turnaround in the near future. The Goromonzi study shows that the new land ownership and tenure patterns under the A1 model have in large part replicated the gendered dimension to land existing in long-standing communal areas. Therefore, both A1 and customary areas in Goromonzi are marked by pronounced patriarchal domination in land access and control. In this respect, the fast track proposal to allocate a 20% quota of land to women is problematic in that it is often linked specifically to female-headed households; in this sense, it leaves out married women, who on a regular basis continue to obtain land in A1 farms through their husbands. In the end, this becomes an explicit admission by the government that if there is a man and a woman competing for land, first choice will be given to the man as almost a patriarchal entitlement. Customary practices remain hegemonic in all rural areas (both on A1 farms and in customary areas).

In Zimbabwe, after having seen the detrimental effects of marginalising women from accessing land and land-based resources, a number of NGOs were formed in a bid to mainstream gender into land issues. The NGO in the forefront for lobbying and advocating for women's land rights has been Women and Land in Zimbabwe (WLZ). In line with this is also the organisation's monitoring of the impact of government land policies and programmes on gender equality. Before WLZ, the then Women and Land Lobby Group spelt out clearly what women wanted:

> To be treated with dignity as full nationals; women's rights to land to be protected through legislation; non-discrimination on the basis of marital status and their rights in marriage to be protected, for example, through joint title; acknowledgement of women's disadvantaged position/weak negotiation base and for special mechanisms to be instituted e.g. quota, special fund, training, monitoring … standardised procedures for accessing land; … participation in decision making structures (task forces, committees); allocation of whole farms to women; sensitisation of men.
>
> (Gumbonzvanda 1999:9)

In many ways, this comment could be made now and have the same applicability. Fast track has not made significant headway in addressing the concerns raised in this commentary from the late 1990s.

There is however some evidence from this study that women's position in terms of land access has improved in fast track areas (where spouses jointly possess land) compared to customary areas where access is, in vastly more cases, through a male; in Gwaze, land is generally given to *de jure* head of households who tend to be males. As well, the livelihoods of women are also better on A1 farms compared to Gwaze, in part because of the richness of the soils on the former commercial farms (leading to larger harvests and the selling of excess crops) and in part because of greater opportunities for a range of alternative livelihoods that go beyond agricultural activities. Women at Dunstan and Lot 3 pursue a range of income-generating activities. They are involved in making and selling peanut butter to nearby communal areas to earn extra income. A great proportion of females also undertake tailoring and vending of clothes. In fact, 60% of women indicated that they are involved in vending of new and second-hand clothing (commonly known as *mabhero*) as a way of generating income to buy salt, relish and other domestic commodities. These women almost perceive themselves as petty traders such that they refer to themselves as self-employed and pursuing livelihoods in their own terms. In this sense, poverty at household level is lesser on A1 farms.

This is not to claim of course that the FTLRP in Goromonzi has become a panacea for women in resettlement areas who came from customary areas as a result of land reform. Certainly, most women at Dunstan and Buena Vista farms originally from nearby customary areas see the move as a blessing. Their testimonies clearly speak to a rise in their socio-economic status and to food security, as well as to a sense of dignity. On the same note, for women in customary areas (such as Gwaze), life continues as before fast track (without even decongestion of these areas taking place, which was the only intent for customary areas under fast track as articulated by government). Women in Gwaze and elsewhere remain trapped in patriarchal structures and practices, on which they blame a significant portion of their poverty and misery; they perceive resettlement as a way out of the cycle of poverty and speak about the need for another (fourth) *Chimurenga*. Due to limited space in customary areas and the depressed local economies, women are failing to engage in other income-generating activities that may lead to an improvement in socio-economic livelihoods.

Though these differences exist, women on A1 farms (whether from customary areas or not) suffer along with their customary counterparts in terms of patriarchal domination. The chieftainship system may not be entrenched on A1 farms, but certainly the instalment of headmen in A1 villages (who fall under the authority of local chiefs) brings to the fore the continued significance of customary forms of obedience throughout the Zimbabwean countryside. In addition, women on A1 farms continue to be subjected to patriarchal discourses focusing on the ideological construction of women and men's crops (with the land space for women's crops tending to be small).

They also suffer a number of disadvantages in terms of the availability of infrastructure such as water facilities and health clinics. Women are the ones responsible for care work and in Dunstan and Lot 3 of Buena Vista there are no clinics – they thus have to walk close to 25 kilometres in search of medication to Goromonzi town. After spending (on some days) more than 5 hours in the fields, they walk these long distances (including pregnant women). Likewise, women are responsible for water collection, and they walk long distances to fetch water on a regular basis (some travel as far as 12 kilometres, to Seke communal lands in search of clean water).

In this context, two points are important. First of all, any differences that exist in relation to land access and socio-economic livelihoods for women in A1 farms and customary areas cannot necessarily be explained in terms of differences in patriarchal practices between the two agrarian spaces. Hence, the improvement in women's livelihoods at Dunstan and Buena Vista farms, compared to Gwaze customary area, is not apparently due to any relaxation of patriarchy on A1 farms (even though relaxation may have occurred). More specifically, despite being in large part insensitive to the land needs and rights of women, fast track nevertheless in some ways – if only inadvertently – improved the lives of women on resettlement farms. In other words, just as colonial dispossession along racial lines led to the further subordination of women, fast track – in de-racialising land in contemporary Zimbabwe – has given scope to women to enhance their livelihoods. A similar argument can be made about disadvantages for women on A1 farms, such as access to infrastructure: though it may be argued that a more gender-sensitive land reform programme would have tackled such problems of access, there is no doubt that the existing problems arose because of fast track per se and the form it took (entailing limited pre-settlement and post-settlement infrastructural support).

Second, and related to the first point, women on A1 farms in particular are not simply objects of domination; they have not stood by idly in the face of patriarchy but have shown evidence of agency in the fluctuating and fluid conditions of fast track. Despite the prevalence of patriarchy as an intertwined system of structures and practices, women have sought to identify and open up gaps (i.e. opportunities) as they manoeuvre their way 'within' (but not against) this system. In doing so, they soften the burden of patriarchy and 'make the best out of a bad situation'.

This is reflected most notably in their pursuit of non-agricultural based livelihood strategies. Men continue to dominate the agricultural system (including decision-making processes) and women are still relegated to the realm of women's crops; but, on A1 farms, women are strategically engaging in a series of activities that they can call their own and that allow them a degree of independence from men (in the case of married women). Again, to reiterate the first point, the possibility of this pursuance cannot be explained in terms of a loosening of patriarchy on A1 farms. Further, women do not necessarily pursue these activities as a conscious effort to undercut patriarchy, though this may be an unintended consequence in the longer-term.

Conclusion and policy insights

Goebel (2005:145) quite rightly argues that "the current 'fast track' practices continue to privilege men as primary recipients of resettlement land, and the emerging role of traditional authorities in the land reform process [on A1 farms] marginalises women." Seeking to overcome entrenched patriarchy in relation to women and land is no easy task and entails systemic change that recognises the many complex and interrelated facets of patriarchy (as structures, practices and discourses). For instance, as noted below, organisational and policy changes in themselves are not sufficient as they do not necessarily tackle the ingrained and embedded character of patriarchy – as developed historically – in Zimbabwe.

In this vein, Oppah Muchinguri, the Manicaland Governor, acknowledged, "all the structures in the land reform programme were headed by men who were favouring other men while depriving women who work very hard in the fields". This particular argument is predicated though on a sweeping assumption that involving women more fully in decision-making organisations (such as district land committees) would effectively remove gender discrimination, enhance women's access to resources, boost agricultural productivity and reduce poverty reduction for women. This tends to falsely imply that altering the gender make-up of organisational structures (or replacing one kind of agent with another – male with female) is tantamount to broader transformative change, when in fact this reformist measure could simply more effectively entrench patriarchy.

Likewise, granting land rights for women on the same basis as for men (nationally through land policy) would not create gender equity overnight, given the complex nature of gender and power relations that operate at local levels. As Izumi (1999:16) has argued, "institutions that govern women's relationship with land cannot be seen simply as a set of rules, norms, policies, and laws: it is the social legitimacy of these which constitutes an institution". Though of some significance, access to land for women cannot be achieved through formalistic and superficial legal change, as patriarchal practices (backed by specific dis-courses) – including customary practices – also need to be challenged as they deny women voice and agency.

If gender inequality in all its manifestations is to be addressed, the first port of call is challenging patriarchy at all levels. Fast track land reform failed to do this in any meaningful manner. Regrettably, the academic critics of fast track fail to bring to the fore the weaknesses of the reform process in terms of addressing the gendered character of the land question. Simultaneously, the academic sup-porters of fast track overemphasise the radical nature of the process in tackling the land question – insofar as fast track did not address gender, it can hardly be labeled without qualification as progressive. It seems then that the land question in Zimbabwe remains unresolved and that a 'Fourth Chimurenga' is indeed required, a struggle that seeks consciously to articulate the needs of women and to undo the patriarchal structures, practices and discourses that continue to mar-ginalise women in the Zimbabwean countryside. It is hoped that this study makes a contribution to the awareness of this.

References

Action Aid, 2009. *Zimbabwe Country Brief, Women and Land Rights*. Harare: University of Zimbabwe Press.

Amanor-Wilks, D. 1996. Invisible Hands: Women in Zimbabwe's Commercial Farm Sector in SAFERE. Sexuality, Identity and Change 2:1. *Southern African Feminist Review (SAFERE)* 1 (1): 1–12.

Blackwells, W. 2003. *Agrarian Change, Gender and Land Rights*. Washington, DC: Wiley Blackwell. DCUSA.

Chimedza, R. 1988. *Women's Access to and Control over Land: The Case of Zimbabwe*. Working Paper AEE10/88. Department of Agricultural Economics and Extension: University of Zimbabwe.

Chingarande, S. 2004. *Gender and Fast Track Land Reform in Zimbabwe*. Harare: AIAS.

Chingarande, S. 2008. Gender and the Struggle for Land Equity. In S. Moyo, K. Helliker and T. Murisa, *Contested Terrain: Land Reform and Civil Society in Contemporary Zimbabwe*. Pietermaritzburg: SS Publishing.

Chitsike, F. 2003. *A Critical Analysis of Land Reform in Zimbabwe*. Harare: University of Zimbabwe Press.

Goebel, A. 2002. Men These Days They Are a Problem. Husband-Taming Herbs and Gender Wars in Rural Zimbabwe. *Canadian Journal of African Studies*, 36 (3): 460–489.

Goebel, A. 2005. Zimbabwe's "Fast Track" Land Reform: What about Women? *Gender, Place & Culture: A Journal of Feminist Geography*, 12 (2): 145–172.

Goebel, A. 2007. We Are Working for Nothing. Livelihoods and Gender Relations in Rural Zimbabwe 2000–2006. *Canadian Journal of African Studies*, 41 (2): 226–257.

Gumbonzvanda, N. 1999. *Women's Struggle for Land Rights: The Zimbabwe Case Study*. Paper presented at the Bonn Conference.

Hellum, A. 2004. Land reform and Human Rights in Contemporary Zimbabwe: Balancing Individual and Social Justice Through an Integrated Human Rights Framework. *World Development*, 32 (10): 1785–1805.

Izumi, K. 1999. Liberalisation, Gender, and the Land Question in Sub-Saharan Africa. *Journal of Gender &Development*, 7 (3): 9–18.

Jacobs, S. 2003. *Democracy, Class and Gender in Land Reform: A Zimbabwean Example?* Harare: University of Zimbabwe.

Jeater, D. 1993. *Marriage, Perversion and Power: The Construction of Moral Discourse in Southern Rhodesia*. Oxford: Clarendon.

Kesby, M. 1999. Locating and Dislocating Gender in Rural Zimbabwe: The making of Space and the Texturing of Bodies. *Journal of Gender, Place and Culture*, 6 (1): 27–47.

Maboreke, M. 1991. Women and Law in Post-Independence Zimbabwe: Experiences and Lessons. In J. Bazilli (ed.), *Putting Women on the Agenda*. Johannesburg: Raven Press.

Marongwe, N. 2008. *Interrogating Zimbabwe's Fast Track Land Reform and Resettlement Programme: A Focus on Beneficiary Selection*. Unpublished DPhil Thesis, University of Western Cape. Institute for Poverty, Land and Agrarian Studies.

McFadden, P. 1996. Editorial: Sexuality, Identity and Change. *Southern African Feminist Review*, 2 (1): vii–ix.

McFadden, P. 2002. *Becoming Post-Colonial: African Women Change the Meaning of Citizenship*. Public Lecture, 2002 Robert Sutherland Lecture. Queen's University. Kingston. Ontario. 24 October.

McCulloch, J. 2000. *Black Peril, White Virtue: Sexual Crime in Southern Rhodesia, 1902–1935*. Bloomington: Indiana University Press.

Moore, D. 2001. Is the Land the Economy and the Economy the Land? Primitive Accumulation in Zimbabwe. *Journal of Contemporary African Studies*, 19 (2): 253–266.

Moyo, S. and Yeros, P. 2007. The Radicalised State: The Zimbabwe's Interrupted Revolution. *Review of African Political Economy*, 111: 103–121.

Murisa, T. 2011. Local Farmer Groups and Collective Action Within Fast Track Land Reform in Zimbabwe. *Journal of Peasant Studies*, 38 (5): 1145–1166.

Presidential Land Review Committee (PLRC). 2003. *Report of the Presidential Land Review Committee* under the Chairmanship of Dr C.M.B. Utete. Vol. 1 Main Report and 11 Special Studies. Harare: Government Printers.

Razavi, S. 2002. *Shifting Burdens: Gender and Agrarian Change under Neoliberalism*. Bloomfield, CT: Kumarian Press.

Rutherford, B. 2001. *Working on the Margins: Black Workers, White Farmers in Post Colonial Zimbabwe*. London and New York: Zed Books.

Schmidt, E. 1992. *Peasants Traders and Wives: Shona Women in the History of Zimbabwe, 1870–1939*. Portsmouth, NH: Heinemann.

Stewart, J. 1992. Inheritance in Zimbabwe: The Quiet Revolution. In J. Stewart (ed.), *Working papers on Inheritance in Zimbabwe*. Women and the Law in Southern African Research Project. Working Paper No. 5, Harare.

Sylvester, C. 2000. *Producing Women and Progress in Zimbabwe: Narratives of Identity and Work from the 1980s*. Portsmouth, NH: Heinemann.

Utete, C. 2003. *Report of the Presidential Land Review Committee on the Implementation of the Fast Track Land Reform Programme, 2000–2002 ("The Utete Report")*. Available at: www.sarpn.org/documents/d0000622/P600-Utete_PLRC_00-02.pdf (Accessed 31 December 2014).

Zinanga, E. 1996. Sexuality and the Heterosexual Form: The Case of Zimbabwe. *Southern African Feminist Review*, 2 (1): 3–6.

Index

Page numbers in *italics* denote tables.

Africa 8, 26, 30, 57, 77–8, 94, 151, 179, 215–16
agency 1, 3–5, 15, 40, 42, 77, 110, 140, 157, 174, 179, 181, 214, 226, 227
agrarian: change 6; economy 5; issues 15; relations 217; spaces 226; structure 213, 220; system 213
agriculture 15–16, 33–4, 38, 40, 48–50, *50*, 54, 75, 78, 92–5, 102–3, 105, 115–16, 118, 121, 154, 165, 167, 171, 199, 201, 203
Archer, Margaret 5, 7, 142
assets 3–7, 16, 19, 45, 53–4, 66, 155, 185–7, 190, 191, 201, 207, 222

Bhaskar, Roy 7
Bourdieu, Pierre 5

capital 3, 5, 7
capitalism 4–5, 7, 155
capitalist 4, 14, 60
Chambers, Robert 2–3, 157
climate 18–19, 66, 107, 140, 142, 148–9, 151; climate change 6, 18, 96, 103–4, 139–42, 150–1, 154; climate variability 1, 18, 139, 148–51
colonial 8–9, 14, 20, 57, 76, 78–9, 92–3, 103, 155, 198, 213, 214, 215–16, 219, 226
commercial agriculture 10; commercial farms 12, 103, 204, 213, 216, 220, 225; commercial farmers 8, 9, 174, 217; commercial resettlement scheme 218
communal areas 8–11, 15–18, 20, 92–4, 107–8, 173, 176, 199–200, 201, 204–5, 207, 209, 213, 215–17, 219–25; communal farmers 8–9, 95, 99, 103, 105, 112, 208; communal land 154, 201, 220, 222, 226; communal tenure 207–9
community 17, 65, 92–3, 110, 113–14, 125–7, 133, 135–6, 154, 159, 171–2, 175, 177–8, 180, 186–7, 189, 196n2, 198, 208; community members 110, 113–14, 130–2, 134, 162; community participation 18, 124–8, 131–4, 136
conflicts 15, 18, 33, 51, 119, 121, 161, 166, 208
conservation farming 95–6, 102, 105, 159
contract farming 100, 156
conventional farming 158, 160, 162–5
Cornway, Gordon 2–3, 157
corruption 12, 19, 74, 170, 223
crises 1, 6, 13, 26, 34, 60, 111, 190
crop production 50, 58, 92–5, 101, 104, 172
cross-border 15, 31, 35–6, *47*, 82, 87
customary 93, 110, 181, 216, 224–5, 241; customary areas 94, 213, 216, 218, 219–22, 224–6; customary law 216, 218, 221

development 2, 4, 8–9, 11, 13, 19, 42, 107–9; agencies 2, 11; initiatives 107, 110, 115; practitioners 40; projects 110–11, 113, 115–16, 119–20; processes 4; system 3–4, 94
diversification 3, 15, 31, 38, 53–4, 118, 120–1, 155, 167

economy 8–10, 13, 17, 30–1, 36–7, 74, 5, 86, 107, 125–6, 198, 224
economic and political environment 125
economic crisis 11, 57, 62, 64, 71, 74, 77, 80–1, 112

employment 1, 10, 16–17, 26, 31, 32, 42, *46*, 46–7, 54, 58, 59–60, 64, 67, 79–80, 83–4, 88n4, 163–4, 166, 171, 203
environment 19, 80, 83, 135, 139, 150, 157, 159–60; authorities 161–2; conservation 157, 165, 173, 208; management 157, 161, 202
ESAP (Economic Structural Adjustment programmes) 9

farming 19, 33, 54, 93, 96–7, 100–1, 103–5, 144–5, 154, 157–60, 162–3, 170, 174, 181, 215 farming community 17
farming systems 142–3, 162
fast track farms 11, 16, 19, 93–4, 201
Fast Track Land Reform Programme 1, 10, 60, 74, 167, 175, 198–9, 213
fast track resettlement areas 11, 198
food security 2, 28, 32–3, 50, 54, 92, 93, 97, 102, 105, 171, 192, 216, 225

gender 16, 20, 45, 53–4, 76, 174, 213–14, 215, 217, 227
gender-based domestic violence 62, 69
gender biases 218
gender inequalities 1
governance 14, 115, 121, 189, 207, 209
Government of National Unity 11, 37
Government of Zimbabwe 9, 36, 210, 213, 217

HIV and AIDS 1, 9, 19, 60, 75, 87, 125, 129, 134, 184–7, 189–91, 193–4, 196
households 3–7, 15, 17, 19–20, 26, 30–4, 36–7, 42–54, 77, 82, 85, 87, 88n6, 92–4, 100, 140, 142, 154–6, 158–60, 165, 166–7, 174, 176, 179, 184–7, 189–92, 194–6, 198–200, 203–4, 209, 217–22, 224–5

informality 81; informal sector 10, 17, 26, 31, 37–9, 42, 54, 58, 128; informal vending 28, 30, 32
infrastructure 8, 15, 42, 107, 133, 171, 209, 226
institutions 3–4, 6, 15, 59, 84, 103, 105, 126, 154–5, 157, 161, 165, 167n1, 186–7, 217, 227
irrigation scheme 19, 170–2, 176; irrigation system 167; irrigation water 173, 179

land crisis 14

land occupations 10, 19, 75, 93, 170, 176, 204, 218
land redistribution 8, 9–10, 93, 198, 200, 213, 217, 224
land tenure 15, 19, 198–203, 207–9; land tenure systems 198, 208–9
livelihood activities, livelihood outcomes 3
livelihoods 1–4, 6–7, 11, 15–20, 26–7, 31, 35, 37, 39–40, 42–3, 47, 52, 54, 57, 60, 71, 74, 76, 86–7, 94, 107, 110, 122, 140, 143, 153, 155–67, 155–66, 167n1, 170, 172, 175, 177, 184–6, 190–1, 199, 201–3, 205, 207, 210, 213, 216, 221, 223, 225–6
livelihoods approach 5–6
livelihoods framework 1–3, 5, 7, 165
local community 129, 187, 208
local government 11, 18–19, 107–8, 113, 115–16, *117*, 117–21, 125–7, 130, 132, 135
local resources 15, 110, 136

macro-economic environment 13
market 9, 16, 26–30, 34, 54, 81–2, 93–4, 98–103, 107, 207, 209
migration 11, 15, 17, 57, 60, 64, 74–80, 82, 84–8, 89n10, 155, 166, 215–16
Moyo, Sam 12–13, 15–16, 94, 111–12, 198, 200–2, 208, 219

national reconciliation 8
natural resources 15, 20, 47, 95, 141, 150, 152, 166, 167, 173, 198, 199, 201–9
non-governmental organisations (NGOs) 1, 11, 17, 18, 51, 70, 105, 107–13, 115, 119–22, 166, 224

Operation *Murambatsvina* 12, 25, 27, 31, 34, 38, 75

participation 18, 102, 104, 107, 110–11, 113–16, 118–21, 124, 126–8, 131–6, 161, 174, 177, 185, 224
participatory methods 18, 107, 110, 111, 114, 120
patriarchy 7, 60, 213, 215, 217, 218, 219, 221, 224, 226, 227
peri-urban areas 15
petty traders 16, 27–31, 33–9, 58, 59, 68, 79–82, 87, 225
political economy 1, 2, 3, 4, 7, 13, 14–16, 44, 125
political violence 12, 16, 74, 77

post-2000 1, 2, 10, 15, 16, 17, 74, 76, 77, 79, 80, 82, 83, 84, 86, 87, 88
post colonial 8, 20, 57, 60, 74, 155, 177, 198, 199, 214, 216, 217
post harvest 91, 97–9, 105, 144
poverty 1, 3, 8–10, 15, 29, 31, 43, 44, 46, 48, 57, 60–4, 70, 75, 87, 111, 113, 126, 155, 157, 166, 171, 177, 180, 181, 200, 207, 216, 217, 224, 225, 227
power 4–13, 18, 19, 38, 42, 50–2, 54, 77, 91, 111, 119–21, 124, 125, 136, 170, 175, 176, 179, 180, 181, 190, 200, 205, 207, 208, 214, 216, 227
primary health care 1, 18, 124, 126, 127, 135, 136

qualitative research 76, 108, 130, 199
quantitative research 27, 43, 44, 91, 108, 109, 113, 139, 140, 142, 185

rainfall 58, 92, 94, 96, 100, 104, 139–47, 150, 151, 155, 157, 179, 199, 203, 223
remittances 16, 32, 38, 51, 52, 54, 74, 85, 189
research 1, 2, 15, 21, 22, 24, 25, 27, 40, 43, 55, 57, 58, 72, 76, 79, 80, 83, 84, 88, 89, 91, 94, 95, 99, 105, 107–9, 115, 116, 122, 127, 128, 130, 131, 137, 139, 140, 152, 156, 161, 167, 174, 179, 186, 190, 194, 195, 199, 203, 218, 220, 229
resilience 6, 151, 154, 159, 184–7, 190, 191, 194, 196
Rhodesia 8, 78, 93, 103

sanctions 8, 10, 13, 42, 74, 126
sex work(ers) 16, 17, 57–71, 191, 192
Scoones, Ian 2–4, 6, 15, 80, 157, 198–202, 210
small-scale farmers/farming 17, 18, 91–5, 97–100, 102–5, 198, 203, 204
smallholder irrigation 19, 93, 170–3, 176
social capital 19, 36, 158, 166, 184, 186, 187, 190, 193–5, 209
social networks 74, 186, 187, 191–3, 195, 209

socio-economic 1, 2, 3, 17, 20, 26, 39, 45, 60, 111, 124, 140, 170, 174, 178, 185, 186, 200, 213, 220, 225, 226
South Africa 15, 17, 28–30, 32, 35, 36, 42, 57, 58, 60, 61, 68, 74, 75, 77–88, 147, 180, 189, 192, 203
Southern African Development Community (SADC) 13, 51
structure-agency 4
survival strategy 62, 74, 76, 85, 87, 88, 154
sustainable livelihoods 1–3, 54, 110, 199, 207
sustainability 3, 4, 18–20, 32, 87, 107, 110, 112, 113, 119–21, 154, 159, 201

top-down approach 18, 132
traditional leaders 95, 174, 195

unemployment 9–11, 74, 75
urban 1, 3, 6, 9–12, 14, 26–8, 31–40, 42, 43, 45, 50, 51, 54, 64, 75, 79, 86, 88, 103, 130, 131, 155, 185, 194, 200, 215, 220

vending 27–32, 34, 36, 38, 47, 48, 225
vendors 27–35, 38, 39
vulnerability 4, 5, 7, 16–18, 50, 60, 75, 110, 119–21, 154, 155, 157, 158, 161, 162, 165–7, 177, 184–6, 193, 215

water 18, 30, 32, 42, 95, 96, 117, 126, 146, 148, 150, 156, 167, 171, 173, 179, 181, 201, 202, 204, 226
wealth index 45, 48–53
wildlife 155, 167, 199, 201, 202, 205, 206, 209
World Health Organisation 75, 124, 131

Zimbabwe African National Union-Patriotic Front (ZANU-PF) 8–13, 39, 74, 75, 112, 119, 170, 172, 177, 178, 217, 218
Zimstat 44–6, 84, 92